TAXATION OF
OIL AND GAS INCOME

by

Clark W. Breeding, C.P.A.

Partner, Peat, Marwick, Mitchell & Co.
Dallas, Texas

and

A. Gordon Burton, F.C.A.

Partner, Peat, Marwick, Mitchell & Co.
Calgary, Alberta, Canada

New York
PRENTICE-HALL, INC.
1954

Preface

This book sets forth the principles in the field of income taxation that control transactions common to the oil and gas producer. It is not possible for economic or political concepts to be applied with mathematical exactitude; nevertheless, the concepts and practices discussed will provide a guide to the person who plans the transactions of oil and gas producers, so that the tax impact can be predicted with reasonable certainty. Although the book is primarily concerned with operations of the industry in the United States, one chapter has been devoted to the corresponding tax concepts applicable to practice in Canada.

It is appropriate that we acknowledge the efforts of our associates, who have contributed so much to preparation and review of the manuscript. Without the considerable assistance of our partners, W. B. Wood of Dallas and T. A. M. Hutchison of Toronto, the completion of the treatise would have been much delayed. Criticism and counsel given by our partners George H. Abbott and Waymon G. Peavy of Dallas and J. A. Martin of Houston have assisted us in formulating the scope of the text and in eliminating inaccuracies and obscurities in the manuscript.

We are also indebted to Arthur B. Wood, Division Geophysicist, Shell Oil Company, Corpus Christi, for critical review of the chapter on Geological and Geophysical Costs; to Robert B. Payne of the firm Shank, Dedman & Payne, Attorneys, Dallas, for reviewing legal terminology used herein; to John A. Goodson, C. P. A., Trustee, Caroline Hunt Trust Estate, Dallas,

iii

for the many suggestions concerning the practical problems of oil and gas producers; and finally to several persons connected with the United States Internal Revenue Service, whose names we are not at liberty to disclose, for their helpful comments and suggestions.

CLARK W. BREEDING
A. GORDON BURTON

Contents

CHAPTER I

Petroleum Production

NATURE OF THE INDUSTRY [1]

1.01   **Introduction.** The federal tax concept of income from the exploration, development, and production phases of the oil and gas industry bears little resemblance to the usual concept

---

[1] The subjects of geology, geophysics, oil well drilling, and operations are highly complex technical subjects within themselves. Only a brief general survey of those subjects is intended here as an introduction to the accounting and income tax problems encountered in petroleum production. For a more detailed discussion of the technical side of this industry the reader is referred to the list of additional readings at the end of this chapter.

1

of income from a business, accounting, or legal standpoint. In large measure the dissimilarity arises from the nature of the industry itself, from its operating practices, and from the specialized terminology used in the industry. As a consequence, it would be difficult to understand the tax concept without a general comprehension of the nature of the business. This introductory chapter is intended to provide the basic orientation necessary to an understanding of the chapters that follow.

1.02   Oil Industry in General. The oil and gas industry is a composite of many functions, ranging from the search for the mineral in its natural underground reservoir to the marketing of refined products. The mineral must be found in the ground, lifted from its natural reservoir to the surface, and transported to refineries, where it is manufactured into more than a thousand different products. The products must then be transported to markets and ultimately sold to consumers. In this book, however, attention will be given only to the so-called production phases of the oil and gas industry, which may be considered to end when the products of the wells, crude oil or natural gas, are delivered to pipelines for transportation to refineries or to consumers.

The business of producing oil and gas is an extractive industry, and is like the mining industry in that oil and gas production is the process of removing a mineral in its natural state from the ground, after which it may be subjected to changes through chemical and physical processes and adapted to a necessary human use. It is also like the mining industry in that its product—crude oil or natural gas—is a limited natural resource that is depleted by production.

1.03   The Search for Oil. Crude oil and natural gas are generally located in porous underground rocks and sands, usually sedimentary in origin. Such formations act as reservoirs for gases and liquids if some geological condition results in the creation of a pocket in which the liquids and gases may accumulate. Such pockets are found in structures of various forms usually associated with anticlines, faults, and stratigraphic traps. An *anticline* (Figure 1) is, in its simplest form, a dome caused by the upfolding of rock strata. A *fault* (Figure 2) is caused by a break or a slip in the earth's rock crust. A *stratigraphic trap* (Figure 3) is caused by differences in the porosity and slope of successive formations of the earth's crust. In many formations, water and gas or oil are found together, and, since oil floats on water and gas is lighter than either oil or water, the oil and gas are found at the top of a given pocket. In each case the oil or gas, or both, are trapped in porous strata between or against impervious strata.

1.04 *Geological and Geophysical Methods.* The various traps for oil and gas sometimes occur only a few hundred feet underground, but in most instances they are found many thousands of feet below the surface. Even where the potentially oil-bearing or gas-bearing strata are far below the surface, there may be surface indications of their presence; some, in fact, may show on the surface in the form of outcrops. Strata which are so exposed may be sampled, analyzed, and classified. The outcrops will usually be great distances from the point at which an oil- or gas-filled pocket may have been formed, so preliminary surveys of such phenomena often cover very broad areas. Sometimes the presence of anticlines and faults may be indicated by surface conditions, but stratigraphic traps, which are not characterized by any up or down folds of rock strata, can rarely be detected in this manner. It will be apparent that a study of surface conditions is only tentative and preliminary, and that it is necessary to study subsurface conditions to locate possibly oil-bearing structures.

Geologists and geophysicists have devised several methods by which such studies can be made. In *core drilling,* small, portable drilling tools are used to take cores or rock samples from the topmost layers, working on the probability that the

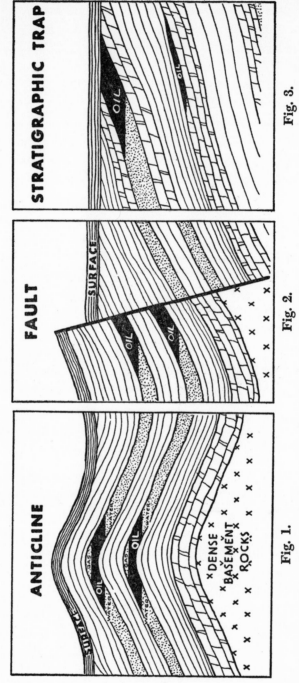

ANTICLINE

FAULT

STRATIGRAPHIC TRAP

Fig. 1.

Fig. 2.

Fig. 3.

(From *Petroleum Discovery and Production*, pamphlet, American Petroleum Institute, New York, N.Y.)

4

pattern of folds in strata found near the surface is indicative of the pattern of folds in the strata at greater depths. In a field where wells have been drilled, similar information can be obtained from the records of the wells drilled in the area. A second method is based on the fact that different geological structures may cause slight variations in the force of gravity, due to the shape and density of the subsurface structure. Gravity meters have been devised to detect such minute differences in the force of gravity and thereby analyze underground formations. Another method of subsurface exploration involves the use of the seismograph, which was originally devised to record earthquakes. In this method of prospecting for oil, a dynamite blast is set off to send shock waves down into the earth. Such waves are refracted and/or reflected by the various formations, and are recorded by sensitive detectors on the surface. Differences in velocity of the reflected shock waves indicate different types of formations. The elapsed time between the blast and the return of the reflected shock waves to the detectors measures indirectly the depth of the particular type of formation. Although all geological and geophysical exploration methods have been improved materially in many years of study, it remains a fact that the only way actually to prove the presence of oil or gas is by exploratory drilling that penetrates the stratum expected to contain petroleum deposits.

1.05 *Exploration Rights.* Preliminary studies of surface conditions that may be indicative of potentially oil-bearing or gas-bearing strata are frequently made on public lands, such as the public highways, or are made from water and airways. If the preliminary surveys indicate the possible existence of petroleum, more intensive surveys become necessary or desirable. In order to make these intensive surveys, it is often necessary to obtain permission from the landowners to enter private or public lands. Permission to enter property for purposes of conducting geological or geophysical surveys is frequently obtained without cost. In some instances such rights are secured by paying the landowner a nominal amount for exploration rights, either with or without an allowance for crop or other surface damages. Frequently an oil and gas lease is acquired before beginning the survey, since such a lease usually grants the right to make geological surveys as well as the right to develop the mineral deposits, if any are found. An *acreage selection clause* in the lease permits a large area to be surveyed geologically, with an option on the part of the lessee to select, within a limited period of time, only a portion of the acreage for leasing. Under such an arrangement the lessee usually pays a relatively small amount for the survey rights and a larger amount for the acreage which is ultimately selected.

1.06   Development of Oil and Gas Properties. Inherent in the ownership of minerals is the right to extract them. This right is frequently granted to another person by means of an oil and gas lease. Extraction of the mineral is then made possible by the drilling, equipping, and operation of one or more wells.

1.07   *The Oil and Gas Lease.* Under the ordinary oil and gas lease, the lessee is given the right to enter upon a property, to survey it and locate a well site, to perform drilling operations, and to remove any minerals found. The lessee is also given, expressly or by implication, the right to perform all acts necessary and incident to this ultimate objective. The term of the lease is most often for a specified number of years, called the primary term, and for as long thereafter as production is obtained from the property. Usually the lease may be terminated by the lessee without penalty.

In consideration of the granting of the lease, the lessee ordinarily (1) pays the mineral owner a bonus in cash, which is usually equal to a specified amount per acre under lease, (2) promises to pay a specified amount per acre in delay rentals, usually annually, until production commences or until the lessee terminates the lease, and (3) promises to deliver to the mineral owner, at no cost to him, a fraction of all oil and gas produced and saved from the property or, at the lessor's option, to pay him the cash value at the well of a fraction of all oil and gas produced and saved from the property. The lessor's share of production is known as the *landowner's royalty* or *fee royalty*, and the interest acquired by the lessee is known as the *working interest.*

The most commonly accepted fraction of production designated as the landowner's royalty in the southwestern United States has, through custom, come to be one-eighth. In other parts of the United States, one-sixth or one-fifth of the production has been specified as the landowner's royalty. The size of the fractional interest representing the landowner's royalty may depend in part upon the relative bargaining positions of the landowner and the prospective lessee.

It might appear, from the relatively small fraction accruing to the landowner's royalty, whether it be one-eighth, one-sixth, or one-fifth, that the landowner is not obtaining an equitable share of the production from the property. However, when it is remembered that the landowner bears no part of the development or operating costs of the property, all of which are borne by the lessee, it becomes apparent that the landowner's royalty may be worth as much as, and in some cases more than, the lessee's working interest. There is nothing to prevent the landowner from developing his own property, or to prevent a person who desires to acquire a mineral property from purchasing the entire mineral interest, so that he owns both royalty and working interest. However, the financial burdens and risks are so great that it is more common to separate these two interests, and it often occurs that the owner of the working interest will induce others to share part of the burdens and risks by transferring to them certain portions of his interest.

1.08 *Drilling Operations.* After a lease has been obtained, the next step in the development of an oil property is the selection of a likely well site and the commencement of drilling. In drilling oil wells, it is necessary to drill through rock, sand, and other types of formations. Those readers who have drilled a hole in wood have probably observed that the drill bit is made in such a way that it carries the cuttings from the drilling out of the top of the hole. In drilling an oil well, this method of removing the cut-away material is not practical, and one of the problems encountered in drilling operations is the removal of cut-away material from the hole. Rigs used for drilling oil and gas wells fall into two general classes: the *cable tool rig* and the *rotary rig*. The cable tool rig operates on a percussion or pounding principle, and pulverizes the formations in the bottom of the hole. The pulverized material is then removed from the hole by the use of a bailer. The more common type of rig in present-day use is the rotary rig, illustrated in Figure 4. In the rotary rig, the drill bit is attached to lengths of drill pipe, additional joints or lengths being added as drilling progresses. As the drill pipe is rotated, the bit is rotated in the hole, thereby cutting or drilling through the various rock strata. The drill pipe and the bit are hollow, and a mud solution, commonly called drilling mud, is pumped down through the center of the drill pipe and bit. It is forced out through the bottom of the drill pipe and bit and up to the surface of the ground through the annulus between the walls of the hole and the drill pipe. As it is forced to the surface, the mud carries the cuttings from the drill bit with it. When the drilling mud reaches the surface of the hole it flows into the mud pits provided for the storage of this material. Also, as the mud flows through the arrangement of pits, the heavy cuttings settle out and the mud can be re-used or recycled.

The drilling mud also serves the additional purpose of sealing the walls of the hole, which tends to prevent caving of the walls and the infiltration of water from the drilling mud into the various formations that are drilled through. The weight of

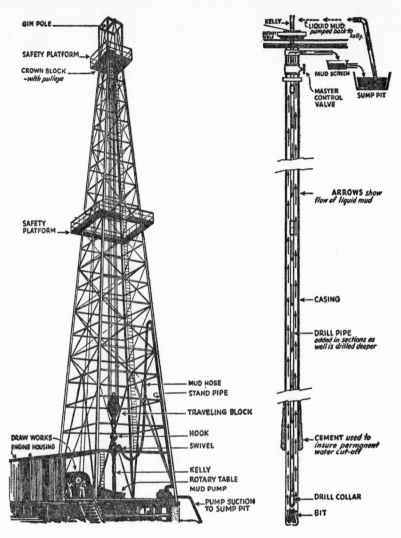

Fig. 4. Rotary drilling rig.

Left: derrick—above ground.

Right: drilling operations—below ground.

"Draw Works" is the collective name for the hoisting drum, shaft, and clutches, and other operating machinery. Power is received from the engine. The rotary table is driven by a chain from the draw works and rotates the hollow drill stem, which drills the well. The drill stem, consisting of drill pipe, drill collar, and bit, is raised from or lowered into the well by a cable, which is wound on the hoisting drum and passes through a series of pulleys in the crown block. Casing, or lining for the well, is raised or lowered in the same manner. (From *Petroleum Discovery and Production,* pamphlet, American Petroleum Institute, New York, N.Y.)

the column of drilling mud in the hole also offsets oil and/or gas pressure in the underground formations and helps to prevent "blow-outs." It is for this reason that heavier muds are used in areas where it is known that gas and/or oil will be found under high pressures.

After the well has reached a predetermined depth, sufficient to have penetrated all fresh water producing zones, a string of *surface casing* is usually set and cemented in place. This surface casing serves two purposes:

1. To prevent the drilling and operation of the well from contaminating natural underground fresh water supplies; and

2. To serve as a conductor for the drill bit and drill pipe as additional hole is being drilled.

After the surface casing is set and cemented in the hole, drilling proceeds to greater depths. If a very deep hole is projected, the operator may set two, three, or more strings of casing in the hole. These additional strings of casing are used:

1. To prevent cave-ins, which might result in loss of the hole;

2. To shut off high pressure water, oil, and/or gas zones that are not desirable; and

3. To shut off zones of lost circulation that may develop as drilling proceeds.

Each successive string of casing is somewhat smaller than the one above it, so that the succeeding string may be run through the string above and set at the desired depth in the well.

If oil and/or gas production is developed and the well is to be completed as a producer, a string of casing, commonly called the *production string*, will be set either above the pay zone or through the pay zone and cemented in place, using such volume of cement as is necessary properly to protect the pay zone from water encroachment and the loss of oil and/or gas to nonproductive zones behind the production string of casing. If the casing is set above the producing zone or sand, the well will be completed in the open hole below the casing seat. If the production string is set through the producing sand or sands, the casing then will be perforated opposite this producing zone or zones.

It has been noted previously that gas, oil, and water may be trapped in the producing zone. The gas, which is compressible, is usually in solution in the oil. However, a zone of free gas may be present above the oil zone. Also, because of the density of the water, there may be a zone below the oil and/or gas zones that will produce only water. The perforations in the casing are placed in relation to these zones to minimize the possibility of producing the undesirable gas or water. Assuming that the producing zone is 20 feet thick, with free gas in the top portion and free water in the lower portion, the middle five feet of casing in the productive zone might be perforated. This arrangement is considered a means of prolonging the flow of oil without the encroachment of either free gas or water in undesirable quantities.

After the perforations have been made in the casing, or after the well has been drilled to the desired total depth from the casing seat, a string of pipe, called *tubing,* is set and sealed into the well. Screens are attached to the tubing at the level of the producing stratum to strain out sand and other particles. At the top or ground level of the well a "Christmas tree" or a pumping engine is connected to the tubing. The "Christmas tree" is a complex set of valves used to control the flow from a well where the underground pressure in the producing formation is sufficient to cause the well to flow naturally. If the natural pressure below the ground is not sufficient, a pump is attached to the lower end of the tubing to force the oil up the well. On the surface a pumping engine, which is attached to the pump by "sucker rods," supplies power for the pump.

A single well may penetrate two or more producing sands or horizons. If the operator elects to produce from two or more sands at the same time, the well is said to be a *dual comple-*

tion. In the case of dual completion, equipment can be installed in the well to produce first from one sand and then from the other, or from both sands simultaneously.

When the "Christmas tree" or the pump is installed, the well equipment is considered complete, but certain lease equipment is also required for the operation of the well. Lines of pipe must be run from the well to separators, which separate water, oil, and gas, and let the oil be carried to batteries of tanks which are usually located on the lease. Since gas is not as readily stored as oil, it will frequently be transported, by gathering lines, from the separators directly to pipelines for transmission to users.

1.09   Operation of Producing Properties. After oil or gas has been found and the well has been completed as a producer, the product of the well must be marketed, and the operating and maintenance expenses of the well must be paid. It was indicated above that gas produced from a well is ordinarily delivered directly to transmission companies, because storage on the lease is difficult. Oil produced from a well is normally stored in tanks, either on the lease or in the field, awaiting delivery to a pipeline for transmission to refineries. Before the oil taken from a particular lease is paid for by the purchaser, division orders are circulated by the purchaser among the various owners of interests in the property for their signatures. Such division orders show the fractional interest of each owner. On the basis of the division orders, the purchaser will make payment directly to each interest owner for his proportionate share of the proceeds, less severance or production taxes. The amount of oil taken from the lease at any particular time, together with its division among the various owners of interests, is generally shown on a *run statement* supplied by the purchaser. Payment for gas produced from the lease may be handled in a similar manner, but more often the purchaser of the gas will pay the lessee for 100 per cent of the gas produced, less production or severance taxes. In accordance with the terms of the lease, the lessee in turn accounts to the royalty owners for their respective shares of the gas sold.

Numerous expenses are incurred by the lessee in connection with the operation of an oil or gas lease. Such expenses include labor and supervision in connection with lease operations, maintenance of equipment, power costs in connection with pumping wells, work-over costs incurred when wells "sand up" in the course of operation and must be cleaned out, repressuring costs incurred in connection with the injection of dry gas, salt water, or other substances designed to maintain reservoir pressure, and so on. All such expenses are the burden of the owner of the working interest in the property.

BASIC PRINCIPLES OF FEDERAL INCOME TAXATION

1.10   General. Since the purpose of this chapter is to provide orientation in the subject of federal income taxes as applied to the production phase of the oil and gas industry, the principles contained in the following paragraphs are stated in their most general terms. Later chapters will be devoted to a detailed consideration of the principles that are outlined below.

1.11   The Search for Oil. In general, all of the costs incurred by the party making geological or geophysical surveys are to be capitalized as a part of the leasehold costs of the property or properties acquired or retained as a result of the surveys. In addition, payments made to landowners in the form of damages or bonuses for the acquisition of a lease may also be capitalized as a part of the cost of the properties acquired. If the landowner receives a cash consideration for the granting of a lease on the property, such cash is a lease bonus, which is treated as ordinary income subject to depletion because it is considered to be an advance royalty.

To illustrate these principles, assume that *L* owns land that has not been leased, developed, or otherwise exploited for oil production. Assume also that O is an oil company that is interested in the area including L's land as a potentially oil-bearing or gas-bearing prospect. O's consideration of this property has resulted in its hiring, for $1,000, a geological survey company to make preliminary surveys on the public highways in the area. The survey company considers it worth while to enter on L's property in order to make more intensive geological studies of the area. As a consequence O pays L $500 in cash, for which it receives the right to enter upon L's land and make geological studies, and also receives an option to select for lease any portion of L's land. Such option provides for the payment of a lease bonus of $10 per acre for any acreage selected. Although the survey made by the geological company covered a more extensive area, as a result of the survey O exercises its option as to 640 acres of L's land. O pays L $6,400 lease bonus for a lease on the property selected by it. In addition, O pays the survey company $5,000 for the survey that resulted in the selection of L's acreage.

O has incurred $6,000 in geological or geophysical survey costs, and has paid $6,400 as a lease bonus. The sum of these costs, plus the $500 paid for the option, are capitalized by it as the cost of the leasehold interest acquired in L's acreage.

The geological survey company, which, of course, has received compensation for services, treats the amounts received by it as ordinary income. L has received $6,900, all of which is treated as lease bonus and is subject to depletion because it is considered to be a payment in the nature of advance royalties. If L had received the $500 payment for granting only shooting rights, he would probably be required to treat that amount as rental income not subject to depletion. Similarly, he would probably have to treat the $500 as rental income if O had not actually selected any acreage from L's tract.

1.12   Development of Oil and Gas Properties. The costs of drilling and completing an oil and gas well are divisible for tax purposes into two classes, intangible drilling costs and equipment costs. The equipment costs must be capitalized and recovered through depreciation. As to intangible drilling costs, the lessee has the option to expense or capitalize such costs; however, an election once made in the first taxable year in which such costs are incurred is binding upon that taxpayer as to treatment of such expenditures on all properties for all future years. Assuming that this is the first year in which the lessee has incurred intangible drilling costs, he has the option to charge them to expense when incurred, or to capitalize them as a part of the cost of the lease and recover such capitalized costs through depletion and depreciation. If similar costs had been incurred in connection with other properties in prior years, the lessee would be bound by the election he had made in the prior year.

The landowner is not considered to have derived any taxable income by reason of the fact that a well has been drilled upon his property. Although there is an enhancement in value of his property, such enhancement is not recognized as taxable income because it has not been realized.

Assume that O, in our previous example, expended $100,000 in intangible drilling costs and $30,000 in equipment costs in drilling and completing a well on the leased property. It should be noted that the entire burden of drilling and equipping the well has fallen on O, the owner of the working interest in the lease. None of the costs are borne by L, the landowner, who retained only a royalty interest in the property. Assuming that O has made or now makes a proper election to expense intangible drilling costs, it may claim as a deduction on its income tax return for the current year the $100,000 of intangible drilling costs incurred in connection with the drilling of the well on L's property. The equipment costs of $30,000 are capitalized by it and are to be depreciated over the useful life of the property. At this point O has an investment of $12,900, which is treated as leasehold cost and which it will recover through depletion, and an equipment cost of $30,000 to be recovered through depreciation. Since the intangible drilling costs are expensed, they are not included in the basis to be recovered through future depletion or depreciation. If, on the other hand, O had elected to capitalize intangible drilling costs, its leasehold cost, all of which is recoverable through depletion charges, would be increased by most of the $100,000, and the balance would be added to equipment cost, which is recoverable through depreciation.

1.13   Operations. Assuming that oil has been found and that the well has been completed as a producer, the income from the well is divided between the landowner, who owns the royalty, and the lessee, who may be referred to as the operator or owner of the working interest. Each of them is entitled to recover by depletion allowance his capital investment, if any, in the property. A taxpayer is entitled to claim the higher amount of depletion computed by two methods. The first method specified by the law is cost depletion, which is computed by dividing the depletable cost of the property by the estimated recoverable reserves to arrive at a unit cost. Such unit cost is then multiplied by current unit sales to arrive at cost depletion for the taxable year. The second method specified by the law is percentage depletion, which is computed at 27½ per cent of the gross income from the property, but which cannot exceed 50 per cent of the net income of the property. Allowable depletion is not limited in amount to the taxpayer's basis in the property, and he may, therefore, continue to claim percentage depletion after the full depletable capital investment in the property has been recovered by prior depletion allowances.

Production or severance taxes levied by the various states on the production of oil or gas are deducted by the purchaser of production from the well, in making remittance to the various owners of interests in the property. This expense is borne by the royalty owner proportionately with the owner of the working interest; the cost of treating the oil on the lease to make it marketable may also be shared by the royalty owner. All other expenses incurred in connection with the operation of the well are borne entirely by the lessee or owner of the working interest in the property.

Assuming that the royalty interest retained by L has no income tax basis in his hands, he would have no basis upon which to compute cost depletion. The fact that he has no basis does not, however, prevent him from claiming percentage depletion based on the gross income from the property for the year. L received $6,900 as a lease bonus and, assuming that his share of production, before deduction of production taxes of $125, amounted to $2,500 for the year, his gross income would be $9,400. His percentage depletion would be 27½ per cent of this amount, or $2,585, and since this amount is not in excess of 50 per cent of his net income from the property ($4,637.50) for the taxable year, the full amount would be allowable as a deduction.

Assuming that O has elected to expense intangibles, it was indicated that its basis for the lease would be $12,900 and that this amount is recoverable through depletion charges over the productive life of the property. The unit cost for depletion is computed by dividing the leasehold cost of $12,900 by the estimated reserves in the lease belonging to the working interest, which we will assume to be 129,000 barrels of oil. The unit cost would, therefore, be ten cents a barrel. Assuming that the lessee's share of current sales was 8,000 barrels, current cost depletion would be $800 (8,000 barrels times ten cents per barrel). Assume that O had gross income from the property of $17,500 before production taxes, and had incurred operating expenses of $3,000 and the intangible drilling costs of $100,000. O therefore had a net loss from operation of the property for the current year. Because of the loss, the net income limitation on percentage depletion prevents the allowance of percentage depletion for the current taxable year. Allowable depletion would, therefore, be cost depletion of $800 as computed above.

FINANCING EXPLORATION AND DEVELOPMENT

1.14   General. Because the exploration and development of oil and gas properties is a risky and expensive undertaking, the owner of the working interest in a property frequently seeks means to spread the risks and reduce his own expenditures. Usually the simplest way to obtain cash for development of the property is by the disposition of some kind of property interest. Various kinds of property interests that may be assigned are described in Chapter 2. The types of conveyances and their tax consequences are described in Chapters 3 through 7.

SUGGESTED ADDITIONAL READINGS FOR CHAPTER I

Ball, Max W., *This Fascinating Oil Business* (New York: The Bobbs-Merrill Company, 1940).

Cloud, Wilbur F., *Petroleum Production* (Norman: University of Oklahoma Press, 1937).

Engineering Committee, Interstate Oil Compact Commission, *Oil and Gas Production* (Norman: University of Oklahoma Press, 1951).

American Association of Oilwell Drilling Contractors, *A Primer of Oil Well Drilling* (Austin, Texas: The University of Texas, 1951).

Glasscock, C. B., *Then Came Oil* (New York: The Bobbs-Merrill Company, 1938).

Perry, Josephine, *The Petroleum Industry* (New York: Longmans, Green and Co., 1946).

Kalichensky, V. A., *The Amazing Petroleum Industry* (New York: Reinhold Publishing Corporation, 1943).

Hollyman, Thomas, *The Oilmen* (New York: Rinehart & Company, Inc., 1952).

Jakosky, *Geophysical Exploration* (Los Angeles, Calif.: Times-Mirror Press, 1950).

CHAPTER II

Kinds of Property Interests

DEFINITIONS AND ATTRIBUTES

2.01   Introduction. Prerequisite to an understanding of the production phase of the petroleum industry is a working knowledge of the various kinds of property interests or rights that, for federal tax purposes, comprise ownership of oil and gas in place. Ownership of land in the United States encompasses both surface and subsurface rights in a clearly defined tract. Subsurface rights include the minerals in and under the tract, and the mineral interest may be separated in whole or in part from the surface right. It is the mineral rights, usually referred to as minerals, and the tax consequences of their exploitation with which this book is concerned.

It must be emphasized that the following discussion of

property interests is concerned with their federal income tax attributes and not with their legal status or characteristics under the property laws of the various states. In general, federal revenue legislation is to be interpreted so as to give uniform application to a nationwide scheme of taxation.[1] As a consequence, the federal income tax rules will be applied more or less uniformly without differentiation based upon differences in local property laws. However, in a few cases, which will be discussed in later chapters, the decision of the court has appeared to depend upon the laws of the state in which the property was located. Such cases may be of doubtful value as precedents except for similar transactions in the same states.

2.02   Minerals. As used herein, minerals may be defined, for federal income tax purposes, as the sum total of all rights to oil and gas in place. Since the owner of the minerals frequently does not own the surface of the land under which the minerals lie, ownership of the minerals carries with it the right to make such reasonable use of the surface as is necessary to develop the property for production of oil and gas. The owner of minerals has the right to reduce the oil and gas to his possession and to remove them from the property. It is the owner of the minerals, not the surface owner, who has the right to grant an oil and gas lease, and it is he who is entitled to any lease bonus and delay rentals that may be payable in connection with a lease. The owner of the minerals may assign all, a segregated portion, or an undivided fraction thereof. Thus, the owner of all the minerals under 160 acres of land may assign all 160 mineral acres, or may assign all the minerals under the northeast 40 acres—a segregated portion—or may assign a one-fourth interest in the minerals under the entire 160 acres—an undivided fraction. He may also make a so-called horizontal assignment by assigning all, or some portion, of the minerals above or below specified depths.

---

[1] *Burnet v. Harmel*, 287 U.S. 103, 11 A.F.T.R. 1085 (1932).

When the mineral rights so assigned are limited in duration, they are called *term minerals,* as contrasted to *perpetual minerals.* The assignor of minerals may reserve to himself the portion of any bonus or delay rentals, arising out of future leasing arrangements, that would otherwise have accrued to his assignee. This restriction causes the interest assigned to be described as *nonparticipating minerals.* The minerals may be regarded as the sum of two major interests, the royalty and the working interest, which are described below.

2.03   Royalty. A royalty interest, for federal tax purposes, is a right to oil and gas in place that entitles its owner to a specified fraction, in kind or in value, of the total production from the property, free of expense of development and operation. It is, therefore, a mineral interest, stripped of the burdens and rights of developing the property. Words of limitation applied to minerals, such as *term* and *nonparticipating,* are sometimes applied to royalties with the same restricting effect. It has been previously noted that the fraction of the oil and gas accruing to the royalty owner may vary between different properties or in different parts of the country. If the bargaining position of the owner of the minerals is particularly favorable, he may be able to retain a relatively larger fraction, or may even be able to reserve a minimum royalty stated in terms of a specified number of dollars a year, regardless of actual production from the property. Such minimum royalty may or may not be chargeable against the royalty owner's share of future production.

A royalty may be created by assignment, as when the owner of the mineral rights conveys an interest therein, reserving to himself all operating rights and burdens. It may be reserved by the owner of the minerals when he grants an oil and gas lease placing in the grantee the exclusive rights and burdens of development. At such time as the lease expires, the leasehold interest reverts to the owner of the minerals.

2.04   Working Interest. The mineral interest minus the royalty equals the working interest in an oil and gas property. The working interest, for federal tax purposes, is an interest in oil and gas in place that is burdened with the cost of development and operation of the property. Because this interest must bear the burden of such expenses, it receives a large share of the total production from the property.

The working interest is created, or carved out of the mineral interest, by the granting of an oil and gas lease. In the usual lease the lessee does not undertake a specific obligation to develop the property or to pay delay rentals, but he agrees that the lease will expire if the property is not developed or rentals are not paid. Ordinarily the lessee can abandon the property without penalty to himself. It is customary, however, for the lessee to release the lease if he desires to surrender the property without development.

The lessee, who is the owner of the working interest, may retain it intact throughout the life of the lease, or he may carve it up into various property interests. In many instances the lessee desires to obtain outside funds for financing, or to spread the risk inherent in developing oil and gas properties. He may accomplish this by assigning some property interests carved out of his working interest. For example, *O,* the owner of the working interest, might assign an oil payment to *D,* a drilling contractor, in return for *D's* promise to drill a well. Or, he might sell an overriding royalty for cash and use the cash to develop the property. Since both of these interests are created from the working interest, they cannot exist beyond the life of the working interest. Hence, if *O* has made the assignments mentioned above and the well proves dry, so that the lease is not held by production, the working interest, the oil payment, and the overriding royalty would all terminate upon abandonment of the lease, or at the end of the primary term of the lease.

In each of the examples above, *O* has retained the working interest and has assigned or carved out the other interests. In other words, he has retained the primary responsibility for development and operation. It is equally possible for him to assign the working interest and retain an overriding royalty, an oil payment, or some other type of interest. Shifting the responsibility of development from the working interest owner to an assignee is known in the industry as a *farm-out*. The lessee may or may not receive a bonus from the assignee at the time of such an assignment.

Whether the interests created from the working interest are carved out or retained, they reduce the share of production accruing to the working interest. Thus, O may own the working interest in a lease that is entitled to receive $\frac{7}{8}$ of the total production from the property. He may assign this working interest to X and retain an overriding royalty equal to $\frac{1}{7}$ of $\frac{7}{8}$, or, in effect, $\frac{1}{8}$ of the total production from the property. The working interest in X's hands is then entitled to $\frac{6}{8}$ of the total production. X in turn may assign the working interest to Y, retaining another overriding royalty, and so on. Even though the share of total production which accrues to the benefit of the working interest is reduced to the extent of each of the interests created therefrom, the working interest is still burdened with all of the costs and expenses of development and operation of the property.

2.05   Overriding Royalty. An overriding royalty is similar to a royalty in that, for federal tax purposes, each is a right to oil and gas in place that entitles its owner to a specified fraction of production, in kind or in value, and neither is burdened with the costs of development or operation. They differ in that an overriding royalty is created from the working interest, and its term is co-extensive with that of the working interest from which it was created.

The overriding royalty may be carved out or retained. It is said to be carved out if the owner of the working interest assigns a right to a fractional share of production free and clear of development and operating expense. It is retained if the lessee assigns the working interest and retains a fractional share of production free of development and operating costs.

2.06   Net Profits Interest. A net profits interest is, for federal tax purposes, an interest in oil and gas in place that is defined as a share of gross production measured by net profits from operation of the property. Like the overriding royalty, a net profits interest is created out of the working interest and has a similar duration. Unlike the overriding royalty, the income accruing to the net profits interest is reduced by specified development and operating costs, but the interest bears such expenses only to the extent of its share of the income, and is not required to pay out, advance, or become liable for such costs, as is the working interest. If there is no net profit from the operation of the property, the net profits interest owner receives nothing. If there is a net loss from operations, he receives nothing, but is not liable for any share of the loss. Until any accumulated net losses are offset by future net profits from operation of the property, the owner of the net profits interest will receive no income. The interest is regarded as a non-operating interest similar to an overriding royalty.

The net profits interest is usually defined as a fraction, perhaps one-third or one-half, of the operator's net profit from the operation of the property. The instrument creating the interest must clearly define such terms as gross income from the property, operating expenses, depreciation, depletion, and so on, and should prescribe in some detail the accounting procedures to be followed by the operator of the property. The net profit account may or may not be chargeable with development and equipment costs, and may be credited with the proceeds from sale of equipment, depending upon the agreement between the parties. The holder of a net profits interest does not, however, have a depreciable interest in equipment, even if the cost is charged to the account. The net profits interest may be carved out by a separate assignment, or it may be retained by the lessee upon his assignment of the working interest. In either case it represents a contractual arrangement between the parties, defining their respective interests in production.[2]

For many years the courts held that a net profits interest was not an interest in gross production but was merely a contractual consideration for the assignment of property based on net profits from its operation.[3] However, as a result of the Burton-Sutton[4] and Kirby[5] decisions, wherein the Court viewed the interest as being a right to gross production measured by net income, it is now established that a net profits interest is an interest in the production. A danger always exists that a disposition of an oil property for a consideration measured by a formula may assume the nature of a contractual obligation and cease to be an interest in the oil in place. For a better understanding of this distinction, see the discussion of economic interest in paragraphs 2.09–2.12.

2.07 **Production Payment.** A production payment, for federal tax purposes, is a right to oil and gas in place that entitles its owner to a specified fraction of production for a limited time, or until a specified sum of money (which may be determined by a formula) or a specified number of units of oil or gas has been received. A production payment, or, as it is more commonly called, a gas payment or an oil payment, is somewhat like an overriding royalty, but, because it is definitely limited in amount and expires when this amount has been paid, different tax consequences attend its creation and disposition (as explained in Chapter 6). Argument has been advanced

---

[2] *Burton-Sutton Oil Co., Inc.* v. *Commissioner,* 328 U.S. 25, 34 A.F.T.R. 1017 (1946).

[3] *Helvering* v. *Elbe Oil Land Development Co.,* 303 U.S. 372, 20 A.F.T.R. 787 (1938), reh. den., 303 U.S. 669, 21 A.F.T.R. 59 (1938).

[4] *Burton-Sutton Oil Co., Inc.* v. *Commissioner, supra.*

[5] *Kirby Petroleum Co.* v. *Commissioner,* 326 U.S. 599, 34 A.F.T.R. 526 (1946).

that an oil payment should not be for an amount so large that it evidently will never pay out, for it may then be treated as an overriding royalty. From a theoretical standpoint, this argument sounds impressive, but it must be remembered that the tax cases making distinctions between oil payments and overriding royalties were construing instruments involving assignments of nonproducing properties where by definition no certainty of payment existed.[6] Although most of the cases involve oil payments reserved upon the assignment of a lease, such payments may nevertheless be carved out of any larger interest.

Reference was made in preceding paragraphs of this chapter to term minerals and term royalties. It should be observed that assignments of certain types of term minerals or royalties may have the same tax effect as assignment of an oil payment. There are two types of such term interests, one for a specified term of years, and the other for a specified term and so long thereafter as oil or gas is produced in commercial quantities from the property.[7] An assignment of the latter type of interest, which is in more common use today, does not have the same effect as assignment of an oil payment. However, where the assignment is only for a specified period of time and the interest is not extended by production, the interest assigned is nothing more than an oil payment, even though called by another name. In later sections of this book, the expressions term mineral or term royalty will refer to the type of interest which is extended by production.

2.08   Carried Interest. The carried interest is an arrangement between two or more co-owners of a working interest, whereby one agrees to advance all or some part of the development costs on behalf of the others and to recover such

---

[6] *See Thomas* v. *Perkins*, 301 U.S. 655, 19 A.F.T.R. 538 (1937); *see also* G.C.M. 24849, 1946-1 C.B. 66; I.T. 4003, 1950-1 C.B. 10.

[7] *Plow Realty Company of Texas*, 4 T.C. 600 (1945), acq., 1945 C.B. 6.

advances from future production, if any, accruing to the other owners' share of the working interest. The owner who advances the costs is known as the *carrying party*, and the owner for whom costs are advanced is called the *carried party*. The carried interest may extend for only one well, for some of the wells on the lease, or for the full development of the property.

The carried interest may arise by agreement between co-owners, but it is generally created in connection with an assignment of a portion of the working interest. For example, *A*, the owner of the entire working interest, may assign a one-half interest in the property to *B* if *B* will pay all the costs of drilling and equipping one well thereon and look only to production, if any, from the grantor's share of the working interest to recover the grantor's share of such costs. This general result has been accomplished under three different types of arrangements, and since the tax consequences differ it is necessary to distinguish the three quite clearly.

1. The owner of the working interest may assign the entire working interest, or an undivided fraction thereof, for a period of time, measured by the recoupment of cost by the assignee, at which time a portion of the working interest assigned reverts to the assignor. This type of assignment was passed on by the Tax Court in the Manahan case.[8]

2. The owner of the working interest may assign an undivided fraction thereof, together with a production payment, measured in terms of dollars of expenditure incurred by the assignee for the benefit of the assignor, and payable out of the assignor's retained fractional interest, as illustrated in the Herndon case.[9]

3. The owner of a fraction of the working interest may mortgage his interest to the other co-owners as security for a loan

---

[8] *Manahan Oil Co.*, 8 T.C. 1159 (1947).

[9] *Herndon Drilling Company*, 6 T.C. 628 (1946), acq. and nonacq. on other issues, 1946-2 C.B. 3, 6.

for which he is not personally liable, as in the Abercrombie case.[10]

Each of these three arrangements produces the same economic result so far as division of income and expense is concerned, and yet each has been held to have a different tax consequence. For a discussion of this difference, see paragraph 8.14 *et seq., infra*. It might be noted that the Commissioner of Internal Revenue has acquiesced in the Abercrombie case, but Revenue Service field practice, almost without exception, considers any carried interest arrangement to amount to an assignment of the entire working interest for a period of time with a reversionary interest in the assignor, as in the Manahan case.

It should also be observed that if one party is, by the terms of the agreement, to be carried for the entire life of the property, and there is no reservation by him of a possibility of reverter, the carried interest resembles very closely a net profits interest. In fact, the similarity may be so great that the Revenue Service will hold that the so-called carried interest is a net profits interest. The later discussion of conveyances will show that this interpretation can materially alter the tax consequences of the assignment.

ECONOMIC INTEREST

2.09   Definition. A term that plagues the tax consequences of every assignment of property in all extractive industries is the mystifying and somewhat illusory "economic interest." The determination of whether a property interest qualifies as an economic interest is important, because the owner of the economic interest ordinarily is taxable upon the income that property produces, is allowed a deduction for depletion against income from production accruing to the interest, and in many cases may be entitled to capital gains treatment upon the sale

---

[10] *Commissioner* v. *J. S. Abercrombie Co.*, 162 F.(2d) 338, 35 A.F.T.R. 1467 (5th Cir. 1947) aff'g 7 T.C. 120 (1946), acq., 1949-1 C.B. 1.

or exchange of that interest. Each of the property interests described above constitutes an economic interest.[11] The regulations contain the following description:

An economic interest is possessed in every case in which the taxpayer has acquired, by investment, any interest in mineral in place . . . and secures, by any form of legal relationship, income derived from the severance and sale of the mineral . . . to which he must look for a return of his capital.[12]

2.10   Acquisition by Investment. An investment in minerals in place may be acquired by purchase for cash,[13] in exchange for other property,[14] for services rendered,[15] by gift,[16] by inheritance,[17] or as a liquidating dividend.[18] An investment in minerals in place may be retained if it is represented by a portion of a previously-owned economic interest.[19] It is not necessary that the taxpayer incur a cost in connection with the acquistion or retention of the investment, nor is it necessary that he have any tax basis in such investment.

2.11   Interest in Mineral in Place. For federal tax purposes an interest in the oil in place is owned if a right exists to share in the oil produced, even if under state law legal title to oil in

---

[11] Mineral interest—*Anderson v. Helvering*, 310 U.S. 404, 24 A.F.T.R. 967 (1940). Royalty interest—*Burnet v. Harmel, supra*, as explained in *Anderson v. Helvering, supra*. Working interest—*Lynch v. Alworth-Stephens Co.*, 267 U.S. 364, 5 A.F.T.R. 5258 (1925), as explained in *Palmer v. Bender*, 287 U.S. 551, 11 A.F.T.R. 1106 (1933). Overriding royalty interest—*Palmer v. Bender, supra*. Net profits interest—*Burton-Sutton Oil Co., Inc. v. Commissioner, supra*. Oil payment—*Thomas v. Perkins, supra*. Carried interest—*Manahan Oil Co., supra*.

[12] U.S. Treas. Reg. 118, Section 39.23(m)-1(b).

[13] *Anderson v. Helvering, supra*.

[14] *Kate J. Crichton*, 42 B.T.A. 490 (1940), acq., 1952-1 C.B. 2, aff'd, 122 F.(2d) 181, 27 A.F.T.R. 824 (5th Cir. 1941); *E. C. Laster*, 43 B.T.A. 159 (1940), acq. and nonacq., 1941-1 C.B. 7, 1952-2 C.B. 5, modified, 128 F.(2d) 4, 29 A.F.T.R. 465 (5th Cir. 1942).

[15] *Dearing v. Commissioner*, 102 F.(2d) 91, 22 A.F.T.R. 632 (5th Cir. 1939), aff'g 36 B.T.A. 843 (1937), acq. 1940-2 C.B. 2.

[16] *R. E. Nail, Exec.*, 27 B.T.A. 33 (1932), nonacq., 1949-1 C.B. 6. But *see* I.T. 3935, 1949-1 C.B. 39 and I.T. 4003, *supra*.

[17] *Commissioner v. Laird*, 91 F.(2d) 498, 19 A.F.T.R. 1127 (5th Cir. 1937).

[18] *Boudreau v. Commissioner*, 134 F.(2d) 360, 30 A.F.T.R. 1132 (5th Cir. 1943).

[19] *Palmer v. Bender, supra*.

place belongs to another person.[20] A right to share in the oil produced does not imply merely an option to take production in kind but includes the right to share in the proceeds from the disposition of the oil.[21] Even if the proceeds are subject to reduction by certain expenditures, one holding such a right shares in the oil produced and is considered to have an economic interest.[22]

Ownership of an interest in mineral in place is a requisite to a finding that an economic interest exists. For example, in the Bankline case [23] the taxpayer was the owner of a gasoline plant and had contracted to extract gasoline from wet gas for a percentage of the proceeds from sale. The Supreme Court held that the taxpayer had no capital investment in the mineral deposit, and thus he did not own an economic interest in the property. On the other hand, the Hudson case [24] held that the assignment of a fractional interest in the heavier hydrocarbons in place, in consideration of the assignee's agreement to construct a plant and extract liquids from the wet gas, did create an economic interest in the assignee. The principal difference between the two cases is that in the latter the transaction took the form of an assignment of an interest in the producing property. That the difference is more than formal is indicated, for example, by the fact that the assignor of only a share of the products could still mortgage the entire producing property, whereas the assignor of an interest in the property could mortgage only what he retains.

A different aspect of the same test was applied in the O'Donnell,[25] Tuttle,[26] and Haynes [27] cases. In these cases the

---

[20] *Thomas v. Perkins, supra,* as explained in *Anderson v. Helvering, supra.*
[21] *Kirby Petroleum Co. v. Commissioner, supra.*
[22] *Burton-Sutton Oil Co., Inc. v. Commissioner, supra.*
[23] *Helvering v. Bankline Oil Co.,* 303 U.S. 362, 20 A.F.T.R. 782 (1938).
[24] *Edward J. Hudson,* 11 T.C. 1042 (1948), nonacq. on this issue, 1949-1 C.B. 5, acq. on another issue, 1949-1 C.B. 2, aff'd, 183 F.(2d) 180, 39 A.F.T.R. 646 (5th Cir. 1950).
[25] *Helvering v. O'Donnell,* 303 U.S. 370, 20 A.F.T.R. 785 (1938), reh. den., 303 U.S. 669, 21 A.F.T.R. 59 (1938).
[26] *Tuttle v. United States,* 101 F. Supp. 532, 41 A.F.T.R. 549 (Ct. Cls. 1951).
[27] *Haynes v. United States,* 50 F. Supp. 238, 31 A.F.T.R. 281 (Ct. Cls. 1943).

taxpayers sold stock of a corporation and the purchaser contracted, among other things, to pay a sum of money equivalent
to a fraction of the income or profits from operation of leases
owned by the corporation. In the O'Donnell and Tuttle cases
the contracts required that the purchaser liquidate the corporation, but no such provision was involved in the Haynes
case. In each case it was held that neither party to the contract
had an investment in the minerals in place because the property was owned by the corporation, a separate entity. As a
consequence, it was held that the contractual consideration
received by the taxpayer was not an economic interest but was
merely a contingent sum to be paid for the sale of the stock.
If the agreement between the parties had contemplated liquidation of the corporation by the seller, and the retention by
him of an interest upon assignment of the properties, a different result might properly have occurred.

Sometimes the distinctions become hairline, and a question
arises as to what circumstances permit the wording of the instruments or the form of the transaction to control tax consequences. Even the Supreme Court has found itself unable to
agree unanimously, as was demonstrated by the concurring
opinion in the Burton-Sutton case.[28] In that case a majority of
the Court found that an economic interest had been retained
when the language of the assignment purported to reserve an
interest in the oil and gas measured by a portion of the net
profits from operation of the property. Several years earlier
the Supreme Court, in the Elbe case, had refused to find that
an economic interest had been retained when additional consideration was given the assignor in the form of a covenant to

---

[28] Mr. Justice Frankfurter commented in his concurring opinion in *Burton-
Sutton Oil Co., Inc.* v. *Commissioner, supra:* "Nothing better illustrates the
gossamer lines that have been drawn by this Court in tax cases than the distinction made in the Court's opinion between *Helvering* v. *Elbe Oil Land Co.,*
303 U.S. 372 . . . and this case. To draw such distinctions, which hardly can
be held in the mind longer than it takes to state them, does not achieve the
attainable certainty that is such a desideratum in tax matters. . . ."

pay a sum of money out of net profits when, as, and if earned.[29] Although the economic results of the two assignments were similar, the former purported to reserve an interest in the minerals in place, whereas the latter did not. This distinction, based on the form of the transaction, may not be substantial, as Justice Frankfurter suggested in his concurring opinion in the Burton-Sutton case.[30] Many practitioners consider the Elbe case overruled, but the decision in the Southwest Exploration case [31] indicates that such a conclusion may be unwarranted. In that case the owner of shoreline property was granted a right to a share of net profits from operation of an offshore lease, in return for use of the shore property as a drillsite. The Court held that his right to a portion of the net profits was not an economic interest. Until the Supreme Court specifically over-rules the Elbe case, it is well to safeguard the tax consequences of a transaction by contractual language expressly reserving or acquiring an interest in the oil and gas in place measured by the net profits.

It has been suggested that the term "economic interest" should be regarded as embracing any contractual right to, and dependent upon, production and sale of minerals.[32] That the Revenue Service is inclined to follow the contractual right theory, at least within limits, is indicated by the nonacquiescence filed in the Southwest Exploration case. If this test were applied, it would appear that the taxpayers in the Bankline and Southwest Exploration cases would have been found to be owners of economic interests. This theory would also support

---

[29] *Helvering* v. *Elbe Oil Land Development Co., supra.* Because the assignee, by its option to reconvey, had the right to cause the lease to terminate without ever paying any net profits to assignor, the assignment might be considered a sale of the entire working interest for a limited period of time.

[30] *Burton-Sutton Oil Co., Inc.* v. *Commissioner, supra; See also* footnote 28, *supra.*

[31] *Southwest Exploration Company,* 18 T.C. 961 (1952), nonacq., 1953-1 C.B. 7, appeal pending to 9th Cir.

[32] See Dale H. Flagg, *Legal Aspects of Depreciation in Natural Resource Industries,* Second Annual Institute on Oil and Gas Law and Taxation (New York: Matthew Bender & Company, 1951), p. 425.

a different result in the O'Donnell and related cases provided that the corporation, the stock of which is sold, is liquidated so that the property comes into the hands of the purchaser of the stock. If the corporation is not liquidated, it remains the owner of its properties, and it would be impossible for persons dealing in its stock to create interests in its properties or even contractual rights to production therefrom. It would not make any difference, from the standpoint of the creation of the depletable interest, whether the seller or the purchaser liquidates the corporation, although problems unrelated to the oil and gas field may arise.[33]

2.12 Income from Severance and Sale of Mineral. A right otherwise classifiable as an economic interest will not be so classified if it can be satisfied in any way other than solely from a share in production. This principle is best illustrated by the Anderson case[34] in which an assignor conveyed certain properties to the taxpayer for a specified amount of cash, and an additional sum payable from the proceeds from production, and/or from sale of fee title to any of the properties conveyed. The Court held that the reservation of the interest in the fee changed the character of the interest retained because the assignor might receive a portion of the deferred payments from sale of fee title; such payments were not dependent entirely upon production of oil or gas. A contractual right to receive a definite sum of money within a definite time, with interim payments measured by production, is not an economic interest, because the right to share in the oil and gas proceeds is incidental to the covenant to pay a sum certain.

---

[33] *See* for example: *Commissioner* v. *Court Holding Co.*, 324 U.S. 331, 33 A.F.T.R. 593 (1945); *United States* v. *Cumberland Public Service Co.*, 338 U.S. 451, 38 A.F.T.R. 978 (1950); *Dallas Downtown Development Co.* (*Dissolved*), 12 T.C. 114 (1949), acq., 1950-1 C.B. 2, appeal dismissed without written opinion (*Nolle Prosse*) (5th Cir. 1950). But see also I.R.C., section 337.

[34] *Anderson* v. *Helvering, supra.*

CHAPTER III

Classification of Conveyances for Federal Tax Purposes

3.01 Introduction. In the preceding chapter, the nature of the various property interests was discussed. It was pointed out that ownership of the minerals encompassed the right to production plus the right to develop and operate. An interest in the production for the life of the property, divested of its right to develop and operate the property, was defined as a royalty interest. The grantee of operating rights may in turn divest himself of these operating rights, and at the same time create other types of property interests. Any owner of a property interest may assign all or a portion of his interest. Regardless of the particular legal forms or instruments by which the various conveyances are accomplished, the federal tax consequence is determined by reference to the interests of the parties involved, and to the consideration for which such interests were transferred. All such transactions will, for federal tax purposes, fall in one of the following classifications:

1. Lease or sublease
2. Sale or exchange

34

3. Anticipation of income
4. Sharing arrangement

The classification of the transaction is important because each type has a different tax consequence to the parties. For example, income derived from a sale or taxable exchange would constitute capital gain unless the taxpayer were a dealer in such properties. Any consideration in cash or property received in connection with a lease or sublease is considered a lease bonus, which is ordinary income subject to depletion. Anticipation of income has the effect of moving ordinary taxable income from a future to a current taxable period. A sharing arrangement involving no cash consideration is not a taxable transaction, and no income or gain arises therefrom. These general observations are not intended to cover all of the tax implications of the various types of conveyances, since this subject is treated in detail in later chapters. They do, however, show that the classification of the conveyances which will be defined and illustrated in this chapter is a matter of considerable significance.

3.02   Leasing or Subleasing Transactions. A transaction will be classified as a lease or a sublease in any case where the owner of operating rights assigns all or a portion of such rights to another person, for cash or its equivalent, and retains a continuing, nonoperating interest in production. Thus, if A, the owner of the working interest, assigns the working interest to B and retains an overriding royalty, he has made a sublease. It is the conjunction of type of interest assigned and type of interest retained that characterizes the transaction. The assignment of any type of interest other than operating rights cannot be a lease or a sublease. So if A had assigned an overriding royalty and retained the working interest, the transaction would not be a sublease because he did not assign the working interest or operating rights. On the other hand, unless a continuing, nonoperating interest is retained, the transaction cannot be a lease or a sublease. Hence, if A had assigned the working interest and retained an oil payment, the transaction would not be a sublease because the interest retained, although nonoperating, is not a continuing interest in production. A continuing interest is one the duration of which is co-extensive with the life of the lease.

If the grantor assigns all or a fraction of the working interest and retains two or more interests, one of which is a continuing, nonoperating interest, the transaction will be a lease or a sublease. Therefore, if A assigned all or a fraction of the working interest and retained an overriding royalty and an oil payment, the transaction would be a sublease. The same result would be achieved if A had retained a net profits interest and an oil payment. In both examples A assigned operating rights and retained a continuing, nonoperating interest, in the form of the overriding royalty in one case and the net profits interest in the other. The fact that the oil payment, which is not a continuing interest, is also retained does not change the tax consequence of the transaction.

3.03   Sales or Exchanges. A transaction will be treated as a sale or exchange under any of the following circumstances, if the consideration received is cash or its equivalent:

1. When the owner of any kind of property interest assigns all of his interest or a fractional interest identical, except as to quantity, with the fractional interest retained.

2. When the owner of a working interest assigns any type of continuing nonoperating interest in the property, and retains the working interest.

3. When the owner of any kind of continuing property interest assigns that interest and retains a noncontinuing interest in production.

The first class above includes a situation where the assignor parts with his entire interest in a property for cash or other property, as well as one where the assignor disposes of a divided or undivided interest in the property. It is characterized by the fact that the assignee receives an interest identical, except as to quantity, with that held by the assignor. Thus, if A owns the working interest and assigns the entire working interest to B, he has made a sale or exchange because B has received all of A's rights and B's interest is identical with that formerly held by A. A will also have made a sale or exchange if he assigns an undivided one-fourth interest to B because B's interest is identical, except as to quantity, with that held by A. The same result would occur regardless of the type of interest owned by the assignor, so long as he disposes of all or a fraction of his interest.

The second class of transactions that would be considered sales or exchanges embraces the carving out of various interests from the working interest. Present Revenue Service policy requires that the carved-out interest be a continuing interest. Hence, if the owner of the working interest carves out by assignment, for cash or other property of unlike kind, an overriding royalty or a net profits interest, he has made a sale or exchange. However, if he carves out an oil payment, a noncontinuing interest, the Revenue Service holds that he has not made a sale but has anticipated future income.

The only type of property or economic interest which is noncontinuing is the oil payment, because its life is limited in duration. Hence the third type of sale or exchange transaction is one where the assignor retains an oil payment upon the assignment of a continuing interest in a property for cash or other property of unlike kind. The interest assigned can be a working interest, a royalty, or an overriding royalty, because each is a continuing interest in the property; in this class of sale transaction it is not material whether the interest assigned is an operating or nonoperating interest.

3.04   Anticipation of Income. The anticipation of income doctrine holds that the sale of a carved-out oil payment results in a present realization of future production income. Since such income would be depletable if received in the future, the amount received currently is also subject to depletion. It has been stated previously that an oil payment is an interest in oil or gas in place, or an economic interest, but that it is not a continuing interest, because it is limited in time or amount and is not co-extensive with the life of the property from which it is created. Because the interest is not continuing, the Revenue Service takes the position that the consideration received for the carved-out oil payment should be treated as immediate income, like prepaid rental receipts.

This doctrine is applied by the Revenue Service if A, the owner of a working interest, assigns an oil payment, carved out of such working interest, to B for cash, without pledging to use the proceeds to develop the property. It would be equally applicable if A owned any other type of interest, including a longer-lived oil payment, from which the oil payment is assigned. It is not applicable if A pledges to use the proceeds for development, or if the oil payment is assigned by the owner of operating rights to one who, in consideration therefor, agrees to supply some service or material necessary to the development of the property. Such transactions constitute sharing arrangements, which are discussed below.

3.05   Sharing Arrangements. In the three preceding sections it was indicated that the principal consideration for the various assignments was cash or its equivalent in other property. If, however, the principal consideration for the assignment is the contractual assumption by the assignee of all or some portion of the burden of development of the property, the transaction is regarded as a sharing arrangement, even though the interests of the parties might otherwise make the transaction appear to be a sublease or a sale.

In a sharing arrangement the grantor conveys some interest in the minerals in return for a contribution of aid in the development of the property. The owner of the operating rights desires someone to share the burden and risk of developing the property. The assignee shares this burden and risk, either by obligating himself to participate directly in the development of the property (by drilling, equipping, furnishing geological information, securing dry hole commitments, or in any other way contributing services or property to such development), or indirectly by contributing cash or unrelated property to the grantor to be used exclusively for the development of the property. For tax purposes the grantor has entered upon neither a sale nor a leasing transaction.

It now becomes apparent that the classification and tax consequence of a particular transaction involving the creation or assignment of interests in oil and gas properties is dependent not only upon the nature of the interests of the parties, but also upon the consideration given by the assignee to the assignor. If cash or its equivalent is given, without restriction as to its use, the transaction might be construed as a lease or sublease, a sale, or anticipation of income, depending upon the interests of the parties in the property both before and after the assignment. If such cash is pledged to the development of the property, a sharing arrangement is created regardless of the interests of the parties. For example, if A owns the entire working interest in a property, and he assigns one-half to B for $50,000 in cash, the principles set forth above would indicate that he has made a sale, upon which he would compute gain or loss. However, if he pledges to use such cash for development of the property, he has entered into a sharing arrangement and would realize income only if his development costs were less than the cash he received. Although the tax consequences of sharing arrangements are discussed in Chapter 7, this brief statement will indicate the necessity for identifying the class of transaction between the parties. Such classification depends first upon the nature of the consideration moving between the parties, and second upon the nature of the interest acquired or retained by the parties. It might be noted, however, that sharing arrangements can be made only between the owner of the working interest or operating rights, on the one hand, and an assignee who assumes some part of the burden of development of the property on the other hand. If the property is already fully developed, the sharing concept is not applicable.

CHAPTER IV

Conveyances–Leasing or Subleasing Transactions

INCOME TAX CONSEQUENCES

4.01   Introduction. The federal tax classifications of conveyances as they are found in the petroleum industry having been set forth, it is necessary to consider in detail the income tax consequences of each type of conveyance. In this chapter the leasing or subleasing transaction will be examined more closely in order to set forth the applicable federal tax rules and to explore the efforts to minimize adverse tax consequences. It will be recalled that a leasing or subleasing transaction occurs when the assignor of all or a part of the operating rights receives cash or its equivalent and retains a continuing non-operating interest in production.[1] Table I illustrates some of

---

[1] G.C.M. 27322, 1952-2 C.B. 62. Cf. *West* v. *Commissioner,* 150 F.(2d) 723,

41

the conveyances which would be classified as a lease or sublease. It should be noted that the Revenue Service considers a
perpetual carried interest the equivalent of a net profits interest.[2] Accordingly, whenever the grantor of operating rights
retains a perpetual carried interest, he has made a lease rather
than a sale. If a transaction involves term minerals or term
royalties, its tax effects will depend upon the nature of the
term. As stated in Chapter 2, term interests which are extended
by production are continuing interests, while those not extended by production are considered oil payments.

4.02   Grantee of Nonproducing Properties. It has been indicated previously that the grantee of an oil and gas lease
ordinarily pays the lessor or grantor a sum of money called a
lease bonus. Since the bonus paid for a lease is an advance
royalty,[3] such sum may be regarded as prepaid royalty by the
grantee. As in the case of rent paid in advance for a period
longer than a year, the payment is not deductible when made
but must be amortized over the life of the property.[4] Since
the life of the property is measured by depletable units, so
likewise is the amortization period,[5] and it becomes academic
whether the recovery of the bonus investment is called amor-

---

34 A.F.T.R. 81 (5th Cir. 1945), cert. den., 326 U.S. 795, reh. den., 327 U.S.
815, second reh. den., 328 U.S. 877, third reh. den., 328 U.S. 881, and *Arthur
N. Trembley,* T.C. Memo. Op., Dkt. No. 16684, 1948 P-H T.C. Memo. Dec.,
Para. 48,270 (1948), where it was held that a leasing transaction was distin-
guishable from a sale by the presence (in a leasing transaction) or absence (in
a sale) of a dominating purpose to secure development of the property. *See also
Arthur E. Moreton,* T.C. Memo. Op., Dkt. No. 29488, 1952 P-H T.C. Memo.
Dec., Para. 52,138 (1952), appeal dismissed on stipulation of parties, 204
F.(2d) 689, − A.F.T.R. −, 1953 P-H, Para. 71,080 (10th Cir. April 1, 1953).
The Revenue Service does not agree with this test. G.C.M. 27322, *supra.*

[2] G.C.M. 22730, 1941-1 C.B. 214.

[3] *Burnet* v. *Harmel,* 287 U.S. 103, 11 A.F.T.R. 1085 (1932); G.C.M. 22730,
supra.

[4] U.S. Treas. Reg. 118, Section 39.23(a)-10.

[5] For years prior to 1939, it was recognized that the bonus paid for a nonproductive property could be amortized over the primary term of the lease.
U.S. Treas. Reg. 103, Section 19.23(a)-10, and U.S. Treas. Reg. 101, 94, and
86, Article 23(a)-10. With the promulgation of U.S. Treas. Reg. 111, Section
29.23(a)-10, the Revenue Service decreed that such a deduction was no longer
allowable.

TABLE I

Transactions Constituting Leases and Subleases *

(Fractions indicate share of gross production)

Property Owned Before Conveyance	Property Retained	Property Conveyed
1. Minerals ($\frac{7}{8}$ of $\frac{7}{8}$)	(a) Royalty ($\frac{1}{8}$ of $\frac{7}{8}$)	(a) Working interest ($\frac{7}{8}$ of $\frac{7}{8}$)
	(b) Net profits interest (40% of net profits from the interest conveyed)	(b) Minerals ($\frac{7}{8}$ of $\frac{7}{8}$) subject to net profits interest
	(c) Royalty ($\frac{1}{8}$ of $\frac{7}{8}$) and overriding royalty ($\frac{1}{8}$ of $\frac{7}{8}$)	(c) Working interest ($\frac{7}{8}$ of $\frac{7}{8}$)
	(d) Royalty ($\frac{1}{8}$ of $\frac{7}{8}$) and oil payment (first $50,000 out of $\frac{3}{8}$ of $\frac{7}{8}$)	(d) Working interest ($\frac{5}{8}$ of $\frac{7}{8}$ until payout of oil payment, then $\frac{7}{8}$ of $\frac{7}{8}$)
	(e) Net profits interest (25% of net profits from the interest conveyed) and minerals ($\frac{7}{8}$ of $\frac{7}{8}$)**	(e) Minerals ($\frac{7}{8}$ of $\frac{7}{8}$) subject to net profits interest
2. Working interest ($\frac{7}{8}$ of $\frac{7}{8}$)	(a) Overriding royalty ($\frac{1}{8}$ of $\frac{7}{8}$)	(a) Working interest ($\frac{7}{8}$ of $\frac{7}{8}$)
	(b) Net profits interest (15% of net profits from the interest conveyed)	(b) Working interest ($\frac{7}{8}$ of $\frac{7}{8}$) subject to net profits interest
	(c) Overriding royalty ($\frac{1}{8}$ of $\frac{7}{8}$) and carried working interest, nonperpetual (no production until payout, then $\frac{3}{8}$ of $\frac{7}{8}$)	(c) Working interest ($\frac{7}{8}$ of $\frac{7}{8}$ until payout, then $\frac{5}{8}$ of $\frac{7}{8}$)
	(d) Net profits interest (20% of net profits from the interest conveyed) and oil payment (first $50,000 out of $\frac{3}{8}$ of $\frac{7}{8}$)**	(d) Working interest ($\frac{5}{8}$ of $\frac{7}{8}$ until payout of oil payment, then $\frac{7}{8}$ of $\frac{7}{8}$) subject to net profits interest
	(e) Overriding royalty ($\frac{1}{8}$ of $\frac{7}{8}$) and working interest ($\frac{7}{8}$ of $\frac{7}{8}$)**	(e) Working interest ($\frac{5}{8}$ of $\frac{7}{8}$)

* This list of transactions is illustrative only, and not all-inclusive. If for cash or its equivalent, the grantor conveys any operating rights and retains any continuing nonoperating interest, he has made a lease. The retention of any additional interest or combination of additional interests of any kind will not change the character of the transaction.

** As indicated in paragraph 12.03 the Revenue Service would probably regard the two retained interests as a single property and, if such view is sustained, the designated transactions would constitute sales or exchanges rather than leases or subleases.

tization or depletion. Common parlance styles the bonus paid as leasehold cost and the recovery of such cost in relation to production as depletion. If the property does not become productive and the lease lapses, expires, or is released, the lessee or grantee charges off his investment as an abandonment loss.

The principles stated above may be illustrated as follows: Assume that A, the owner of minerals, grants a lease to B, retaining a one-eighth royalty, and that B pays A $10,000 for the lease. B, the grantee, capitalizes as leasehold cost the $10,000 lease bonus paid to A. If the property becomes productive he will recover such cost through depletion allowances as explained in Chapter 11. If the property does not become productive, B may claim a $10,000 loss at the time of termination or expiration of the lease.

As explained in paragraph 11.02, however, it is not necessary that B have a depletable basis to claim depletion computed by the percentage of income method. Any expenditure he makes that must be capitalized as leasehold cost may be of no tax benefit to him if the property becomes productive. Consequently, it is to B's interest from a tax standpoint, as well as from a business standpoint, to keep the bonus payment as low as possible.

4.03   Grantor of Nonproducing Properties. A lease bonus, the payment received for granting a lease, is considered an advance royalty, which is ordinary income in the year of receipt, and which is subject to depletion.[6] If the grantor had any income tax basis in the mineral property prior to the assignment, such basis is carried over and becomes the basis of

---

[6] U.S. Treas. Reg. 118, Section 39.23(m)-10. I.R.C., Section 452, under certain circumstances, grants an accrual-basis taxpayer an election to defer the reporting, for income tax purposes, of items representing prepaid income. The statutory language is such that a lease bonus might be included in the definition of prepaid income, in which event the taxpayer may have the election to defer the reporting of the income in accord with the statutory rule. However, present Revenue Service policy does not interpret Section 452 as having any application to a lease bonus.

his retained royalty interest.[7] The theory underlying this transfer of basis is that, after adjustment for the amount of the bonus received, the royalty or overriding royalty interest retained, freed of the burdens of development and operation, is equivalent in value to the interest owned before the grant, which was subject to such burdens. The depletion claimed in respect of the bonus is applied to reduce the basis of the interest retained.

The principles stated above may be illustrated if it is assumed that A has acquired ownership of all the minerals in a tract of land at a cost of $15,000. He grants a lease, retaining a royalty, to B for a cash consideration of $10,000. The cash received is a lease bonus, so A realizes taxable income of $10,000 upon the granting of the lease. Since such income is subject to depletion,[8] it may be assumed for the purpose of this illustration that A claims depletion of $2,750; his net taxable income from the transaction is $7,250. The basis of his mineral interest is carried over to the retained royalty, but it must be reduced by depletion claimed; hence the adjusted basis of the retained royalty would be $12,250.

Because the lease bonus constitutes ordinary income, the grantor is confronted with conflicting motives. From a business standpoint he wants to get as large a bonus as possible, but from a tax standpoint he wants to prevent the concentration of ordinary income in a single year. The grantor and grantee of a lease may find a common interest in minimizing taxes by the use of plans such as those discussed in paragraphs 4.06 through 4.09, below.

4.04   Grantee of Producing Properties. If a property has been partially or fully developed before the assignment, part of the cash consideration paid by the grantee is for equipment. It is apparent that such consideration must be apportioned

---

[7] G.C.M. 22730, *supra.*

[8] For methods of computing depletion on lease bonuses, see paragraph 11.05.

equitably between leasehold cost or bonus and equipment.[9] For example, assume that the value of a property is $150,000, consisting of $30,000 worth of equipment and $120,000 of leasehold value. If the entire interest were sold for $150,000 it is clear that the purchaser should treat $30,000 as equipment cost and $120,000 as leasehold cost. If the property is subleased rather than sold, the assignor retains a continuing, nonoperating interest in production, and the interest acquired by the assignee is worth less to the extent of the value of the interest retained. The same principle of equitable allocation is applicable, but such allocation must be based upon the respective values of the separate rights acquired by the grantee. Thus, if the owner of the property described above subleased the property to B for $100,000 in cash, retaining an overriding royalty, B would treat $30,000 of his expenditure as equipment cost, and $70,000 as leasehold cost. As in the case of a sale, B in this transaction has acquired the entire interest in the equipment, which is stated to have a value of $30,000. Since the total value must equal the sum of the values of the component parts, it follows that the value of the leasehold burdened with the overriding royalty is the difference between the aggregate consideration and the value of the equipment.

If some additional consideration passes from grantee to grantor, such as an obligation of the grantee to develop the property or an obligation of the grantee to operate the property for an insufficient share of production, the foregoing principles are also applicable, because such obligations would tend to reduce the value of the interest acquired. If a portion of the consideration is the undertaking of a development obligation, the transaction is a sharing arrangement, which is discussed in Chapter 7. If the grantee undertakes to operate the property

---

[9] U.S. Treas. Reg. 118, Section 39.23(e)-4; *Grain King Manufacturing Co.,* 14 B.T.A. 793 (1928), appeal dismissed for lack of jurisdiction, 47 F.(2d) 608, 9 A.F.T.R. 951 (2nd Cir. 1931); Cf. *Hazeltine Corporation,* 32 B.T.A. 4 (1935), nonacq., XIV-1 C.B. 30.

for an insufficient share of production, the cash consideration cannot be less, in an arms-length transaction, than the net fair market value of the property. It might, however, be less than the fair market value of the equipment, and under such circumstances it might appear that the lease should have a negative value. A negative basis for the lease would not be recognized for tax purposes, but under such circumstances the lease should carry only a nominal value, and most of the cash consideration paid should be allocated to equipment. Thus, if A, in the preceding illustration, had retained the overriding royalty, and in addition had retained a large oil payment payable from the major portion of production accruing to the assigned interest, and B had paid only $10,000 in cash, it would appear that B should allocate all but a nominal amount of the consideration to equipment.

4.05   Grantor of Producing Properties. When a leasing or subleasing transaction occurs after production commences, and the grantor owns equipment on the property, a part of the consideration received is applicable thereto.[10] The Revenue Service has contended for many years that any cash consideration must be applied first to the recovery of basis of equipment, and any excess of cash received must be treated as lease bonus.[11] On the other hand, the Choate [12] case held that a loss on the sale of equipment could be incurred, and it would follow that a gain could likewise be realized. It should be emphasized that in the Choate case the evidence showed that the equipment was sold for the highest price obtainable, and the case cannot be relied upon as authority for claiming a loss where the stated consideration for assignment of the equipment is less than the true value of the equipment. If the grantor has suffered a loss on the sale of the equipment, he should procure and retain

---

[10] *Columbia Oil and Gas Company,* 41 B.T.A. 38 (1940), acq. on other issues, 1943 C.B. 5, aff'd, 118 F.(2d) 459, 26 A.F.T.R. 715 (5th Cir. 1941).

[11] G.C.M. 23623, 1943 C.B. 313.

[12] *Choate* v. *Commissioner,* 324 U.S. 1, 33 A.F.T.R. 297 (1945).

adequate factual evidence as to the value of, and sales price allocable to, equipment.

If the consideration received is less than the basis of the equipment assigned and no loss can be proved on its disposition, a question arises as to the proper method of extinguishing the remaining basis of the property. Prior to the Choate case, the Revenue Service had maintained that the remaining basis should be transferred to the basis of the depletable royalty or overriding royalty interest retained, and thereafter extinguished by depletion.[13] The Supreme Court in the Choate case recognized that a loss existed in the facts presented to it, but by way of dictum implied that depreciable cost could never become depletable cost. Such a conclusion appears to be contrary to those provisions of the regulations that require a reallocation of basis between depreciable and depletable property upon an exchange of properties of like kind.[14] Despite this fact, for a few years the Revenue Service accorded partial recognition to the dictum in the Choate case by permitting the excess of the depreciable basis over the cash received upon granting of a sublease to be amortized over the life of the property on a unit-of-production or on a straight-line method. Now, however, separate amortization will no longer be allowed, and any excess market value of equipment conveyed over consideration received must be transferred from depreciable to depletable basis.

When the cash consideration received exceeds the basis of the depreciable property, it was the viewpoint of the Revenue Service that such excess constitutes lease bonus. This rule has been modified so that the excess of the cash consideration over the fair market value of the equipment conveyed is treated as bonus, and the difference between fair market value and basis of equipment is treated as gain or loss on sale. Where the intent of such a transaction is to secure a cash consideration

---

[13] G.C.M. 23623, *supra*.
[14] U.S. Treas. Reg. 118, Section 39.113(a)(6)-1(c)(1).

equivalent to the market value of the equipment transferred, such intent should be expressly stated in the assignment so that form, in addition to substance, favors the taxpayer. In many instances, the equipment is assigned separately so that the amount paid therefor is clearly stated.

MINIMIZING TAX CONSEQUENCES

4.06   Introduction. It was indicated above that the receipt of a lease bonus by a grantor and the payment of one by a grantee pose some tax problems to both. The grantor realizes immediate ordinary income, and even though he may claim depletion on the bonus, there may be a concentration of income in one year. The grantee must capitalize the bonus and recover it through depletion, but his over-all depletion may not be increased by such capitalized cost. These facts have led to efforts to minimize the bonus or to spread the bonus over a period of years.

4.07   Increased Royalty. One means by which the adverse effect of a large bonus can be avoided is by retention of a larger royalty or override by the grantor. It has been stated that no sanctity attached to the usual one-eighth royalty, and the owner of the minerals may reserve as royalty any fraction to which his lessee will agree. If the property is in a proven area so that there is a good possibility of obtaining production, the grantor will make no economic sacrifice by foregoing or reducing the usual bonus to reserve a larger royalty. He will thereby reduce the concentration of income in a single year. The grantee gains to the extent that he will have little or no bonus which must be capitalized as leasehold cost, but he does reduce his share of future income.

Thus, if a property is particularly valuable, the grantor might reserve a three-sixteenths royalty rather than a one-eighth royalty and receive a smaller bonus or no bonus at all.

Should the grantor in a subsequent, unrelated transaction convey all, or a fractional interest, of his retained royalty for a cash consideration, he would realize capital gain, because the transaction would be a sale rather than a leasing transaction.

4.08   Deferred Bonus. If the income from the bonus payment can be spread over a period of years, the grantor's problem is reduced considerably, although the grantee's problem is not affected. A method of deferring the income created by a substantial bonus was illustrated by the Kleberg[15] case, in which the grantee contracted to pay a bonus over a twenty-year period and a cash-basis taxpayer was permitted to report it as income when received. Although the Titus[16] case might indicate that the same conclusion would apply to an accrual-basis taxpayer, such a result seems inconsistent with the present concept of the accrual method of accounting, in the absence of some contingency that might obviate payment. A subsequent Kleberg[17] case recognized that a sale of such bonus contract constituted a sale of a property right, which was a capital asset. The Cowden[18] case reached the conclusion under Texas law that if the contractual rights were assigned the day following the execution of the contract, there was a sale of a property interest held for more than six months. Such reasoning treats a bonus as income from production attributable to the royalty retained, and an assignment thereof as a conveyance of a substantial property right. While the case was on appeal, the Commissioner reached an agreed settlement with the taxpayer compromising the disputed tax, thus leaving

---

[15] *Alice G. K. Kleberg*, 43 B.T.A. 277 (1941), nonacq. on this issue, 1952-1 C.B. 5, acq. and nonacq. on other issues, 1941-1 C.B. 6, 16.

[16] *C. W. Titus, Inc.*, 33 B.T.A. 928 (1936), nonacq., XV-1 C.B. 46, appeal dismissed on stipulation of parties, 88 F.(2d) 1007, 19 A.F.T.R. 242 (10 Cir. 1937).

[17] *Alice G. K. Kleberg*, 2 T.C. 1024 (1943), nonacq. on this issue, 1952-1 C.B. 5, acq. on other issues, 1944 C.B. 16.

[18] *R. B. Cowden*, T.C. Memo. Op., Dkt. No. 23,246, 1950 P-H T.C. Memo. Dec., Para. 50,304 (1950), remanded on stipulation of parties, 202 F.(2d) 748, 43 A.F.T.R. 439 (5th Cir. 1953).

the question unsettled, but leaving the Tax Court decision on the record.

4.09   Minimium Royalty. One means of accomplishing the desired objective of reducing the tax impact on both grantor and grantee is a lease with the usual royalty reservation but with the additional provision that a minimum royalty, expressed in dollars, be payable regardless of production, such minimum royalty to be chargeable against future production, if any, accruing to the royalty interest. The regulations [19] provide that the grantor receiving the minimum royalty has depletable ordinary income, but such income obviously is spread over a period of years. The regulations [20] also provide that the grantee may expense such minimum royalties as paid or deduct them at the time they are recovered from production, upon proper exercise of the option by the grantee.

It will be apparent that a minimum royalty provision most nearly fulfills the desires of both grantor and grantee from a tax standpoint. The grantor spreads over a period of years what might otherwise be a large amount of income in a single year, although he does expose himself to the risk of surrender of the lease by the grantee. The grantee, if the aggregate minimum royalty does not exceed by too much the amount of bonus which would otherwise be payable, achieves the optimum tax result, because upon proper election he is permitted to deduct the minimum royalty payments. If, therefore, he can substitute a minimum royalty provision for a lease bonus, payments of the minimum royalty would not increase his leasehold cost.

---

[19] U.S. Treas. Reg. 118, Section 39.23(m)-10(b).
[20] U.S. Treas. Reg. 118, Section 39.23(m)-10(e).

CHAPTER V

Conveyances–Sales or Exchanges

INCOME TAX CONSEQUENCES

5.01   Introduction. It was indicated in Chapter 3 that there are a great variety of transactions that, for income tax purposes, are sales or exchanges. In general, neither the tax nor the accounting concepts applicable are as abstruse as in the other types of grant or assignment of interests in oil and gas properties. Hence, the principal problem is one of classification of the transaction, and if it is properly classifiable as a sale or exchange, the general principles of income tax law will control the results. As a consequence, less attention will be devoted to the development of principles in this chapter and more will be given to illustrations of the tax consequences of different types of sales or exchanges. Table II lists transactions that are considered sales or exchanges. When using the table, the distinctions discussed in Chapter 2 should be kept in mind. A carried interest for the entire duration of the property will be treated as a net profits interest. Therefore, in Items 1(c), 1(e), 3(b), and 3(e), the carried interest retained must be nonperpetual if the transaction is to qualify as a sale and not as a lease. Net profits interests and perpetual carried working interests are considered types of royalties, and can therefore be substituted for royalty or overriding royalty in the table. If a transaction involves term minerals or term royalty, its tax effect depends upon the type of the term. It was pointed out in Chapter 2 that term interests that are extended by production are continuing interests, whereas those not so extended are treated as oil payments.

Item 6 also may deserve separate mention because it introduces a concept not previously discussed. The listed transaction involves a "vertical cut" oil payment. The term means that the interest assigned will pay out simultaneously with the property retained, and it constitutes a sale because it is not carved out of a longer-lived interest. A "horizontal cut" oil payment refers to the assignment of the front end of an oil payment, such as the first $50,000 out of $\frac{1}{8}$ of $\frac{7}{8}$ of production, carved out of a payment of the first $100,000 out of $\frac{1}{8}$ of $\frac{7}{8}$. In such case the assigned payment will pay out before the retained interest, and the consideration received is therefore considered to represent an anticipation of future income.[1]

5.02 *Segregation of Property Interests.* It should be noted that property interests may be segregated in transactions constituting sales or exchanges. Thus, rights to oil may be disposed of and rights to gas retained.[2] Rights to minerals below a specified depth may be assigned while rights above such depth are retained.[3] Rights to property interests in a geographical area,

---

[1] I.T. 4003, 1950-1 C.B. 10; *See also* G.C.M. 24849, 1946-1 C.B. 66 and Chapter 6.

[2] *Gray v. Commissioner,* 183 F.(2d) 329, 39 A.F.T.R. 750 (5th Cir. 1950).

[3] *Mascot Oil Company,* 29 B.T.A. 652 (1933), appeal dismissed on stipula-

TABLE II

Transactions Constituting Sales or Exchanges

(Fractions indicate share of gross production)

Property Owned Before Conveyance	Property Retained	Property Conveyed
1. Minerals ($\frac{8}{8}$ of $\frac{8}{8}$)	(a) Minerals ($\frac{5}{8}$ of $\frac{8}{8}$)	(a) Minerals ($\frac{3}{8}$ of $\frac{8}{8}$)
	(b) Working interest ($\frac{7}{8}$ of $\frac{8}{8}$)	(b) Royalty ($\frac{1}{8}$ of $\frac{8}{8}$)
	(c) Carried working interest, non-perpetual (no production until payout, then $\frac{3}{8}$ of $\frac{7}{8}$)	(c) Royalty ($\frac{1}{8}$ of $\frac{8}{8}$) and working interest ($\frac{8}{8}$ of $\frac{7}{8}$ until payout, then $\frac{5}{8}$ of $\frac{7}{8}$)
	(d) Oil payment (first $50,000 out of $\frac{7}{8}$ of $\frac{8}{8}$)	(d) Minerals ($\frac{7}{8}$ of $\frac{8}{8}$ until payout of oil payment, then $\frac{8}{8}$ of $\frac{8}{8}$)
	(e) Any combination of minerals, working interest, nonperpetual carried interest, and oil payment	(e) Any continuing interest or combination of continuing interests
2. Royalty ($\frac{1}{8}$ of $\frac{8}{8}$)	(a) Royalty ($\frac{3}{32}$ of $\frac{8}{8}$)	(a) Royalty ($\frac{1}{32}$ of $\frac{8}{8}$)
	(b) Oil payment (first $50,000 out of $\frac{1}{8}$ of $\frac{8}{8}$)	(b) Royalty (no production until payout of oil payment, then $\frac{1}{8}$ of $\frac{8}{8}$)
3. Working interest ($\frac{7}{8}$ of $\frac{8}{8}$)	(a) Working interest ($\frac{8}{8}$ of $\frac{8}{8}$)	(a) Working interest ($\frac{2}{8}$ of $\frac{7}{8}$) or Overriding royalty ($\frac{8}{8}$ of $\frac{8}{8}$)
	(b) Carried working interest, non-perpetual (no production until payout, then $\frac{4}{8}$ of $\frac{7}{8}$)	(b) Working interest ($\frac{8}{8}$ of $\frac{7}{8}$ until payout, then $\frac{4}{8}$ of $\frac{7}{8}$)
	(c) Working interest ($\frac{8}{8}$ of $\frac{7}{8}$ until payout, then $\frac{4}{8}$ of $\frac{7}{8}$)	(c) Carried working interest, nonperpetual (no production until payout, then $\frac{4}{8}$ of $\frac{7}{8}$)

(d)	Oil payment (first $50,000 out of $3/8$ of $7/8$)	Working interest ($5/8$ of $7/8$ until payout of oil payment, then $7/8$ of $7/8$)
(e)	Any combination of working interest, non-perpetual carried working interest, and oil payment	Any continuing interest or combination of continuing interests
4. Overriding royalty ($1/8$ of $7/8$) (a)	Overriding royalty ($1/16$ of $7/8$)	Overriding royalty ($1/16$ of $7/8$)
(b)	Oil payment (first $50,000 out of $3/32$ of $7/8$)	Overriding royalty ($1/32$ of $7/8$ until payout of oil payment, then $1/8$ of $7/8$)
5. Net profits interest (30% of net profits) (a)	Net profits interest (10% of net profits)	Net profits interest (20% of net profits)
(b)	Oil payment (first $50,000 out of 25% of net profits)	Net profits interest (5% of net profits until payout of oil payment, then 30% of net profits)
6. Oil payment (first $50,000 out of $1/8$ of $7/8$)	Oil payment (first $30,000 out of $3/40$ of $7/8$)	Oil payment (first $20,000 out of $2/40$ of $7/8$)
7. Any property interest	Nothing	Entire property interest

such as "the SW ¼ of section 10," may be conveyed without any effect on similar interests in contiguous areas.

5.03 **Nontaxable Exchanges.** If a transaction is properly classifiable as an exchange, it is possible that it may fall within the general income provisions covering nontaxable exchanges of property.[4] Exchanges of property of like kind held for investment, or for use in a trade or business, are nontaxable,[5] and if boot is received on the exchange of such properties, the gain, if any, is taxable only to the extent of the boot received.[6] There have not been very many cases involving exchanges of oil or gas properties, but it has been held that the following were exchanges of property of like kind: producing leases exchanged for producing leases,[7] city lot for minerals,[8] ranch land and improvements for working interest,[9] and minerals for surface.[10] The exchange of an oil payment for any type of continuing interest in oil and gas is viewed by the Revenue Service as a taxable exchange, and this view finds support in the Midfield case [11] where the exchange of an oil payment for an overriding royalty was held taxable and in the Vaccaro [12] and Kimbell [13] cases, where the exchange of a lease for an oil

---

tion of parties, 75 F.(2d) 1009, 15 A.F.T.R. 361 (9th Cir. 1935); *Berry Oil Co.* v. *United States,* 25 F. Supp. 96, 21 A.F.T.R. 1046 (Ct. Cls. 1938), cert. den., 307 U.S. 634 (1939).

[4] I.R.C., Section 1031(a) [1939 I.R.C., Section 112(b)(1)].

[5] U.S. Treas. Reg. 118, Section 39.112(b)(1)-1.

[6] I.R.C., Section 1031(b) [1939 I.R.C., Section 112(c)(1)]; U.S. Treas. Reg. 118, Section 39.112(c)-1 and (e)-1.

[7] *E. C. Laster,* 43 B.T.A. 159 (1940), acq. on other issues, 1941-1 C.B. 7, nonacq. on another issue, 1952-2 C.B. 5, modified on another issue, 128 F.(2d) 4, 29 A.F.T.R. 465 (5th Cir. 1942).

[8] *Kate J. Crichton,* 42 B.T.A. 490 (1940), acq., 1952-1 C.B. 2, aff'd, 122 F.(2d) 181, 27 A.F.T.R. 824 (5th Cir. 1941).

[9] I.T. 4093, 1952-2 C.B. 130.

[10] I.T. 4093, *supra.*

[11] *Midfield Oil Company,* 39 B.T.A. 1154 (1939), acq., 1939-2 C.B. 25.

[12] *John Vaccaro,* T. C. Memo. Op., Dkt. No. 111858, 1943 P-H T.C. Memo. Dec., Para. 43,433 (1943), appeal dismissed on stipulation of parties, Dkt. No. 11080, 33 A.F.T.R. 1672 (5th Cir. 1944).

[13] *Kay Kimbell,* 41 B.T.A. 940 (1940), acq. and nonacq. on other issues, 1940-2 C.B. 5, 12.

payment was held taxable. This question is unsettled, however, because of a decision in the Fleming case,[14] which held that under Texas law the exchange of royalties for carved-out oil payments was an exchange of properties of like kind. This problem is discussed in more detail in Chapter 6.

5.04   Grantor. The grantor of a mineral property in a sale or taxable exchange realizes income or incurs loss to the extent of the difference between the fair market value of the consideration received and the basis of the property conveyed. Such basis would include both depreciable and depletable costs, if any. For example, assume that A owns a producing oil property, and that his records disclose the following information:

```
Original cost:
    Leasehold  ..........................$ 10,000
    Equipment  ..........................  50,000
    Intangible drilling costs
        (expensed for tax purposes) ........ 200,000
Depreciation allowed or allowable .........  20,000
Depletion allowed or allowable ............  75,000
Sales price ...........................  300,000
```

Two points should be remembered in determining his gain or loss. First, intangible drilling costs which have been expensed are not included in either depletable or depreciable basis.[15] Second, depreciable and depletable bases must be reduced respectively by the depreciation and depletion allowed or allowable, except that neither basis is reduced below zero.[16] In other words, if the allowed or allowable depletion exceeds the depletable basis, as it well may, the depleted basis becomes

---

[14] *Fleming* v. *Campbell,* 205 F.(2d) 549, — A.F.T.R. —, 1953 P-H, Para. 72,611 (5th Cir. June 26, 1953).

[15] *Continental Oil Co.* v. *Jones,* 177 F.(2d) 508, 38 A.F.T.R. 815 (10th Cir. 1949), cert. den., 339 U.S. 931.

[16] This point may be inferred from a careful reading of G.C.M. 17760, 1937-1 C.B. 102 and G.C.M. 22239, 1940-2 C.B. 105; *See also Beulah B. Crane,* 3 T.C. 585 (1944), rev'd on other issues, 331 U.S. 1, 35 A.F.T.R. 776 (1947), involving a zero depreciable basis of property inherited subject to a mortgage not assumed. If the depletion allowed or allowable has exceeded the depletable basis, subsequent expenditures, which are ordinarily added to depletable basis, must be reduced by such excess. G.C.M. 22239, *supra.*

zero and not a negative figure. A will therefore compute his gain as follows:

Sales price			$ 300,000
Deduct basis:			
Depletable:			
Leasehold cost	$ 10,000		
Depletion allowed or allowable, but not more than cost	10,000		
	0		
Depreciable:			
Equipment	$ 50,000		
Depreciation allowed or allowable.	20,000	30,000	30,000
Gain			$ 270,000

5.05 *Nature of Income Realized.* The income realized by the grantor in a taxable sale or exchange may be ordinary income, capital gain, or gain subject to the provisions of Section 1231 of the Internal Revenue Code [1939 I.R.C., Section 117(j)]. Some taxpayers are dealers in oil properties, just as some taxpayers are dealers in real estate.[17] A large number of purchases and sales without engaging in the development of properties is indicative of a trader's business. If a taxpayer is so classified, any gain or loss on a sale or exchange of a property is included in his ordinary income. With that exception, oil and gas leases, developed or undeveloped, are real property used in trade or business,[18] and equipment is depreciable property used in trade or business. If held for more than six months, both are Section 1231 assets. Aggregate gain from the sale or exchange of such assets in any one taxable year is treated as long-term capital gain. Aggregate loss is reported as ordinary loss. Unless held for sale, oil and gas interests other than leases are capital assets if held for investment,[19] and Section 1231 assets if held for use in trade or business for more than six months.

---

[17] *See* I.R.C., Section 1221(1) [1939 I.R.C., Section 117(a)(1)(A)]; *Greene v. Commissioner,* 141 F.(2d) 645, 32 A.F.T.R. 459 (5th Cir. 1944) cert. den., 323 U.S. 717.

[18] I.T. 3693, 1944 C.B. 272.

[19] *J. E. Thompson,* T.C. Memo. Op., Dkt. No. 14201, 1948 P-H T.C. Memo. Dec., Para. 48,164 (1948); *P. A. Davis,* T.C. Memo Op., Dkt. No. 26090, 1952 P-H T.C. Memo. Dec., Para. 52,216 (1952), taxpayer's appeal dismissed for want of prosecution, — F.(2d) —, — A.F.T.R.—, 1953 P-H, Para. 72,464 (5th Cir. 1953).

5.06 *Transfers Without Consideration.* Certain types of transfers of mineral properties occur which have the form of a sale or exchange except that no real consideration for the assignment moves to the grantor. Such assignments may occur by gift, by devise or inheritance, by partial or complete liquidation of corporations, or as dividends in kind. In general, such transfers are without income tax consequence to the grantor, and he derives no taxable gain or loss from the transfer.

5.07 *Basis in Case of Nontaxable Exchanges.* Like the grantor in other nontaxable exchanges the grantor of a mineral property, in a nontaxable exchange, prorates the basis of the property he assigns to the various types of property he receives in the proportion of their respective fair market values. For example, assume that A owns a royalty in which he has a basis of $100,000 after deduction of depletion allowed or allowable. He transfers this royalty to B in exchange for a producing lease, the total value of which is $200,000 including equipment with a value of $50,000. He will assign $25,000 of his basis to equipment and $75,000 to leasehold.

The allocation of basis required in such exchanges can have an adverse tax consequence if producing leases are exchanged. For example, A owns a producing property with an adjusted basis for depreciation of $100,000 and a zero adjusted basis for depletion. He exchanges this property for a producing lease valued at $500,000, of which $100,000 is the value of equipment. He must allocate $20,000 of his basis to equipment and $80,000 to leasehold.[20] Because of percentage depletion he will probably derive no tax benefit from the basis which was allocated to leasehold, and he has, in effect, lost the tax benefit of $80,000 in deductions. It is probable that this adverse effect could be avoided by exchanging equipment for equipment and lease for lease in separate exchanges.

5.08 **Grantee.** The grantee of a mineral property in a sale

---

[20] *E. C. Laster, supra.*

or exchange is confronted with no unusual tax problems. In a taxable exchange he will assign his cost to the various properties acquired, and if property other than cash is given up in the exchange, he is, as to such property, the grantor and may realize income or incur loss. If the exchange is nontaxable, he prorates the basis of the property given up to the various properties received. In the illustration stated above, *B* would apply all of his basis, both depletable and depreciable, to the royalty received in the exchange. It might be noted that his depreciable basis becomes depletable basis after the exchange.

MINIMIZING TAX CONSEQUENCES

5.09   Introduction. The principal adverse tax consequence arising from a sale or exchange is the grantee's high depletable basis in the property acquired. It has been previously stated that the owner of a mineral property is entitled to percentage depletion, even though he has no depletable basis in the property. As a consequence, he may gain no long-term tax advantage because he has a depletable cost. In addition, if the purchaser is planning to pay for the property out of its production, income taxes may absorb a substantial part of the income available for payment of the purchase obligation. These problems are met frequently by the use of a retained production payment.

5.10   Retained Production Payment. It has been stated that the grant of any type of property interest subject only to a retained production payment constitutes a sale or exchange. Thus, *A* may own a producing oil property worth $1,000,000, which he wants to sell and *B* wants to buy. If *B* purchases the property for cash, assume that $200,000 of the purchase price would be allocable to equipment and $800,000 to the leases. *A* may sell the property, subject to a retained oil payment of $700,000, for $300,000 in cash. In determining gain or loss on sale, A would allocate his basis between the interest sold and the interest retained in the proportion of their respective fair market values, and compute the gain or loss as the difference between the cash received and the basis of the interest sold. A could, if he so desired, then sell the retained oil payment to another party and derive gain, or loss, from such sale.

This plan, involving the retention of an oil payment and its immediate sale, is commonly called the ABC plan and is frequently executed through a broker, who purchases the entire property, sells it subject to a retained oil payment, and then sells the oil payment. If A sells his retained interest also, he is in the same position as though he had sold the entire property outright. B's position is substantially different, however, from what it would have been if he had purchased the entire property. B would have an equipment cost of $200,000 and his leasehold cost would be only $100,000. To accomplish this result, B has, of course, given up a substantial share of the production, but he has gained another material advantage. The production going to satisfy the production payment does not constitute taxable income to B, and in effect he pays for the property from income before taxes. The advantage becomes clear if the above-described result is compared with B's situation if he had bought the entire property with borrowed funds, or subject to a mortgage of $700,000. He would then receive the oil proceeds which would otherwise have been paid to the oil payment owner, but these proceeds would increase B's taxable income. The resulting increase in B's income tax liability would reduce materially the amount available for payment of the purchase obligation. The advantage in this type of arrangement does not all rest with the purchaser of the property. A, the seller, may also get a better price for his property by making it possible for the buyer to obtain the property under more favorable tax circumstances.

CHAPTER VI

Conveyances–Anticipation of Income

6.01   Introduction. Unlike the subject matter of the preceding two chapters, the anticipation of income theory is applicable to only one type of transaction in the oil and gas business. That transaction involves the assignment of a production payment (hereinafter referred to as an oil payment) for a consideration which is not pledged to the development of the property. As stated in paragraph 2.07, an oil payment, for federal income tax purposes, is a right to oil and gas in place which entitles its owner to a specified fraction of production for a limited period of time, or until a specified sum of money or a specified number of units of oil or gas has been received. It has been noted previously that a term mineral interest and a term royalty interest, if the term is not extended by production, are types of oil payments, because they are limited in time. More commonly, however, an oil payment is defined in terms of a certain dollar sum or a sum determined by a formula. The characteristic that distinguishes the oil payment from an overriding royalty is the fact that the oil payment is limited in time or amount so that its duration is not co-

62

extensive with the producing life of the property from which it is payable. Presumably because of this difference, the Revenue Service has adopted, relative to the nature of income derived on assignment of a carved-out oil payment, a theory that is entirely different from the rules applicable in the case of assignment of an overriding royalty. The tax consequences of the assignment of an oil payment are discussed in this chapter only in so far as they relate to the assignor, because the assignee of an oil payment is confronted with no special problems as a result of the assignment.

6.02   *Retained Oil Payments.* Oil payments may be created in one of two ways. An oil payment is said to be retained if the owner of any interest in an oil or gas property assigns his interest and retains an oil payment, payable out of future production from the property interest assigned. An oil payment is said to be carved out if the owner of any interest in an oil or gas property assigns an oil payment to another person but retains his interest in the property from which the oil payment is assigned. The tax consequences attaching to a retained oil payment do not fall within the anticipation of income theory, and hence do not properly belong within the scope of this chapter. However, for the sake of completeness, and to differentiate the tax consequences attaching to the two types of oil payments, it appears desirable to consider this question briefly.

Excluding the possibilities of sharing arrangements as discussed in the following chapter, the grantor of an oil or gas property who retains an oil payment will be required to allocate the income tax basis of the property prior to the assignment between the interest assigned and the oil payment retained in proportion to their respective fair market values.[1] The cost so allocated to the retained oil payment will then become the basis for depletion and for computation of gain or

---

[1] *Columbia Oil & Gas Co.*, 41 B.T.A. 38 (1940), acq. on other issues, 1940-1 C.B. 2 and 1943 C.B. 5, aff'd, 118 F.(2d) 459, 26 A.F.T.R. 715 (5th Cir. 1941); G.C.M. 23623, 1943 C.B. 313.

loss on sale. If the retained oil payment is subsequently sold, any gain would be treated as capital gain unless the seller is a dealer in such properties.

6.03   *Carved-out Oil Payments.* An oil payment may be carved out of any larger interest in an oil property, including a larger oil payment. It is in respect of the carved-out oil payment that the Revenue Service has developed the anticipation of income theory. In effect this theory holds that where the owner of an oil property carves out an oil payment and sells it for a consideration not pledged to development of the property, he has realized immediate income from the oil property. The Revenue Service regards such income as ordinary income subject to depletion in the year of receipt. The computation of depletion on such income is discussed in Chapter 11.

6.04   Revenue Service Policy. In 1946 the Revenue Service publicly advanced the argument that the sale of a short-lived oil payment carved out of a larger interest in an oil or gas property constituted an anticipation of income, except when such assignment was in the nature of a sharing arrangement, as discussed in the following chapter.[2] At the time of this ruling the Revenue Service did not indicate what it considered to be a short-lived oil payment, but in 1950 the Revenue Service ruled that a short-lived oil payment was any payment which had a duration less than the life of the property from which it was carved.[3] In effect, therefore, the Revenue Service held that any oil payment was a short-lived oil payment, since if the oil payment extends for the life of the property out of which it is carved, it is not an oil payment but constitutes an overriding royalty.

It was stated in Chapter 2 that an oil payment is an economic interest in a property that is very similar to an overriding royalty, except that it is for a limited term measured by

---

[2] G.C.M. 24849, 1946-1 C.B. 66.
[3] I.T. 4003, 1950-1 C.B. 10.

time, dollars, or units of production. The similarity is so great that the oil payment is frequently referred to as a limited override, and conveyancing instruments may describe the assignment of an oil payment as a transfer of an overriding royalty for a term of years or for a period measured by production. It was stated in Chapter 5, and the position is supported by decisions of the courts and by Revenue Service policy, that the sale of an overriding royalty carved out of a working interest or a larger royalty interest is to be treated as a sale, and the proceeds therefrom, less any basis applicable to the interest sold, may be treated as capital gain income. Despite this fact, the Revenue Service takes the position that the sale of a carved-out oil payment results in ordinary income subject to depletion.[4] The Revenue Service also holds that the gift of a carved-out oil payment is not a gift of a property interest, but is nothing more than an assignment of future income. As a result, production applied in satisfaction of the oil payment is taxable to the donor at the time that it is paid to the donee.[5]

The Revenue Service policy relies for its authority upon the Rhodes [6] case, in which the Court held that the sale of the right to future dividends on stock without transfer of the stock itself was ineffectual in transferring the liability for tax on such dividends to the transferee. Additional support for this policy might be found in the Clifford [7] case. In that

---

[4] I.R.C. Section 452 gives an accrual basis taxpayer the right, under certain circumstances, to defer the reporting, for income tax purposes, of certain types of prepaid income. If the Revenue Service position regarding sale of carved-out oil payments is sustained by the Courts, it is possible that the resulting income might, in some instances, fall within the statutory definition of prepaid income. If so, the taxpayer would, upon proper election, have the right to defer a portion of such income. However, present Revenue Service policy does not interpret Section 452 as having any application to the sale of a carved-out oil payment.

[5] I.T. 3935, 1949-1 C.B. 39; I.T. 4003, *supra*.

[6] *Herman M. Rhodes*, 43 B.T.A. 780 (1941), aff'd, 131 F.(2d) 50, 30 A.F.T.R. 220 (6th Cir. 1942).

[7] *Helvering v. Clifford*, 309 U.S. 331, 23 A.F.T.R. 1077 (1940).

case the asset was assigned for a relatively short period of time and control was retained by the grantor. These facts made it clear that there was no real intent to vest control in the assignee; hence, no transfer of property interest was intended. However, the Clifford case and the so-called Clifford Regulations,[8] which followed the decision in that case, left room for assignments of property interests for a term of years which would effectively place income in the assignee. It might be noted that the duration of the assignment in relation to the total estimated life of the property assigned is important in this type of case. The assignment for a period of 50 years of a building with a life of 100 years may embrace a relatively shorter period than the assignment of an oil payment which is estimated to pay out in five years. The term is important, however, only insofar as it reflects upon the intent of the parties to transfer a property interest. If the period of payout is extremely short, it tends to show that the parties did not actually intend a transfer of a property interest. Such was the implication of the Rudco [9] case, where the company carved out an oil payment as a dividend. The oil payment in this case paid out in less than three months, and the court held that there was no intent to transfer a property interest.

The view of the Revenue Service finds support indirectly in the Midfield,[10] Vaccaro [11] and Kimbell [12] cases, in which the courts held that the exchange of an oil payment for other types of mineral interests constitutes a taxable exchange. In these cases the courts distinguished the oil payment, because it was not a continuing right to a share of production, from

---

[8] U.S. Treas. Reg. 118, Section 39.22(a)-21.

[9] *Rudco Oil & Gas Co.* v. *United States,* 82 F. Supp. 746, 37 A.F.T.R. 1099 (Ct. Cls. 1949).

[10] *Midfield Oil Company,* 39 B.T.A. 1154 (1939), acq., 1939-2 C.B. 25.

[11] *John Vaccaro,* T.C. Memo. Op., Dkt. No. 111858, 1943 P-H T.C. Memo. Dec., Para. 43,433 (1943), appeal dismissed on stipulation of parties, Dkt. No. 11080, 33 A.F.T.R. 1672 (5th Cir. 1944).

[12] *Kay Kimbell,* 41 B.T.A. 940 (1940), acq. and nonacq. on other issues, 1940-2 C.B. 5, 12.

other property interests that did have a duration co-extensive with the producing life of the property.

On the other hand, there are several cases which call into question the policy adopted by the Revenue Service. In the Ortiz [13] and Majestic [14] cases, it was held that sale of carved-out oil payments was a sale of oil and gas in place, i.e., of a property interest; that no depletion was allowable on the sales proceeds; and that the gain from the sale was the sales proceeds less the basis allocable to the oil and gas in place sold. In the Kimbell case, an oil payment carved out of a larger oil payment was exchanged for a working interest in another lease. The Commissioner considered the exchange taxable and treated the gain as capital gain. The taxpayer claimed the exchange was not taxable but did not otherwise object to the Commissioner's computation of gain. The Board upheld the Commissioner. While these cases were decided before the adoption of the present Revenue Service policy, they certainly raise doubt as to its validity. It should be noted that in many cases involving taxable years prior to 1942 it was the Commissioner who contended that a sale had taken place, and the taxpayer who claimed a depletion deduction. Since the capital gains provisions of the Internal Revenue Code were liberalized in 1942,[15] the roles have been reversed.

6.05   The Caldwell, Lake, and Fleming Cases. The policy of the Revenue Service was directly at issue in the Caldwell [16] case, where a taxpayer sold an oil payment carved out of a royalty interest. The District Court for the Northern District

---

[13] *Ortiz Oil Company*, 37 B.T.A. 656 (1938), acq. and nonacq. on other issues, 1938-2 C.B. 24, 54, aff'd, 102 F.(2d) 508, 22 A.F.T.R. 908 (5th Cir. 1939), cert. den., 308 U.S. 566.

[14] *Majestic Oil Corporation*, 42 B.T.A. 659 (1940), acq. and nonacq. on other issues, 1940-2 C.B. 5, 12.

[15] The Revenue Act of 1942 added subsection (j) to Section 117 of the 1939 Internal Revenue Code, and reduced the required holding period from 18 to 6 months. See 1954 I.R.C., Section 1231.

[16] *Caldwell* v. *Campbell*, − F. Supp. −, − A.F.T.R. −, Dkt. No. Civil 5257 (N. D. Tex., October 15, 1953), appeal pending to 5th Cir.

of Texas held that the taxpayer realized ordinary income subject to depletion. At the time of this writing the case is on appeal to the Court of Appeals for the Fifth Circuit, which, incidentally, is the same court that rendered the decision in the Ortiz case. If the Fifth Circuit should follow its previous opinion in the Ortiz case and reverse the decision of the District Court, the validity of the Revenue Service policy would be questionable; if it should affirm the District Court opinion, the Revenue Service policy would be strengthened. The validity of the Revenue Service policy is also at issue in the Lake [17] case, which is now pending before the Tax Court.

The Fleming [18] case indirectly involved the Revenue Service policy. In that case the Court of Appeals for the Fifth Circuit held that under Texas law an exchange of carved-out oil payments for royalty interests in different oil and gas properties constituted a nontaxable exchange. This decision is in conflict with the Midfield, Vaccaro and Kimbell cases referred to in preceding paragraph 6.04. Although the Court in the Fleming case did not rule directly on the Revenue Service position as to the sale of a carved-out oil payment, the decision raises some doubt of its validity, because if the exchange of an oil payment for a continuing interest in an oil and gas property is an exchange of properties of like kind, the Court is saying, in effect, that the limitation of an oil payment in time or in dollars is not a significant factor in differentiating the oil payment from any other interest in an oil or gas property.

6.06   Conclusion. Until the cases now pending are decided, the tax treatment of proceeds from the sale of a carved-out oil payment is uncertain. In the meantime, while this question remains unsettled, the Revenue Service will rule, at the taxpayer's request as to a prospective transaction, that the carv-

---

[17] *P. G. Lake, Inc.*, T.C. Dkt. No. 48684, filed May 22, 1953, pending before Tax Court.

[18] *Fleming* v. *Campbell*, 205 F.(2d) 549, — A.F.T.R. —, 1953 P-H, Para. 72,611 (5th Cir. June 26, 1953).

ing out and sale of an oil payment results in ordinary income subject to depletion. It has been the Revenue Service policy that a ruling once given will not be reversed retroactively in the absence of a retroactive change in the law. It appears that the taxpayer who desires that the sale of an oil payment should result in ordinary income subject to depletion can obtain that result by securing a ruling from the Revenue Service. If, on the other hand, he desires to realize a capital gain from the sale of an oil payment, it would appear that he must file his return on that basis and may have to litigate the question at the time of examination of his return.

CHAPTER VII

Conveyances–Sharing Arrangements

7.01   Introduction. In the three preceding chapters various conveyances of oil and gas properties have been described and identified as leases or subleases, sales or exchanges, or anticipation of income; it was stated that the consideration for such conveyances must be cash or property other than the assumption of all or part of the burden of developing the property assigned or retained. If a contribution to, or assumption of, all or part of the burden of development is the entire consideration for the assignment, the transaction is a sharing arrangement. If a contribution to, or assumption of, all or part of the burden of development is only part of the considera-

70

tion, the transaction should be regarded as divisible. The portion of the transaction regarded as a sharing arrangement will have one set of tax consequences; the consequences attending the remaining portion of the transaction will depend upon its classification.

A *sharing arrangement* is a transaction wherein one party makes a contribution to the acquisition, exploration, or development of an oil or gas property and receives as consideration an interest in the property to which the contribution is made.[1] It is essential to the sharing concept that the interest received by the contributor be in the property to which the contribution was made. If the contribution is made to one property and the interest received is in another property, a taxable transaction occurs. The contribution to development may be made in cash pledged either expressly or possibly by implication,[2] to the development of the property, or in property or services used in connection therewith. The grantor in a sharing arrangement must be the owner of the operating rights in the property prior to the assignment, and hence will be the owner of minerals or of the working interest. The grantee, on the other hand, can receive any type of interest in the property to which he makes the contribution. As a consequence, any of the transactions listed in the tables on pages 43 and 54 that involve conveyances by the owner of minerals or by the owner of the working interest will be considered sharing arrangements, if the consideration for the transfer is a contribution toward development. Thus, the owner of the working interest might assign (a) an oil payment for cash, which he pledges to use in drilling a well, (b) an overriding royalty, for which the grantee renders geological services,[3] or (c) an undivided share of the working inter-

---

[1] G.C.M. 22730, 1941-1 C.B. 214.

[2] *Transcalifornia Oil Company, Ltd.*, 37 B.T.A. 119 (1938), nonacq., 1942-1 C.B. 30; but *see Vern W. Bailey*, 21 T.C. — (No. 76) (February 9, 1954), acq., I.R.B. # 27 p. 4 (July 6, 1954).

[3] This statement appears to be in conflict with the decision in *Schermerhorn*

est, for which the grantee promises to drill and equip a well. Each of these transactions constitutes a sharing arrangement. In addition, two or more persons, none of whom have an interest in a property, may by a sharing arrangement agree to acquire and develop a property.

7.02   *Farm-out.* The term "farm-out" is in common use in the oil and gas industry, and it is significant in this connection because all farm-outs are sharing arrangements, although not all sharing arrangements are farm-outs. The term does not appear to be susceptible of precise definition, but in the oil and gas industry it has substantially the same connotation as it has in the more familiar baseball vernacular. Like the rookie ballplayer who may be "farmed out" to a minor league team for further training, an oil and gas lease may be "farmed out" for development. In baseball the major league team frequently retains some kind of interest in the player, and the grantor in a farm-out transaction retains some kind of property interest in the oil and gas lease.

The essential characteristic of a farm-out is that some part of the burden of development of an oil or gas property is transferred to another person and, in consideration of the assumption of that burden, the person receives an interest in the property. The term is applied to transactions in which all or some part of the operating rights are transferred to the assignee. This fact prevents the accepted usage of the term from including all types of sharing arrangements, since under a sharing arrangement the grantee may receive any type of interest, whether operating or nonoperating. In the most common type of farm-out, the owner of a working interest in an oil or gas property assigns the working interest, retaining an

---

Oil Corporation, 46 B.T.A. 151 (1942), but this case involved a contractual right to a share of net profits not in the form of an interest in the property; in addition, it was decided before the Supreme Court held, in *Burton-Sutton Oil Co., Inc.* v. *Commissioner,* 328 U.S. 25, 34 A.F.T.R. 1017 (1946), that a net profits interest constituted an economic interest.

overriding royalty, in consideration of the assignee's undertaking to develop the property. This is, however, by no means the only type of farm-out transaction; the owner of the working interest may retain any type of interest upon his assignment of the property, so long as the assignment is conditioned upon the assumption of all or some part of the development obligation by the assignee.

7.03 *General Principles—Nonrealization of Income.* A simple or unmixed sharing arrangement is a nontaxable transaction, but it is not in the nature of a nontaxable exchange. In its inception it is closely akin to the formation of a partnership or joint venture to which the participants make different contributions, but it does not result in the formation of a partnership or joint venture unless other attributes of such organizations are present.[4] If no consideration passes between the parties to a sharing arrangement except a contribution to, or assumption of, some portion of the development obligation, neither grantee nor grantor realizes taxable income or loss from the transaction.

The sharing principle, although not specifically so named, was officially recognized in 1925, when the Revenue Service ruled that the assignor of a fraction of a working interest, in return for the assignee's promise to drill a free well, realized no gain or loss.[5] It was recognized that the drilling of the well was a benefit to the assignor, but that the benefit was represented merely by an appreciation in the value of the property he owned. No taxable income or loss would be recognized until such appreciation was realized.[6] Support for this conclusion is also found in the Detroit Edison case,[7] which is discussed in more detail later in this chapter. In this case it was held that a utility company that received contributions from

---

[4] *See* Chapter 13.
[5] S.M. 3322, IV-1 C.B. 112 (1925).
[6] *Eisner* v. *Macomber*, 252 U.S. 189, 3 A.F.T.R. 3020 (1920).
[7] *Detroit Edison Company* v. *Commissioner*, 319 U.S. 98, 30 A.F.T.R. 1096 (1943).

customers to expand its facilities had no basis in the property acquired with such contributed funds and, by inference, that it realized no taxable income from the contributions. A similar conclusion was reached in the case of a partnership that received sums of money, which it pledged to use in development of a property, and gave the payers ownership certificates entitling them to a specified share of net earnings derived from two wells that were to be drilled.[8] In a later case this conclusion was specifically limited to the situation where the funds received were actually expended on the properties for which the contribution was received.[9] In each case, however, it was found by the court that no income was realized by the assignor if the property or funds were used for the development of the property.

The assignee's position in the sharing arrangement was covered in 1927 when the Revenue Service ruled,[10] in accordance with the law then in effect, that costs incurred by the assignee were capital in nature, that such costs represented his investment in the property, and, by implication, that he had purchased a property interest. Where the assignee drilled a well in consideration of an interest in a property, it was held by the courts that he did not realize taxable income to the extent of the value of the interest received, but rather had made an investment in the oil and gas in place.[11]

In 1941, the Revenue Service promulgated a ruling [12] that summarized and rationalized the tax consequences of a variety of oil and gas transactions. Although this ruling was not con-

---

[8] *Thompson* v. *Commissioner*, 28 F.(2d) 247, 7 A.F.T.R. 8178 (3rd Cir. 1928).

[9] *Rogan* v. *Blue Ridge Oil Company, Ltd.*, 83 F.(2d) 420, 17 A.F.T.R. 981 (9th Cir. 1936), cert. den., 299 U.S. 574.

[10] G.C.M. 932, III-1 C.B. 241 (1927).

[11] *Dearing* v. *Commissioner*, 102 F.(2d) 91, 22 A.F.T.R. 632 (5th Cir. 1939), aff'g 36 B.T.A. 843 (1937) acq., 1940-2 C.B. 2; *See also Commissioner* v. *Edwards Drilling Co.*, 95 F.(2d) 719, 20 A.F.T.R. 1172 (5th Cir. 1938), aff'g 35 B.T.A. 341 (1937), acq. on this issue, 1939-1 C.B. 11, nonacq. on deductibility of costs incurred in drilling, 1940-2 C.B. 10.

[12] G.C.M. 22730, *supra*.

fined to sharing arrangements, it embodied most of the basic principles governing such transactions in the oil and gas industry. For example, it was held that one who furnishes money that is pledged to be used for development of an oil and gas property, receiving therefor an oil payment payable from such property, has made an investment representing an addition to the reservoir of capital invested in oil or gas in place. He does not realize taxable income from making such investment, and the assignor of the interest does not realize taxable income, because the funds received were subject to a restriction. This ruling also held that a driller who drills a well, or an equipment dealer who supplies equipment for a well in return for an interest in the property, makes an investment by which he acquires an interest in the minerals. He is not taxable upon receipt of his interest any more than he would be in the purchase of any type of investment, and his assignor is not taxable upon his contribution, because it represents an unrealized appreciation in the value of the interest retained.

It is important to observe that the rules stated above are applicable only in the case of parties who make some contribution to the acquisition or development of the property. In such case they are contributing to the reservoir of capital investment.[13] If the property is fully developed, the reservoir of capital is complete, and the so-called contributions do not add to it but effect a substitution for a portion of the reservoir.[14] Hence, the cash, property, or services contributed must relate to development of the property, and may include equipment for a well, the property on which the well is to be drilled, any materials directly related to development (such as drilling materials), and also any services of the geologist, the driller, the leasemen who assemble the block, the attorney who clears title, and the accountant who sets up the records. Services rendered or supplies furnished in connection with operation

[13] *Palmer* v. *Bender*, 287 U.S. 551, 11 A.F.T.R. 1106 (1933).
[14] *Rawco, Inc., Ltd.*, 37 B.T.A. 128 (1938).

of the property after it has been fully developed would not qualify as a sharing arrangement.[15]

It is also necessary that the contribution to acquisition or development be made, or agreed to, before the costs have been incurred. Thus, if a well has been drilled on a property before any sharing arrangement has been made, no such arrangement could be made which would affect the drilling costs previously incurred. A contributor, under such circumstances, would not be contributing to the pool of capital but would be substituting his capital for that invested by the party who drilled the well. However, if a well has been started, a sharing arrangement should be possible in respect of costs of that well, or of other wells, subsequently incurred.

The position of the contributor to the reservoir of capital in a sharing arrangement must be differentiated from that of the person who performs services or furnishes supplies with the understanding that he is to be paid a sum of money for such services or supplies, but who accepts an interest in the property in discharge of the money obligation. Such persons do not intend to contribute to the reservoir of capital and hence are not parties to a sharing arrangement. They intend rather to be compensated for their services or supplies, and, if they accept an interest in the property therefor, they are considered to have had a taxable transaction; they would recognize income or loss to the extent that the value of the property interest received differs from the cost of the services or supplies furnished.[16]

7.04.   *General Principles—Basis.* The determination of the nature and amount of income tax basis applicable to the interests of the various parties to a sharing arrangement has some unusual facets. Excepting the determination of basis where property is received by gift or inheritance, the as-

---

[15] *Rawco, Inc., Ltd., supra.*
[16] U.S. Treas. Reg. 118, Section 39.22(a)-3.

signee of an interest in an oil or gas property will have a basis (1) if its receipt constitutes taxable income to him, (2) if he incurred a cost in its acquisition, or (3) if there is a carry-over of basis from some property given up by him in connection with the assignment. Since the sharing principle involves no realization of income, the first of the above methods of acquiring a basis will not be applicable. The Detroit Edison case [17] held that a taxpayer has no basis where he has incurred no cost for his interest in a property. In that case, the taxpayer expended funds in the acquisition and construction of new facilities of which it was the owner, but the taxpayer had derived such funds from contributions for that purpose from its customers. The Court held that since the company had made no investment in the property it had no depreciable basis therein. It follows that only the person contributing funds, or properties or services that of themselves have a basis, would have any basis in the property interest acquired as a result of a sharing arrangement. For example, if A, who owns the working interest, receives cash that he pledges to the development of the property, he is required to reduce his total development expenditures by the amount of such cash. If A assigned an overriding royalty for such cash, his assignee would have a basis in the override equal to the cash paid to A. Or if A carved out an oil payment to be assigned to a driller as consideration for drilling a well on A's lease, A would have no basis as a result of the expenditures made by the driller. The driller, on the other hand, would treat as cost of the oil payment all expenses incurred in drilling the well.[18]

For income tax purposes, the nature of the basis acquired does not necessarily follow the nature of the outlay made by the assignee. If the owner of a working interest carves out an oil payment that is assigned to the driller for drilling an oil well, neither party will be entitled to a deduction for in-

---

[17] *Detroit Edison Company* v. *Commissioner, supra.*
[18] G.C.M. 22730, *supra.*

tangible drilling and development costs. The working interest owner did not incur such costs, so he has no right to a deduction,[19] and the driller has no operating rights, so he cannot claim the deduction.[20] The costs incurred by the driller become his depletable basis in the interest received. Similarly, if the owner of the working interest assigns an oil payment for the equipping of the well, neither party has any depreciable investment—the supplier of equipment capitalizes as depletable cost the expenditures made by him, and the owner of the working interest has made no investment in depreciable property.

7.05   *General Principles—Mixed or Divisible Sharing Arrangements.* The general principles stated above regarding nonrealization of income and effect on basis are applicable to the unmixed sharing arrangement, which includes only those transactions where the sole consideration passing between the parties is the contribution to, or assumption of, a portion of the development burden. Frequently some additional consideration passes between grantor and grantee, either in the form of cash that is not pledged to development, or cash pledged to development but in excess of the cost thereof, or property of unlike kind not related to the development project. For convenience, such additional consideration will be referred to as excess cash, but it should be remembered that the observations would be equally applicable to the fair market value of unrelated property transferred in connection with the transaction.

These mixed transactions have some of the attributes of a sharing arrangement and some of the attributes of other kinds of transactions. It is believed that such mixed arrangements should be treated as though the separate elements are divisible, and they will be referred to as divisible sharing arrangements. The term divisible is not used in the sense that the contract

---

[19] *Detroit Edison Company* v. *Commissioner, supra.*
[20] U.S. Treas. Reg. 118, Section 39.23(m)-16(a)(1); *See also* para. 10.06.

or agreement between the parties is legally divisible, but rather is used in the sense that the economic results and the tax consequences are separately determinable. The portion of such a transaction that has the attributes of a sharing arrangement should have the same tax consequences as a simple or unmixed sharing arrangement, and the portion that has the attributes of some other type of transaction should be attended by the tax consequences ordinarily associated with that type of transaction. In the discussion later in this chapter it will be seen that the other types of transactions that may be combined with a sharing arrangement are a lease or sublease, a sale or exchange, anticipation of income, or a sale of materials or services.

7.06   When Contribution to Development Is Sole Consideration. In instances where the only consideration for an assignment is the contribution to development, the transaction is a sharing arrangement in its simplest form. In such cases no gain or loss is recognized by either grantee or grantor as a result of the transaction. Usually, tax problems arise only in determining the basis and the right to deductions. The general principles that are applicable to these problems have been set forth above, but it appears desirable to clarify the rules by applying these principles to a variety of transactions.

7.07   *Grantor of Nonoperating Interest.* The grantor in a sharing arrangement who assigns a nonoperating interest in exchange solely for a development contribution has no problems regarding allocation of basis. Whatever basis he had before the assignment remains the same, as to both type and amount, after the grant. Assume that A owns the working interest in a property in which he has a lease cost of $10,000 and an equipment cost of $25,000, and that he assigns a $100,-000 oil payment to B in consideration of B's drilling another well on the lease. B spends $90,000 drilling the well, and A pays $25,000 for equipment to complete the well. A's basis in the lease remains $10,000, despite the outstanding oil payment. His basis in equipment is increased from $25,000 to $50,000 by the equipment costs that he paid for the new well. A is not entitled to deduct any intangible costs, because he paid none.

It might be reiterated that the grantor in a sharing arrangement is not entitled to depreciate, deplete, or expense the development and equipment costs incurred by another as consideration for the interest assigned. Where the grantor receives cash that is pledged to the development of the property, he must treat the cash as a reduction of the total expenditures in making the development. If both depletable and depreciable costs are involved, and the funds are pledged to be used for both, each must be reduced ratably by the amount of the cash received.[21]

7.08 *Grantor of Operating Interest.* The tax problems confronting the grantor become somewhat more complex if all or some part of the operating rights are assigned. These problems may be illustrated by considering the position of the grantor in the following transactions.

For example, assume that A is the owner of the working interest in a partially developed lease in which he had unrecovered costs of $10,000 and $25,000 for leasehold and equipment, respectively. He assigns to B the entire working interest, retaining an overriding royalty, in return for B's promise to drill and equip a well. A will probably be required by the Revenue Service to transfer all of his unrecovered costs, whether depletable or depreciable, to the cost of the overriding royalty retained, and will recover such cost through depletion.[22]

The grantor's problem is changed considerably if he assigns only a fraction of the working interest for a free well. If the

---

[21] *Transcalifornia Oil Company, Ltd.*, 37 B.T.A. 119 (1938), nonacq., 1942-1 C.B. 30.

[22] G.C.M. 23623, 1943 C.B. 313.

property is nonproducing at the time of the assignment, the grantor would have only leasehold or depletable investment, if he has any, and that basis would become the basis of his retained share of the working interest. If the property has been partially developed, the grantor will have assigned to the grantee a portion of his interest in equipment, and it might appear logical to transfer to depletable basis the portion of his equipment cost applicable to the interest transferred. However, he might be permitted to retain, and depreciate, his unrecovered equipment cost, in view of the fact that he is securing an interest in the equipment placed on the lease by the grantee.

A common transaction in the oil business is one in which the owner of a property assigns a fraction of the working interest in exchange for the grantee's agreement to pay a larger fraction of the costs of acquisition and development. For example, A may have an option to acquire a lease, and may agree with B that B is to receive a one-half interest upon B's payment of 70 per cent of the costs of acquisition and development; A pledges to use the funds received for the specified purposes. This transaction is a typical simple sharing arrangement. In such case, A realizes no taxable income from the transaction but would be required to credit B's contribution ratably against his costs of acquisition and development. The following tabulation illustrates the result based upon assumed data.

	A's Expenditures	B's Contribution	A's Cost
Leasehold	$ 10,000	$ 7,000	$ 3,000
Intangibles	40,000	28,000	12,000
Equipment	10,000	7,000	3,000

In this illustration the cost of the lease was also shared because of the agreement of the parties and because A had not incurred such costs prior to the agreement with B.

7.09 *Grantee of Nonoperating Interest.* As has been previously stated, the grantee in a sharing arrangement may contribute cash pledged to development, or property or services connected with the development, and may receive therefor any type of economic interest in the property. If the interest that he receives is a nonoperating interest his problems are few and simple. He will capitalize, as the cost of the interest acquired, the cash contributed, the cost or other basis of property supplied, or services rendered. Thus, if *B*, as grantee, provides the equipment for a well in return for an interest in the property, the cost of such equipment becomes the basis of his interest in the property. If he provides services, such as those of the geologist in exploration for the property, the leaseman in assembling the acreage, the attorney in clearing title, the accountant in setting up the records, or the driller in drilling the well, he will capitalize the cost, if any, of such services as the basis of his interest. Since the interest is non-operating, he has no problem of allocation between leasehold cost and equipment, even though the property may be producing at the time he acquires his interest. Although this concept may apply to partially developed producing properties, it is not applicable to fully developed properties because there must be a contribution to development, which obviously cannot be made after the property is fully developed.[23]

7.10   *Grantee of Operating Interest.* If the grantee receives an operating interest in the property his problems are generally more complex. In large measure, these additional problems arise from the option to expense intangible drilling and development costs [24] and from the regulations, which provide that, if the drilling of a well or development of a property is undertaken in consideration of the assignment of an interest in the lease, only that portion of the intangibles applicable to the share of the working interest acquired is subject to the option.[25] Depending upon the circumstances, the grantee of an

---

[23] *Rawco, Inc., Ltd., supra.*
[24] *See* Chapter 10.
[25] U.S. Treas. Reg. 118, Section 39.23(m)-16(a)(7.); *See also* para. 10.06.

operating interest may be entitled to some intangibles deduction, may have some leasehold cost, may have some equipment cost, or may have a combination of all three.

One of the most simple sharing arrangements of this type occurs when *A*, the owner of the working interest in a nonproducing property, farms out the lease to *B*, retaining an overriding royalty, in return for *B*'s promise to drill and equip a well on the property. In such case *B* has acquired the entire working interest, even though it is burdened with the override. Assume that *B* spends $100,000 for intangibles and $30,000 for equipment, and that he has elected to expense intangibles. He will be permitted to deduct the entire $100,000 of intangible drilling costs, since he has acquired the entire working interest. He will have no leasehold cost, because no other consideration passed to *A*, and he will have a depreciable basis in the equipment of $30,000.[26]

If *A* had assigned only three-fourths of the working interest, then *B* would be permitted to deduct only $75,000 or three-fourths of the intangibles and would be permitted to capitalize as equipment cost only $22,500. The balance of the intangibles ($25,000) and of the equipment ($7,500) or $32,500 would be capitalized as leasehold cost, because such costs are applicable to *A*'s retained share of the working interest.[27] The leasehold cost, as so determined, is recoverable through depletion. *A*'s basis in the property, if any, is not changed because of the fact that *B* was required to capitalize a portion of his expenditures.

Assume that *A* owns another property, which had been partially developed prior to any assignment, and that the fair market value of the lease, excluding equipment, was $125,000 and that of the equipment, $25,000. *A* assigns three-fourths of the working interest to *B*, without retaining an override, in exchange for *B*'s promise to drill and equip a well, which he

---

[26] U.S. Treas. Reg. 118, Section 39.23(m)-16(a)(1) and (c)(1).
[27] U.S. Treas. Reg. 118, Section 39.23(m)-16(a)(1).

does at a cost of $100,000 and $30,000, respectively. In that case B would capitalize as the cost of the interest received that portion of his expenditures attributable to A's one-fourth working interest, or $32,500. B would allocate the cost of his interest between lease and equipment as follows:

Leasehold:
$$\left(\frac{\$125,000}{\$125,000 + \$25,000}\right) \times \$32,500 = \$27,083$$

Equipment:
$$\left(\frac{\$25,000}{\$125,000 + \$25,000}\right) \times \$32,500 = \$5,417$$

The $5,417 allocated to equipment, when combined with the $22,500 of additional equipment expenditures, would give B a total depreciable basis of $27,917. The basis of $27,083 allocated to the leasehold would be recoverable through depletion allowances.

Changing the circumstances of this illustration, assume that A retained one-fourth of the working interest plus an override payable out of B's three-fourths working interest, and that the value of the retained overriding royalty out of B's three-fourths working interest is $25,000. The fair market value of the working interest assigned to B would be measured by three-fourths of the fair market value of the lease reduced by the fair market value of the overriding royalty (¾ of $125,000 less $25,000, or $68,750). The fair market value of the equipment transferred to B would be $18,750 (¾ of $25,000). In that case B would allocate the $32,500 which he is required to capitalize as the cost of his interest between leasehold and equipment as follows:

Leasehold:
$$\left(\frac{\$68,750}{\$68,750 + \$18,750}\right) \times \$32,500 = \$25,536$$

Equipment:
$$\left(\frac{\$18,750}{\$68,750 + \$18,750}\right) \times \$32,500 = \$6,964$$

The $6,964 when combined with the $22,500 of additional equipment provided by him would give B a total depreciable basis of $29,464.

If the grantee's contribution to development is property or services that would not themselves qualify as intangible drilling and development costs, then he would not be entitled to any deduction therefor. Thus, if B, the grantee, supplied well equipment in exchange for one-fourth of the working interest, he would not be entitled to any deduction for intangibles, since he did not incur such expenses. He would capitalize one-fourth of his expenditure as equipment cost to be recovered through depreciation, and the other three-fourths would be treated as the cost of his investment in the lease to be recovered through depletion.

If the grantee of an operating interest pays cash to the grantor, and such cash is pledged to development of the property, the grantee may lose his right to an intangibles deduction if it is held that he did not undertake the drilling of the well.[28] The Revenue Service has been known to argue that the payment of cash pledged to development for a share of the working interest is tantamount to the purchase of an interest with a completed well on it. In such case the entire expenditure by the grantee would be capitalized as leasehold and equipment cost. As a precaution, it appears desirable that the agreement between the parties specify the portion of the consideration paid for assignment of the interest and the portion applicable to development costs. If the agreement does not break down the consideration, the intention of the parties should control the consequences, and it is believed that in any case where the cash paid is pledged to development there is a clear intention that the grantee be entitled to claim his share of development costs. In the remainder of this chapter it will be assumed that the agreement is in appropriate form, or that

[28] Sidney Platt, 18 T.C. 1229 (1952), aff'd, 207 F.(2d) 697, — A.F.T.R. —, 1953 P-H, Para. 72,736 (7th Cir. Oct. 26, 1953). See discussion at para. 10.06.

other evidence establishes the intent so that the grantee may claim his share of development costs.

The grantee who contributes cash pledged to development of the property approximately in proportion to his share of the operating rights should be permitted to allocate his expenditure in proportion to the various costs and expenses toward which the contribution is made. Thus, if A, the grantor, assigns a one-third working interest to B for $50,000, which A pledges to use for development, and such amount is approximately equal to one-third of the actual costs of development, then B should be permitted to allocate that expenditure between intangible and equipment costs in proportion to the amounts that an independent contractor would reasonably charge in drilling and equipping a well. However, if B's contribution is substantially in excess of his proportionate share of the total costs, he will probably be required to capitalize a portion as leasehold cost. Thus, if A expended $125,000 in drilling and equipping the well, B's contribution would be reasonably close to one-third of the total cost and he would allocate the $50,000 he paid between intangible drilling costs and equipment costs in proportion to A's expenditures. If, however, A had expended only $60,000 drilling and equipping the well, so that B's contribution was substantially in excess of one-third of A's cost, then it would appear that a portion of B's investment should be treated as leasehold cost. This principle is not susceptible of precise definition, and it is frequently difficult of application because of the wide variety of circumstances which can surround this type of transaction. It should be observed, however, that if the cash is not pledged to the development of the property, there is no sharing arrangement, in which event B will be considered to have made a purchase of a leasehold interest with a completed well and will have to capitalize his entire expenditure as leasehold and equipment cost, unless it is established that B purchased an undivided interest in an undeveloped lease and concurrently contracted with *A* for the drilling and equipping of the well.

Another type of sharing arrangement which is frequently found in the oil industry may produce quite unintended tax consequences. Assume that *A* owns the working interest in a 640-acre tract and that he assigns the entire working interest in a 40-acre drillsite and one-half the working interest in the remainder of the 640 acres in return for *B*'s promise to drill and equip one well free of cost to *A*. It has been indicated previously that if *B* drills a well for an interest in a property he may expense only that portion of the intangible drilling costs applicable to his share of the working interest. Hence, if *B* had received a one-half interest in the entire tract for the free well, he would have been permitted to deduct only one-half of his intangible costs. Is his situation changed by giving the entire working interest in a small portion of the acreage together with a one-half interest in the balance? The Revenue Service may contend that *B* has received two properties—one in the 40-acre drillsite and one in the surrounding acreage—and that the second is a contribution toward drilling in the nature of a bottom-hole contribution.[29] The value of the surrounding acreage at the date of the contract would be capitalized by *B* with a corresponding decrease in drilling costs applicable to the drillsite. In the unusual circumstance where such value exceeds *B*'s development costs, it might be held that the contribution of the surrounding acreage would offset the development costs and that the excess would constitute ordinary income not subject to depletion, but it appears preferable to regard the transaction as a bargain purchase that does not result in taxable income.

7.11   Divisible Sharing Arrangements. When some consideration in addition to the development contribution passes between grantee and grantor, the transaction may, to the extent of such additional consideration, be taxable.[30] This type of

---

[29] *See* discussion at para. 8.06.

[30] *Rogan* v. *Blue Ridge Oil Company, Ltd., supra.*

transaction has been previously referred to in this chapter as a divisible sharing arrangement, and the additional consideration has, for convenience, been designated excess cash. In divisible sharing arrangements either the grantor or the grantee may receive the excess cash. The treatment of the cash paid or received depends upon the nature of the portion of the transaction that is not a sharing arrangement. The tax treatment of divisible sharing arrangements has not been the subject of Revenue Service rulings or of decisions by the courts. As a consequence, the examples given in the following discussion must be based on the general principles applicable to sharing arrangements and other types of transactions. The reader should recognize, however, that the area being explored is, for all practical purposes, uncharted, and should be alert for development of the subject in cases and rulings that are yet to be handed down.

7.12   *Grantor of Nonoperating Interest.* The grantor in a divisible sharing arrangement has, in addition to the problems discussed in paragraphs 7.07 and 7.08, the problems of determining the nature and amount of income or loss arising from the transaction. In general, the nature of the income will depend upon whether the nonsharing portion of the transaction is in substance a lease or a sale of property, an anticipation of income, or a sale of materials or services. If the owner of a lease assigns a nonoperating interest for excess cash and a contribution to development, the cash will be treated as anticipation of income or as proceeds of sale, depending upon the nature of the interest assigned. If he assigns an oil payment, the entire amount of excess cash received would constitute an anticipation of future income from the property and would represent ordinary income subject to depletion.[31]

If the owner of a lease assigns any type of nonoperating interest other than an oil payment, the excess cash represents

_____

[31] G.C.M. 24849, 1946-1 C.B. 66; But *see* discussion at para. 6.04 and 6.05.

the proceeds of sale of an interest in the property, and he would compute gain and loss as the difference between the cash received and the basis properly allocable to the interest sold. For example, assume the following facts:

A (grantor) Owns	Basis	Fair Market Value
Leasehold	$20,000	$100,000

A assigns a one-quarter overriding royalty to B for $10,000 in cash and B's promise to drill and equip a well on the lease. It is estimated that the cost of drilling and equipping will be $30,000. Assume also that the fair market value of A's retained interest is $60,000 and that of the assigned override is $40,-000. A has assigned the overriding royalty for a total consideration of $40,000, $10,000 in cash and $30,000 in drilling and equipment costs.

Allocation of basis: Based on the relative values of the assigned and retained interests, 40 per cent of A's basis in the lease is applicable to the assigned override; such basis must be allocated between the cash of $10,000 and the drilling and equipment costs of $30,000, even though the development contribution and the basis allocable to it have no tax consequences because this portion of the transaction is in the nature of a sharing arrangement. The basis allocable to the cash received is determined as follows:

Override:

$$\left(\frac{\$10,000}{\$10,000 + \$30,000}\right) \times (40\% \text{ of } \$20,000) = \$2,000$$

Income and basis: A's gain on the sale of the overriding royalty will be as follows:

	Cash Received	Basis Allocable	Gain Realized
Override	$10,000	$2,000	$8,000

A's basis in the leasehold after the transaction will be $20,000, less $2,000, which was allocated to the interest sold, or $18,000. The basis applicable to the sharing portion of the transaction remains as part of A's basis in the retained interest in accordance with the principles outlined in paragraph 7.07.

There might appear to be some theoretical objection to the use of present fair market values, in the circumstances discussed above, as a means of allocating the taxpayer's basis in the

property between the interest assigned and the interest retained. It might be said that such allocation should be made
as of the date of acquisition of the property rather than as of
the date of assignment. As a practical matter, there would not
ordinarily be sufficient data to make such an allocation at the
date of acquisition. It also appears to be a reasonable assumption that the proportionate values would not change materially,
even though the total value of the property may have increased
substantially. The same theoretical objection cannot be raised
regarding the use of present values in determining the proportion of the assigned interest that is attributable to the sharing
arrangement and the proportion attributable to the nonsharing
part of the transaction, because the parties are then dealing in
terms of present fair market values.

The principles applied in the preceding example would also
be applicable if A had assigned the overriding royalty for
$40,000 in cash, which he pledged to use in development of
the property, if such development had cost only $30,000. In
such case A has, in effect, made a sharing arrangement as to
the $30,000 and sold a portion of the overriding royalty for
cash of $10,000. The $30,000 received would be offset against
his development costs, and he would compute the gain from
receipt of the $10,000 in exactly the same manner as outlined
above. In neither case would A be entitled to a deduction for
intangibles or to recognize equipment costs, because he did not
incur any.

If A's basis in the lease had been so high that the portion
properly allocable to the interest sold exceeded the amount of
cash received, A should be entitled to recognize and deduct
the loss. For example, if the basis of A's lease had been
$150,000 prior to the assignment, the basis allocable to the
interest sold would be determined as follows:

Override:
$$\left(\frac{\$10,000}{\$10,000 + \$30,000} \right) \times (40\% \text{ of } \$150,000) = \$15,000$$

Since A received only $10,000 of excess cash, he should be permitted to recognize the loss of $5,000. There is some question whether the Revenue Service would approve the deduction of the loss. Whether this view will be sustained by the courts is unknown, but the Revenue Service may argue that the excess cash received in such a case should merely be applied against the taxpayer's basis, and that a loss deduction must be postponed until the entire property is disposed of for less than its basis.

Although the examples discussed above have dealt with undeveloped properties, the same results would apply to partially developed properties, because A retained the entire working interest and assigned nonoperating interests. If the property had been partially developed, A would have some basis in the equipment on the property. By retaining the entire working interest he has also retained the entire interest in the equipment, and no part of the basis of such equipment should be allocated to the interest assigned in the transaction.

In the preceding examples the grantor of the nonoperating interest received excess cash in a divisible sharing agreement. It may also occur that the grantor pays rather than receives the excess cash. In such case he will not have income or loss from the transaction, but he will be required to add the cash expenditure to his basis in the property or, in some instances, to treat the expenditure as intangibles. For example, assume that A owns the working interest in a lease which has a basis of $20,000 and a total value of $100,000, and that he assigns a one-eighth overriding royalty (with a value of $20,000) to B and pays B $20,000 in cash, which B pledges to use in drilling and equipping a well on the property. B spends $30,000 drilling and $10,000 equipping the well. A does not realize any income or loss from the transaction. Since he owns all of the operating rights in the property, he will be permitted to treat the cash paid to B as intangibles and equipment costs in the proportion that such amounts were expended by *B*. *A*'s expenditures for intangibles and equipment costs are as follows:

Intangibles:

$$\left(\frac{\$30,000}{\$30,000 + \$10,000}\right) \times \$20,000 = \$15,000$$

Equipment:

$$\left(\frac{\$10,000}{\$30,000 + \$10,000}\right) \times \$20,000 = \underline{\$\ 5,000}$$
$$\overline{\underline{\$20,000}}$$

The assignment of the override constitutes a sharing arrangement, which is of no tax consequence to *A*. The same result would occur if *A*'s property had been partially developed prior to assignment.

7.13 *Grantor of Operating Interest.* Where the grantor assigns all or part of the operating interest for excess cash and a development contribution, the cash may be treated as a lease bonus or as proceeds of sale depending upon the nature of the interest retained or it may be treated as payment for materials or services. Thus, if *A* assigns the working interest in a property, retaining an overriding royalty, for cash and *B*'s promise to drill a well, the cash received would be treated as a lease bonus. If he assigned the working interest and retained an oil payment, or simply assigned a fraction of the working interest, for cash and *B*'s promise to drill a well, the cash would be treated as proceeds of sale. Gain would be recognized to the extent that the cash received exceeded the basis properly allocable to the interest sold, but here again there is some question as to whether any loss would be allowed.

Although the general principles previously stated will also govern the allocation of basis where operating rights are assigned in a divisible sharing arrangement, the application of those principles presents a few new problems, which it seems desirable to illustrate. In general, the problems are divisible into three phases: (1) the allocation of cash received, (2) the allocation of basis, and (3) the determination of income and remaining basis. For example, assume the following facts:

A (grantor) Owns	Basis	Fair Market Value
Leasehold	$20,000	$124,000

He assigns one-fourth of the working interest to B for $10,000 in cash and B's promise to drill and equip a well, the costs of which are estimated to be $20,000 and $8,000 respectively. Because B receives a one-fourth working interest in the property, one-fourth of the total cost of drilling and equipping the well represents the costs applicable to his own interest and does not constitute part of the consideration passing to A. As a consequence, A has received a total consideration of $31,000, $10,000 of which was in cash and $21,000 of which was his share of the development costs.

Allocation of basis: One-fourth of A's basis in the lease is applicable to the fraction of the working interest assigned, but such basis must be allocated between the cash of $10,000 and A's share of development costs of $21,000. The basis allocable to the cash will be computed as follows:

Leasehold:

$$\left(\frac{\$10,000}{\$10,000 + \$21,000} \right) \times (\tfrac{1}{4} \text{ of } \$20,000) = \$1,613$$

Income and basis: A's gain on the sale of the assigned working interest will be as follows:

	Cash Received	Basis Allocable	Gain Realized
Leasehold	$10,000	$1,613	$8,387

A's basis in the retained working interest will be $20,000 less $1,613, which was allocated to the interest sold, or $18,387.

If the transaction in the above example had been in the form of a sublease, that is, if A had retained an overriding royalty upon his assignment to B, the income would be treated as a lease bonus of $10,000, because no basis would be offset against the cash received in a subleasing transaction. The bonus income would, of course, be subject to depletion, and A's basis would be $20,000 less the allowed or allowable depletion in respect of the bonus.

A somewhat different result may occur where A assigns a one-fourth working interest to B but receives cash pledged to development and is permitted to retain the excess, if any, of cash received over the development costs. For example, assume that the basis and the fair market value of A's lease are $20,000 and $124,000 respectively, but that B paid A $38,000, which A pledged to use to the extent necessary in drilling and equipping the well. If A subcontracts the drilling and equipping of the well at a cost of $28,000, the tax consequences should be identical with those outlined above. However, if A drills and equips the well himself at a smaller cost, the possibility exists that A has enjoyed some profit on a drilling contract, or, in other words, has received part of the consideration as payment for materials and services. If A were able to drill and equip the well for a cost of $24,000, when the reasonable cost, or fair market value, on a subcontracting basis would have been $28,000, it might appear that A had realized contract drilling income of $4,000. However, only one-fourth of that amount was realized by a transaction with others, that is the one-fourth attributable to B's share of the working interest. It appears, therefore, that A has actually realized $1,000 of contract drilling income. It seems clear that A should not treat the other $3,000 as income, because if he owned the entire working interest he would not be permitted to treat as income any savings effected by drilling his own well as compared with subcontracting such drilling. As a consequence, A must be regarded as having received $13,000 for the sale of one-fourth of the working interest; he received a total of $38,000 from B, of which $7,000 was for B's share of the drilling costs, including a $1,000 drilling contract profit to A. $18,000 was the contribution to A's drilling costs (¾ of the actual cost of $24,000), and $13,000 was for the assigned interest.

Allocation of basis: One-fourth of *A*'s basis in the lease is applicable to the entire working interest assigned, and such basis must be allocated between the cash of $13,000 and *A*'s share of the development costs of $18,000. The basis allocable to the cash will be determined as follows:

Leasehold:

$$\left(\frac{\$13,000}{\$13,000 + \$18,000} \right) \times (\tfrac{1}{4} \text{ of } \$20,000) = \$2,097$$

Income and basis: *A*'s gain on the sale of the assigned working interest would be computed as follows:

	Cash Received	Basis Allocable	Gain Realized
Leasehold	$13,000	$2,097	$10,903

A would also have contract drilling income not subject to depletion of $1,000. *A*'s basis in the retained working interest would be $20,000 less $2,097, which was allocated to the interest sold, or $17,903. *A* would have no basis in the equipment placed in the well under the sharing arrangement, because the entire cost was paid by *B*.

Still different results occur where the grantor assigns both an operating interest and a nonoperating interest for cash and a contribution to development. For example, assume the following facts:

A (grantor) Owns	Basis	Fair Market Value
Leasehold	$20,000	$100,000

He assigns to *B* one-fourth of the working interest, plus an oil payment payable from his retained three-fourths working interest and valued at $15,000. In return, *B* pays $17,500 in cash and agrees to drill and equip a well, which is estimated to cost $30,000. Again, one-fourth of the development costs represents *B*'s expenditure for his own share of the working interest, so the total consideration received by *A* is $40,000, consisting of three-fourths of the development costs, or $22,500, plus cash of $17,500.

Allocation of cash: The cash consideration must be allocated to determine separately the portions applicable to the leasehold interest and the oil payment. The respective values of the leasehold and the oil payment are $25,000 and $15,000, and the cash allocable to each is determined as follows:

Leasehold:

$$\left(\frac{\$25,000}{\$25,000 + \$15,000} \right) \times \$17,500 = \$10,938$$

Oil payment:

$$\left(\frac{\$15,000}{\$25,000 + \$15,000} \right) \times \$17,500 = \underline{\$\ 6,562}$$
$$\underline{\$17,500}$$

Allocation of basis: One-fourth of A's basis in the lease is applicable to the entire working interest assigned, but such basis must be allocated between the cash of $17,500 and the drilling contribution of $22,500. Although the basis of the oil payment may be similarly allocated, under the present Revenue Service rulings the entire cash allocable to the oil payment constitutes ordinary income subject to depletion. The basis of the leasehold applicable to cash is determined as follows:

Leasehold:

$$\left(\frac{\$17,500}{\$17,500 + \$22,500} \right) \times (\tfrac{1}{4} \text{ of } \$20,000) = \$2,188$$

Income and basis: A's gain on the sale of the assigned working interest will be as follows:

	Cash Allocable	Basis Allocable	Gain Realized
Leasehold	$10,938	$2,188	$8,750

In addition, A has ordinary income subject to depletion of $6,562, which represents the cash allocable to the oil payment sold. A's basis in the leasehold after the transaction will be $20,000 less $2,188, which was allocated to the interest sold, and less the depletion allowed or allowable on the oil payment.

If the grantor's property has been partially developed at the time he enters into the divisible sharing arrangement the problem of allocation is somewhat more complex. For example, assume the following facts:

A (grantor) Owns	Basis	Fair Market Value
Leasehold	$20,000	$124,000
Equipment	16,000	20,000

He assigns to B one-fourth of the working interest and equipment, and an oil payment valued at $20,000. B pays $14,000 in cash and agrees to drill and equip two wells at an estimated total cost of $56,000. Because one-fourth of the development cost is applicable to B's interest, A has received a total consideration of $56,000, of which $14,000 is in cash and $42,000 is a contribution to drilling.

Allocation of cash: The cash consideration must be allocated to determine separately the portions applicable to the leasehold interest, the equipment, and the oil payment. The respective values of the three rights are $31,000, $5,000, and $20,000, and the cash allocable to each is determined as follows:

Leasehold:

$$\frac{\$31,000}{\$56,000} \times \$14,000 = \$\ 7,750$$

Equipment:

$$\frac{\$\ 5,000}{\$56,000} \times \$14,000 = \$\ 1,250$$

Oil Payment:

$$\frac{\$20,000}{\$56,000} \times \$14,000 = \underline{\$\ 5,000}$$
$$\underline{\underline{\$14,000}}$$

Allocation of basis: One-fourth of A's basis in the lease and the equipment is applicable to the entire working interest assigned, but such basis must be allocated between the cash of $14,000 and the drilling contribution of $42,000. Although a similar allocation may be made to the oil payment, under present Revenue Service rulings the cash allocable to the oil payment represents ordinary income subject to depletion. The basis allocable to the cash received is determined as follows:

Leasehold:

$$\frac{\$14,000}{\$56,000} \times (\tfrac{1}{4} \text{ of } \$20,000) = \$\ 1,250$$

Equipment:

$$\frac{\$14,000}{\$56,000} \times (\tfrac{1}{4} \text{ of } \$16,000) = \$\ 1,000$$

Income and basis: The gain to A on sale of the assigned interest will be as follows:

	Cash Allocable	Basis Allocable	Gain Realized
Leasehold	$7,750	$1,250	$6,500
Equipment	1,250	1,000	250
	$9,000	$2,250	$6,750

The cash allocable to the oil payment sold will be treated as ordinary income subject to depletion. A's basis in the leasehold after the transaction will be $20,000, less $1,250 that was allocable to the interest sold, and less the depletion allowed or allowable on the oil payment. His basis in equipment will be $16,000, less $1,000 allocated to the interest sold.

In this type of transaction a loss will be suffered in any case where the fair market value of the property is less than its basis to the grantor. Ordinarily the problem would arise only as to equipment, but it could also happen if the value of the leasehold interest is less than its basis. It has been indicated that the Revenue Service would probably deny the loss deduction and argue that the loss should be added to depletable basis of the retained interest. However, since the accounting for the transaction requires that fair market values be determined, and it may be assumed that there is satisfactory evidence of such value, the loss should be allowable. If a loss will occur, the taxpayer might improve its argument by dealing separately as to the equipment transfer, but such separation would normally be difficult to arrange.

7.14   *Grantee of Nonoperating Interest.* The grantee of a nonoperating interest in a divisible sharing arrangement has very few problems. His entire net expenditure will constitute the basis of his interest in the property. Hence, if B, the grantee, pays cash and agrees to drill and equip a well in exchange for an overriding royalty, all of the amounts that he spends will be treated as his depletable investment in the property. The fact that he purchased equipment as part of his contribution does not alter the result, and he does not have any depreciable basis in the equipment. The result is also the same whether the interest received is an overriding royalty, an oil payment, or a net profits interest. If the grantee receives cash from the grantor, he treats such sums as a reduction of his expenditures in determining his basis in the property. If the grantee receives two or more nonoperating interests, he must allocate his basis to each in proportion to their relative fair market values.

7.15   *Grantee of Operating Interest.* The grantee in a divisible sharing arrangement who receives an operating interest, or both an operating and a nonoperating interest, is confronted with a more involved allocation problem. The regulations provide [32] that if a person drills a well for the assignment of an interest in a lease, he may elect to deduct only those intangibles applicable to the interest acquired; the balance of the intangibles, plus the share of equipment costs paid by him but attributable to other shares of the working interest, must be capitalized as the cost of the interest acquired. The same rule should be applied whether the grantee pays cash that is pledged to the development of the property or pays the drilling costs himself, although, as has been previously indicated,[33] the Revenue Service may take a different position. It might be observed that the amount to be capitalized is not necessarily that fraction of his total expenditures equal to the share of the working interest owned by others. For example, if *B*, the grantee, agrees to pay 75 per cent of the drilling costs for a one-half interest in the lease, he is not required to capitalize 50 per cent of his expenditure but will be required to capitalize one-third of his expenditure, since that is the amount applicable to the other owners of the working interest.

In determining the basis allocable to the interests received in the divisible sharing arrangement, the grantee first determines the amount of his expenditure that can be treated as

---

[32] U.S. Treas. Reg. 118, Section 39.23(m)-16(a)(1).
[33] *See* para. 7.10.

intangibles or as equipment cost, and the balance of his expenditure must be capitalized as the cost of the interests acquired. Thus, if *B* pays $12,000 in cash and drills and equips a well, at a cost of $40,000, in exchange for a one-fourth interest in a nonproducing property, he may treat one-fourth of the $40,000 as intangibles and equipment cost. The balance of drilling and equipping costs, plus the cash paid, or a total of $42,000, would be capitalized as the cost of his share of the working interest. If the property had been productive prior to the assignment, he would allocate the $42,000 between lease and equipment in proportion to their respective fair market values at the date of the transaction. If he had also received a nonoperating interest, a portion of the $42,000 would be allocated to that interest on the basis of its fair market value.

A different question may arise if the grantee is assigned a fraction of the working interest and pays cash to the grantor, which is pledged to the development of the property but which exceeds such development cost. If the cash paid is not in excess of the reasonable costs of such development, although it exceeds the actual costs, the grantee should be permitted to treat the entire amount as a contribution to development. In such case he would capitalize only the portion applicable to other shares of the working interest, and the balance would be treated as intangible or equipment cost. To that extent the transaction is a simple sharing arrangement. It is only when the cash exceeds the reasonable cost of development that a divisible sharing arrangement occurs, and it is the excess cost that must be directly capitalized as part of the cost of the interest acquired.

If the grantee receives cash pledged to development in the transaction, it appears that he should credit the cash ratably against the development costs incurred, and the balance of such costs should be allocated in accordance with the principles stated above.

7.16 **Summary.** It must be reiterated that the rules that will ultimately be held applicable to sharing arrangements are presently only in the formative stage. Although transactions of the type described in this chapter are very common in the industry, they are frequently not recognized or treated as such. It is believed that the law on the subject will develop, and an effort has been made here to set forth the principles that are considered appropriate. The income tax principles which appear to be applicable to sharing arrangements may be summarized as follows:

1. Fundamentally, the sharing arrangement, which must involve a contribution to acquisition or development of a property in exchange for an interest in the same property, is a nontaxable transaction.

2. The contribution to acquisition or development must be made, or agreed to, before the costs that are to be shared are incurred.

3. A divisible sharing arrangement is one in which there are two elements, one of which is a sharing arrangement and the other a taxable transaction of some kind.

4. Where cash is received by either the grantee or the grantor, such cash must be pledged, either expressly or possibly by implication, to development, if that portion of the transaction is to qualify as a sharing arrangement.

5. The nonsharing element of a divisible sharing arrangement may result in

    (a) a lease bonus, if the form of the transaction is a lease or sublease;

    (b) proceeds of sale of a property interest, if the form of the transaction is a sale or exchange;

    (c) anticipation of income, if the grantor assigns an oil payment;

    (d) payment for materials or services; or

    (e) a combination of the foregoing.

6. One party to a sharing arrangement, or to a divisible sharing arrangement, does not have depreciable or depletable basis, nor a right to deductions, because of the expenditures of other parties to the transaction.

CHAPTER VIII

Ownership and Operation of Oil and Gas Properties

8.01   Introduction. In the preceding chapters consideration was given to the nature of various interests in oil and gas properties and to the tax consequences of acquisition and disposition of such interests. In this, and in the remaining chapters, the tax problems attending the ownership and operation of oil and gas properties will be discussed. There is no necessity for devoting attention to the general provisions of the Internal

103

Revenue Code and regulations dealing with taxable income and allowable deductions, since most of such provisions are applicable equally to all businesses, including the oil and gas industry. In some instances, however, such provisions create special problems when applied to the oil and gas industry. These special problems, and also the provisions of the Internal Revenue Code and regulations that are specifically applicable to the oil and gas industry, will be considered in the remaining chapters. This chapter will deal with some of the less involved problems; each of the later chapters will be devoted to one of the more complex problems that confront the owner of oil and gas properties, such as the treatment of geological and geophysical costs and intangible drilling and development costs, the allowance for and computation of depletion, the determination of the property unit, and joint operation of oil and gas properties.

8.02   Commissions Paid by Grantor. In regular leasing transactions any commissions paid by transferor-lessor are capital expenditures recoverable over the life of the lease.[1] This rule was applied in the Bonwit Teller case,[2] where such expenditures were made by a lessee in obtaining a sublease. It has also been held that a broker's commission, paid by the fee owner of certain property to obtain an oil and gas lease, was a capital expenditure and not an ordinary and necessary business expense.[3] In the Cockburn case [4] the taxpayers were dealers in oil and gas leases and also were lessees of a producing oil and

---

[1] *Central Bank Block Association,* 19 B.T.A. 1183 (1930), acq., X-1 C.B. 12, aff'd, 57 F.(2d) 5, 10 A.F.T.R. 1495 (5th Cir. 1932); *Tonningsen v. Commissioner,* 61 F.(2d) 199, 11 A.F.T.R. 914 (9th Cir. 1932).

[2] *Bonwit Teller & Company,* 17 B.T.A. 1019 (1929), acq., IX-1 C.B. 6, rev'd on other issues, 53 F.(2d) 381, 10 A.F.T.R. 656 (2nd Cir. 1931), cert. den., 284 U.S. 690; *See also Evalena M. Howard,* 19 B.T.A. 865 (1930).

[3] *L. S. Munger,* 14 T.C. 1236 (1950); *San Fernando Mission Land Co.,* B.T.A. Memo. Op., Dkt. No. 107149, 1942 P-H B.T.A. Memo. Dec., Para. 42,296 (1942), aff'd on another issue, 135 F.(2d) 547, 31 A.F.T.R. 19 (9th Cir. 1943).

[4] *Dorothy Cockburn,* 16 T.C. 775 (1951).

gas lease. The taxpayers assigned the producing property for cash and retained an overriding royalty and an oil payment. The transaction was, for federal income tax purposes, a sublease, and the sole question involved was whether the taxpayers could deduct as ordinary and necessary business expenses certain expenses of sale, which included engineering fees, revenue stamps, and commissions. Despite the argument advanced by the taxpayers that they acquired nothing that they did not already own, the Court held that these sums represented capital expenditures by the taxpayer in acquiring certain rights under the contract, and they could not be deducted as business expenses.

In the Naylor case,[5] on the other hand, a taxpayer held certain oil and gas leases that he transferred, retaining an overriding royalty. In connection with the transfer he paid a brokerage commission. The Court, in an oral opinion without citation of authority, held that such commission was deductible as an ordinary and necessary business expense because the taxpayer received no benefit from what he paid out. The Naylor case is in direct conflict with the Cockburn case, but it appears likely that the latter case will be followed in the future, since it relied upon the leading case of Bonwit Teller,[6] which the Court considered controlling even though oil and gas leases were not involved. The viewpoint that commissions paid by the grantor to obtain an oil and gas lease are capital expenditures is usually acceded to by the oil and gas industry.

8.03   Payments for Exploration Rights. In the usual form of oil and gas lease, the lessee is given the right to make exploratory surveys as well as the right to develop the property.[7] However, it is frequently necessary to pay a substantial bonus to obtain an oil and gas lease, whereas exploration rights can usually be obtained for a smaller sum. Particularly where large

---

[5] *Naylor* v. *Dunlap,* Dkt. No. 3330, 40 A.F.T.R. 1387 (N.D. Tex. 1949).

[6] *Bonwit Teller & Company, supra.*

[7] *See* Chapter 4 for a more detailed discussion.

areas are to be surveyed for the purpose of selecting likely prospects, an operator may acquire only exploration privileges, or shooting rights, by contract with the landowners. Such contracts usually provide for the payment by the operator of a certain sum per acre as compensation to the landowner for the use of his land, or for surface damages, or for both. In return, the operator obtains the right to make exploratory surveys on the land for a limited period of time. If the payments are only for the use of the land, the landowner should report them as ordinary income, not subject to depletion, because essentially the payments represent rent.[8] The operator, as grantee of the exploratory rights, should treat the payments as geological and geophysical costs, the treatment of which is discussed in Chapter 9.

If the contract for exploration rights also grants the operator an option to take leases, at a specified bonus per acre, on all or any part of the acreage surveyed, the contract is commonly called a *shooting option,* and the provisions granting such option are referred to as *acreage selection clauses.* Informally, the Revenue Service has taken the position that initial payments under a shooting option, together with any amounts paid for the granting of leases on acreage selected, represent a lease bonus, which is depletable income to the landowner and a capital investment in the lease or leases to the grantee.[9] If no leases are taken under the option, the consideration for the contract should be treated as geological and geophysical costs by the grantee and as ordinary income in the nature of rents by the grantor.

[8] Letter to Condray, Pratas and Smith, Lubbock, Texas, dated June 18, 1951, and signed E. I. McLarney, Deputy Commissioner, 1952 P-H, Para. 76,166.

[9] But *see Houston Farms Development Company* v. *United States,* 131 F.(2d) 577, 30 A.F.T.R. 328 (5th Cir. 1942), reh. den., 132 F.(2d) 861, 30 A.F.T.R. 698 (5th Cir. 1943), where the Court held the initial payment to be a lease bonus but, under the facts of the case, construed the payments made upon the execution of the lease to be delay rentals that were in the form of selection rentals. The Court found that under the particular facts involved, the money paid upon selection of the acreage was merely for holding the lease for a year without the necessity of drilling.

8.04   Damages. The Revenue Service has held that amounts received by a landowner as consideration for the privilege of conducting exploration on his land are ordinary rental income, even though damage to the land may result from such activities. In such a case no deductible loss will be allowed, nor may any part of the consideration received be treated as a return of capital.[10] In holding that no loss is allowable, the Revenue Service relied on the Pugh case,[11] in which the Board of Tax Appeals found as a fact that damages of $50,000 had been caused to the surface of the land because it had become impregnated with oil and salt water from producing oil wells. The Board held that, although there had been a shrinkage in value of the land, the taxpayer was not entitled to a loss deduction in the absence of a sale or other disposition of the property. This case supports the theory that no loss deduction is allowable, but it is not authority for the ruling that consideration received for damages may not be treated as a return of capital. It appears, therefore, that if the landowner can prove that some part or all of the consideration received is in payment for damages sustained and is not compensation for the use of his land, he should be permitted to treat such amounts as a nontaxable return of capital. If, however, the payments exceed the basis of the land, the excess would constitute taxable income.[12]

8.05   Delay Rentals. During its primary term, the usual oil and gas lease may be maintained by (1) payment of annual delay rentals, (2) commencement of continuous drilling operation, or (3) production of oil or gas from the property. At the expiration of the primary term the usual oil and gas lease may be extended only by (1) prior commencement of continuous

---

[10] Letter to Condray, Pratas and Smith, Lubbock, Texas, dated June 18, 1951, and signed E. I. McLarney, Deputy Commissioner, *supra*.

[11] *Mrs. J. C. Pugh, Sr.*, 17 B.T.A. 429 (1929), acq., IX-1 C.B. 45, aff'd, 49 F.(2d) 76, 9 A.F.T.R. 1280 (5th Cir. 1931), cert. den., 284 U.S. 642.

[12] Compare *Inaja Land Company, Ltd.*, 9 T.C. 727 (1947), acq., 1948-1 C.B. 2; *See also* I.T. 2621, XI-1 C.B. 67 (1932).

drilling operations, or (2) prior production of oil or gas from the lease. In effect, therefore, a delay rental is paid for the privilege, during the primary term of the lease, of deferring development of the property. A payment that is made to maintain an existing lease may be regarded as a delay rental, but in one case it was held that where the payment extended the lease for a period of more than one year, it should be considered as a lease bonus.[13] The lessor must report delay rentals as ordinary income not subject to depletion,[14] and the lessee may expense or capitalize such payments, as explained more fully below.

If the lessee is committed to make annual payments and he cannot avoid the payments by abandoning the lease, commencing drilling operations, or obtaining production from the property, such payments will be regarded as a lease bonus payable in installments and not as a delay rental.[15] The payment of ad valorem property taxes, for which the lessor is liable, by the lessee of an oil and gas property prior to production is considered to be in the nature of delay rentals.[16] After production is obtained from the property, the payment of taxes by the lessee is considered to be in the nature of additional royalties to the extent of the production from the property for the year, and any excess of taxes paid over production is treated as delay rental.[17]

The Revenue Service has taken the position that delay rent-

---

[13] *Houston Farms Development Company v. United States, supra; Bennett v. Scofield,* 170 F.(2d) 887, 37 A.F.T.R. 570 (5th Cir. 1948). But *see Dougan v. United States,* — F. Supp. —, — A.F.T.R. —, 1953 P-H, Para. 72,732, (D. Utah Aug. 6, 1953), appeal pending to 10th Cir., *Hagood v. United States,* — F. Supp. —, — A.F.T.R. —, 1953 P-H, Para. 72,760, (D. Wyo. Oct. 26, 1953), and Olen F. Featherstone 22 T.C. — (No. 96) (June 30, 1954) where the respective courts permitted deduction of first-year rental payments on noncompetitive government leases that extended the lease for a three-year period.

[14] *Houston Farms Development Company v. United States, supra; Bennett v. Scofield, supra; J. T. Sneed, Jr.,* 33 B.T.A. 478 (1935), acq. on another issue, XV-1 C.B. 21.

[15] *Bennett v. Scofield, supra.*

[16] G.C.M. 26526, 1950-2 C.B. 40.

[17] G.C.M. 26526, *supra;* Rev. Rul. 16, 1953-1 C.B. 173.

als are not materially different from carrying charges on non-productive property,[18] and that they may, therefore, at the election of the taxpayer, be either expensed [19] or capitalized.[20] The taxpayer may make a new election each year [21] as to nonproductive properties owned by him, and also may make a different election as to each nonproductive property.[22] For example, a taxpayer may elect to expense delay rentals paid on property A and to capitalize delay rentals paid on property B, or he may elect to expense taxes on a property and capitalize delay rentals and other carrying charges on the same property.

Because of the option to expense or to capitalize delay rentals, the taxpayer may be able to reduce or to eliminate a net operating loss for federal income tax purposes. For example, if the taxpayer anticipates that he will suffer a net operating loss for a given year and that such loss cannot be availed of as a carryover or carryback, he might elect to capitalize delay rentals to reduce or eliminate the loss. If the property becomes productive, the capitalization of delay rentals may be of no tax benefit, because the taxpayer is entitled to claim percentage depletion even though he has no basis in the property.[23] However, if the property does not become productive, the capitalization of delay rentals and other carrying charges may produce some tax benefit by increasing a later abandonment loss.[24] In general, however, if the taxpayer has net taxable income, it will be to his advantage to expense all delay rentals.

8.06   Bottom-Hole and Dry-Hole Contributions. The operator of an oil or gas property who contemplates drilling a well may seek bottom-hole or dry-hole contribution agreements

---

[18] G.C.M. 11197, XII-1 C.B. 238 (1933).

[19] I.R.C., Section 162(a) [1939 I.R.C., Section 23(a)].

[20] I.R.C., Section 266 [1939 I.R.C., Section 24(a)(7)]; U.S. Treas. Reg. 118, Section 39.24(a)-6(b)(1)(i).

[21] U.S. Treas. Reg. 118, Section 39.24(a)-6(b)(3).

[22] U.S. Treas. Reg. 118, Section 39.24(a)-6(b)(3) and (4).

[23] See Chapter 11 for more detailed discussion.

[24] See paragraphs 8.09 et seq.

from the owners of surrounding acreage. In the dry-hole contribution agreement the adjoining property owner agrees to make a contribution, either in the form of cash or other property, in the event that the well to be drilled reaches an agreed upon depth and is found to be dry. A bottom-hole contribution agreement is made under similar circumstances, except that the contribution in cash or property is due when the well reaches a predetermined depth, regardless of whether the well is dry or productive. The contribution frequently will be in the form of an interest in the adjoining acreage, in which event the recipient takes into account the fair market value of the interest as of the date of the contract.

In essence, the bottom-hole and dry-hole contribution arrangements are sharing arrangements, the characteristics of which were discussed in Chapter 7. They differ from sharing arrangements in general because the contributor receives, instead of an interest in the property to which the contribution is made, geological information that will be helpful to him in connection with his own property. In any event, the general principles regarding tax consequences of sharing arrangements are applicable to this type of contribution. The Revenue Service has ruled [25] that a dry-hole contribution is deductible as an ordinary loss because no real value is received by the contributor. This ruling also stated that a bottom-hole contribution should be capitalized by the contributor if the well to which the contribution was made is productive, but is deductible as a loss if a dry hole results. The recipient of the contribution, like the grantor in any sharing arrangement, should reduce his costs by the amount of cash or by the fair market value of the property received. Ordinarily the contribution will be applied in reduction of intangible drilling costs.

8.07   Minimum Royalties. In some cases, the bargaining

---

[25] Revenue Service letter dated May 4, 1945, and signed by Joseph D. Nunan, Jr., Commissioner, 1945 P-H, Para. 76,209.

position of the lessor may be so strong that he is able to require the lessee to agree to make annual payments of a specified minimum amount, regardless of production from the property. Depending upon the provisions of the lease, annual payments may be classified as installment bonus payments, as delay rentals, or as minimum royalties. It is necessary to distinguish the three types of payments, because the tax consequences may differ.

If the lessee is required to pay the lessor certain annual payments for a fixed number of years regardless of production, and if the lessee is unable to avoid such payments by terminating the lease, the annual payments will be regarded as a lease bonus payable in installments.[26] In such case the payments represent depletable income to the lessor, and an additional leasehold cost to the lessee. If the lessee may terminate the lease at the end of any annual period by failing to make the annual minimum payment, the payments made prior to production are considered to be delay rentals.[27]

Similar payments made after production occurs may be classified as minimum royalties.[28] The tax consequences of a minimum royalty depend upon whether it is recoverable from future production.

A minimum royalty clause may provide that any payments that are in excess of production accruing to the royalty interest for the current year are recoverable from future production accruing to the royalty interest in excess of the specified minimum. Payments under such a minimum royalty clause, whether or not represented by earned production, would be treated by the lessor as royalty income subject to depletion.[29] The lessee

[26] *Minerva King Patch*, B.T.A. Memo. Op., Dkt. No. 98852, 1941 P-H B.T.A. Memo. Dec., Para. 41,552 (1941); *See also Alice G. K. Kleberg*, 43 B.T.A. 277 (1941), nonacq. on this issue 1952-1 C.B. 5, acq. and nonacq. on other issues, 1941-1 C.B. 6, 16; *James Lewis Caldwell McFaddin*, 2 T.C. 395 (1943), acq. 1943 C.B. 16.

[27] *Continental Oil Company*, 36 B.T.A. 693 (1937).

[28] *Continental Oil Company, supra.*

[29] *James Lewis Caldwell McFaddin, supra.*

is granted the option of deducting such payments, to the extent
that they exceed the current share of production accruing to
the royalty interest, as a deduction against gross income, either
in the year the payments are made or in the year such amounts
are earned and recovered from production.[30] The election is
made by the lessee on his return for the first year in which
payments are made under a minimum royalty clause, and such
election is binding upon him for all subsequent years and as to
all properties. A failure to deduct such minimum payments in
the year paid constitutes an election to deduct the payments
in the year earned by the royalty interest.[31]

Payments received by a lessor, pursuant to a minimum royalty provision, that are not earned by production but that are
recoverable from future excess production accruing to the
lessor, constitute royalty income subject to depletion.[32] The
same rule is applied even though the lessor may ultimately be
required to repay an excess amount of receipts in the event
that the field does not produce the specified minimum.[33]

If the minimum royalty payments are not recoverable from
future production, and the lessee may forfeit the lease by nonpayment of the minimum royalties, the Revenue Service will
probably consider payments made prior to production as delay
rentals.[34] If such payments are made subsequent to obtaining
production, but the production accruing to the royalty interest
is less than the specified minimum, it appears that the earned
portion of the minimum payment would be treated as royalty,
and the unearned portion of the minimum payment would be
treated as delay rental.[35] If the lessee is not permitted to re-

---

[30] U.S. Treas. Reg. 118, Section 39.23(m)-10(e).

[31] U.S. Treas. Reg. 118, Section 39.23(m)-10(e).

[32] *Logan Coal & Timber Association*, 42 B.T.A. 529 (1940), aff'd, 122
F.(2d) 848, 27 A.F.T.R. 927 (3rd Cir. 1941).

[33] *Crossett Timber & Development Company, Inc.*, 29 B.T.A. 705 (1934).

[34] Compare G.C.M. 26526, *supra*, where the Revenue Service ruled that payments by the lessee of the lessor's taxes were delay rentals prior to production,
and royalties subsequent to production if the gross production equaled the taxes.

[35] Compare G.C.M. 26526, *supra*, and Rev. Rul. 16, *supra*, where the Revenue

cover excess payments from future production, and if he cannot terminate the lease and thereby terminate his obligation to make the minimum payments, it appears that the earned portion of such minimum payments would be treated as royalty, whereas the unearned portion would be treated as a lease bonus.

8.08   *Shut-in Royalties.* Leases sometimes provide for the payment of shut-in royalties, which are usually relatively nominal amounts payable after a producing well has been drilled on the property if the well is shut in for some reason such as lack of marketing facilities. If, as is usually the case, the payment of the shut-in royalty extends the lease for a period of one year or less, and, if the payment is not recoverable from future production, it appears that the payment should be treated as a delay rental. If the payments are recoverable from future production they should probably be treated as minimum royalties.

8.09   Loss from Worthless Properties. The Internal Revenue Code allows a deduction as an ordinary loss for losses not compensated for by insurance or otherwise, if incurred in a trade or business, or in any transaction entered into for profit though not connected with the taxpayer's trade or business.[36] The regulations require that such losses be evidenced by closed and completed transactions or fixed by identifiable events. The loss must be, in substance and not merely in form, a bona fide loss actually sustained during the taxable period for which the deduction is claimed. The allowable loss must be determined by giving full consideration to any salvage value and to any insurance or other compensation received.[37] These items are deducted from the adjusted basis of the property to arrive at the amount of the loss deduction.

Service held that payment of lessor's taxes by the lessee constituted royalty payments to the extent of gross income, with any excess payment treated as a delay rental.

[36] I.R.C., Section 165(a) and (c) [1939 I.R.C., Section 23 (e) and (f)].

[37] U.S. Treas. Reg. 118, Section 39.23(e)-1(b).

The Revenue Service formerly held that all of the taxpayer's right, title, and interest in an oil and gas property must be relinquished in a given taxable year to establish a loss deduction in that year.[38] The Board of Tax Appeals also once held this view.[39] In 1928 the Revenue Service modified its position by holding that formal disposal of the interest was not required if its worthlessness was established by some other means.[40] The earlier rule, although it may have appeared strict, had the virtue of certainty. With the liberalization of the policy a number of questions were created, some of which have come before the courts. The decisions of the courts have not set forth a clearly defined set of principles but, with a few notable exceptions, the decisions appear to be following a discernible pattern.

If the taxpayer claims a deduction for a worthless oil or gas property, but he does not relinquish his interest therein, he is required to attach to his income tax return a statement on a form prescribed by the Revenue Service.[41] This statement, on Form 927, must be executed by the taxpayer separately from the execution of the income tax return. It includes the presentation of all facts pertinent to the decision that the mineral property became worthless during the taxable year. The form also includes an attestation that the property is worthless and an agreement by the taxpayer that he will forego depletion, to the extent of the loss allowed, if the property should in the future become productive. This agreement is required in order to prevent the taxpayer from first recovering his depletable basis through a loss deduction and then, through percentage depletion, obtaining what would amount to a double deduction if the property should later prove productive.[42]

---

[38] S.M. 5700, V-1 C.B. 241 (1926).
[39] *Roy Nichols*, 17 B.T.A. 580 (1929), acq. on other issues, IX-1 C.B. 40.
[40] G.C.M. 3890, VII-1 C.B. 168 (1928).
[41] *Proof of Worthlessness of Mineral Rights*, Treasury Department Form 927.
[42] *Louisiana Iron & Supply Company, Inc.*, 44 B.T.A. 1244 (1941), acq., 1941-2 C.B. 8.

8.10 *Nonproductive Properties.* A loss deduction is not allowed for a mere shrinkage in value but only for complete or practically complete worthlessness. The Board of Tax Appeals and two Circuit Courts of Appeals have held, on the basis of this rule, that no loss deduction is allowable to the owner of both surface and minerals at the time it is determined that the land is barren of oil and gas. The courts so held despite the fact that the land had been purchased solely as an oil prospect.[43] Although the rule that no loss is to be allowed for mere shrinkage in value appears sound under the law and regulations, the result reached in the cited cases appears questionable, because the basis applicable to the mineral right was agreed upon or determinable. All of such value had been proven worthless by the failure to find oil and gas. There appears to be no sound reason why the owner of both surface and minerals should be denied a loss deduction for the worthlessness of the minerals if he is able to prove the basis properly allocable to the minerals, particularly if he acquired the land principally for the mineral content. The courts did not state, and it should not be inferred, that the failure to find oil or gas proved that the allocation of basis to the minerals was not justified. Nor should it be inferred that the taxpayer had no right to allocate the basis between the surface and mineral rights, since it has long been recognized that the purchase price of fee land with growing timber may be allocated between surface and timber rights.[44] There is no sound basis for distinction between minerals and timber in this regard.

A view contrary to that of the above cases is found in a more

---

[43] *The Louisiana Land and Exploration Company,* 7 T.C. 507 (1946), acq. on other issues, 1946-2 C.B. 3, aff'd, 161 F.(2d) 842, 35 A.F.T.R. 1388 (5th Cir. 1947); *Coalinga-Mohawk Oil Co.* v. *Commissioner,* 64 F.(2d) 262, 12 A.F.T.R. 389 (9th Cir. 1933), cert. den., 290 U.S. 637; *Fred C. Champlin,* 1 B.T.A. 1255 (1925).

[44] *Oregon Mesabi Corporation,* 39 B.T.A. 1033 (1939), acq., 1944 C.B. 22, appeal dismissed on stipulation of parties, 109 F.(2d) 1014, 24 A.F.T.R. 458 (9th Cir. 1940).

recent decision of the Court of Claims.[45] In this case the decedent, at the date of death, owned in Texas a one-half interest in a tract of land, subject to a mineral lease. For estate tax purposes, a separate value was established for the mineral interest. Thereafter the lessee drilled a dry hole and surrendered its lease, and the estate claimed a deduction for the value of the mineral interest. The Court allowed the deduction, observing that it was the custom in oil-producing areas to regard the mineral interest as separate from the other rights to the tract, that Texas law recognized ownership of minerals separate from the land, and that the government had recognized a separate property by valuing it separately from the land.

Granting that the property must be worthless, as distinguished from having shrunk in value, the taxpayer has the burden of proving that a bona fide loss was actually sustained during the taxable year.[46] As stated above, losses must be evidenced by closed transactions or identifiable events that establish that the property has become worthless. The taxpayer must actually prove two facts: (1) that some event during the taxable year established the worthlessness of the property, and (2) that no event had occurred in a prior year which had established its worthlessness in such prior year. Thus, in general, a taxpayer cannot defer the deduction beyond the year in which the property becomes worthless. The taxpayer can, however, obtain the deduction in an earlier year by disposing of the property through a bona fide sale or abandonment.[47]

Whether a property is worthless must be judged on the basis

---

[45] *Pool* v. *U.S.*, 119 F. Supp. 202, — A.F.T.R. —, 1954 P-H, Para. 72,406 (Mar. 2, 1954).

[46] *Grass Creek Oil and Gas Company* v. *Reynolds*, Dkt. No. 2106, 15 A.F.T.R. 920 (D. Wyo. 1933), appeal dismissed (*Nolle Prosse*), 71 F.(2d) 1007, 14 A.F.T.R. 367 (10th Cir. 1934); *Tennessee Consolidated Coal Company*, 24 B.T.A. 369 (1931), nonacq. on another issue, XI-1 C.B. 11; *C. H. Goodwin*, 9 B.T.A. 1209 (1928), acq. VII-1 C.B. 12.

[47] *Royalty Corporation of America*, T.C. Memo. Op., Dkt. No. 11058, 1947 P-H T.C. Memo. Dec., Para. 47,170 (1947).

of the facts known by the end of the taxable year, and not in the light of subsequent developments. Thus, a taxpayer claimed a loss in 1935 because a dry hole drilled that year on an adjoining tract had apparently condemned his royalty interest, but he retained title to his interest. In 1936, he executed a lease and received a bonus. In 1937, the lessee completed a well from which the taxpayer received a small amount of royalties. In 1938, the well was abandoned. The Board of Tax Appeals found that the taxpayer was justified in claiming a loss in 1935.[48] On the other hand, where the taxpayer overlooked an event which proved his property worthless in a prior year, he was not allowed a loss deduction for a later year in which another dry hole confirmed the worthlessness.[49]

The closed transaction that most clearly establishes worthlessness of oil and gas properties is relinquishment of title, which can be accomplished by nonpayment of delay rentals, surrender of a lease, and so on. Abandonment of the property is ordinarily sufficient to establish the loss,[50] unless the property had already become worthless in some prior year. Therefore, if the taxpayer claims a loss when he relinquishes title, he may be called upon to prove that the worthlessness of the property was not demonstrated by other evidence in a prior year.

The identifiable event other than abandonment that may prove an oil and gas property worthless is the drilling of a dry hole on or near the property. In each case, however, it is a question of fact whether the dry hole does indeed condemn the property as worthless. For example, a dry hole on a small tract would probably be held to condemn it, particularly in a wildcat area. If the tract is in semi-proven territory and the dry hole is drilled on the edge of the property farthest from the

---

[48] *Chaparral Oil Company*, 43 B.T.A. 457 (1941), acq. 1943 C.B. 4, appeal dismissed on motion of Commissioner, 122 F.(2d) 933, 27 A.F.T.R. 947 (10th Cir. 1941); *Pilot Royalty Company*, T.C. Memo. Op., Dkt. No. 107654, 1942 P-H, T.C. Memo. Dec., Para. 42,665 (1942).

[49] *Pilot Royalty Company, supra.*

[50] *S. W. Forrester*, 23 B.T.A. 942 (1931), acq., X-2 C.B. 24.

producing area, there is a distinct possibility that a productive well might be drilled on the same property closer to production. A large block of acreage is less likely to be proved worthless by a single dry hole, though one such hole in or near the center of the block in a wildcat area might condemn the entire block. If the block is near a producing field, the effect of a dry hole will depend upon its location in relation to the field and to the acreage on which it is drilled. The worthlessness of a property may be demonstrated by dry holes on adjoining tracts. Here, the location of the dry hole, in relation to the property and to any nearby producing areas, is usually the decisive factor. For example, a dry hole drilled between the property and the productive area would probably condemn the property. If the property lies between two productive areas, the limits of both such areas would probably have to be determined by dry holes before the taxpayer would be permitted to charge off his property interest as worthless.

In the Harmon case,[51] the Tax Court set forth certain principles governing the treatment of losses from the worthlessness of oil and gas interests. These principles, which have been followed in other more recent cases,[52] are as follows:

1. A loss is allowable when the property becomes unsalable in the ordinary channels of trade.

2. In ascertaining worthlessness, the same standards should be used for all classes of property.

3. Worthlessness may be caused by
    (a) Exhaustion of oil and gas underlying the property;
    (b) The proven nonexistence of oil and gas under the property; or

---

[51] *C. C. Harmon*, 1 T.C. 40 (1942), acq. on this issue, 1943 C.B. 11, nonacq. on another issue, 1943 C.B. 33, rev'd on another issue, 323 U.S. 44, 32 A.F.T.R. 1411 (1944), reh. den., 323 U.S. 817.

[52] For example *see Harvey A. Heller*, 1 T.C. 222 (1942), acq., 1943 C.B. 11; *The Louisiana Land and Exploration Company, supra; Foster Investment Corporation*, T.C. Memo. Op., Dkt. No. 109387, 1942 P-H T.C. Memo. Dec., Para. 42,664 (1942); *Pilot Royalty Company, supra.*

(c) The mere improbability that oil and gas in profitable quantities will be found under the property.

4. Losses may be allowed even though the taxpayer does not relinquish title to the property.

5. A loss may be allowed even though all sedimentary beds have not been penetrated by drilling, provided the known productive horizons in the area have been so penetrated.

6. The mere speculative possibility of future production is not, by itself, sufficient ground for disallowing a loss deduction.

The tests listed above are objective in the sense that they represent an effort to appraise the property as it might be appraised in the market. The holder of any nonoperating interest, such as a royalty, overriding royalty, net profits interest, or oil payment, has no control over the development of the prop erty, and he is likely to be held to an evaluation of the property such as it would receive in the market. Since market value would probably be destroyed by the drilling of a dry hole, which effectively condemns the property, such a taxpayer will be well advised to claim a loss deduction in the first year in which any dry hole is drilled on or near his property. If he waits until a later year, he may lose the deduction.

The holders of operating rights do have some control over development, and the courts have held that where the lessee pays rentals or drills another well after a dry hole the property is demonstrated to have some value, even though it might otherwise be considered in the market to have lost its value. Thus, a lessee was not allowed a loss deduction for the year in which he drilled a dry hole, because thereafter he continued to pay delay rentals on the property.[53] In another case, the taxpayer charged off his leasehold interest in 1943, during which year a dry hole was drilled on his property, and during which year he was advised by geologists that the property was worth-

---

[53] A. T. *Jergins Trust,* 22 B.T.A. 551 (1931), nonacq. on another issue, X-2 C.B. 91, aff'd and rev'd on other issues, 288 U.S. 508, 12 A.F.T.R. 22 (1933).

less. However, in 1944 the taxpayer participated in the drilling of a second well on the property which also proved dry. On these facts, the Tax Court held that the loss was not allowable in 1943, because the taxpayer and others apparently regarded the property as having sufficient value in a subsequent year to justify another drilling attempt.[54]

On the basis of the foregoing decisions it appears that the holders of nonoperating rights may be required to take a loss deduction in an earlier year than the holders of the operating rights in the same property. It also appears that a lessee may, in fact, defer the loss deduction to a later year by continuing, in good faith, to pay delay rentals on the property. It is believed, however, that the difference in result arises from the fact that if the lessee is willing to expend more money on the property, either for the payment of rentals or for drilling, he demonstrates that the property is not worthless, regardless of how much it may have shrunk in value.

8.11   *Depleted Properties.* If the taxpayer has not recovered his full depletable basis in a producing property when it ceases producing and is abandoned, a loss deduction will probably be disallowed by the Revenue Service on the theory that the taxpayer should have recovered his basis through depletion. As more fully explained in Chapter 11, the taxpayer is entitled to deduct depletion based either on cost or on a percentage of income, whichever is higher in each taxable year. The Revenue Service will probably contend that if cost depletion had been properly computed in past years, the taxpayer would have recovered his entire basis by the time the mineral deposit was exhausted. To be allowed a loss deduction, the taxpayer would have to be able to prove that for each year he has claimed the higher of cost or percentage depletion, computed on the basis of data known at the end of each such year.[55] However, if pro-

---

[54] *L. M. Fischer,* 14 T.C. 792 (1950), acq. on other issues, 1950-2 C.B. 2.
[55] U.S. Treas. Reg. 118, Section 39.23(m)-2(a) and (c), and 9(b).

duction ceases suddenly for causes not reasonably foreseeable, the Revenue Service should allow either an abandonment loss in the year production ends, or a cost depletion deduction for that year equal to the entire remaining basis. A loss deduction has been denied where a lease was held by production, even though such production was not commercially profitable. The Board of Tax Appeals determined that in such a case the loss was deductible in the year in which the lease was surrendered to the lessor.[56]

8.12   Oil and Gas Sales. The owner of an economic interest in an oil and gas property, as defined in paragraphs 2.09-2.12, is entitled to a depletion allowance in respect of income derived from such interest.[57] The owner of an oil and gas property excludes from his income the share of production accruing to other owners of economic interests in such property.[58] For example, if a working interest is burdened with an oil payment, the owner of the working interest does not include in his income the share of production accruing to the owner of the oil payment.

A taxpayer who receives a portion of the proceeds of sale of oil and gas, but who does not own an economic interest in the property producing such oil and gas, realizes income that is not subject to depletion allowances. For example, in one case [59] an attorney entered into a contingent fee arrangement with his client providing that, if he were successful in establishing his client's right to an oil royalty interest, the attorney would become entitled to one-half of his client's interest in the royalty and to one-half of any income which accumulated during the period of litigation. Upon successful settlement of litigation,

---

[56] *Macon Oil and Gas Company,* 23 B.T.A. 54 (1931), acq. on another issue, X-2 C.B. 44.

[57] *Palmer* v. *Bender,* 287 U.S. 551, 11 A.F.T.R. 1106 (1933); U.S. Treas. Reg. 118, Section 39.23(m)-1(b).

[58] *Thomas* v. *Perkins,* 301 U.S. 655, 19 A.F.T.R. 538 (1937).

[59] *Leland J. Allen,* 5 T.C. 1232 (1945), acq., 1946-1 C.B. 1.

the attorney received and reported as depletable income his
share of the proceeds of production that accumulated during
the controversy. The Tax Court held that he was not entitled
to depletion on such income, because he did not own an economic interest in the oil during the period when the income
accumulated. In another case,[60] the Supreme Court held that
the owner and operator of a natural gasoline plant who had a
contractual right to receive a fractional share of the proceeds
of sale of plant products could not claim a depletion allowance,
because he had no economic interest in the properties that
produced the gas run through the gasoline plant.

The producers of oil and gas are ordinarily paid on a
monthly basis for the number of barrels of oil or thousands of
cubic feet of gas run from their wells or field tanks into a
gathering system. Generally, the purchasers of oil and gas are
refiners, utility companies, crude-oil purchasing companies, or,
in some instances, pipe-line companies. The price paid for the
oil or gas may be established by contract between the parties,
or it may be determined by a posted field price for the product.
The principal purchasers in a particular area set the posted
field price in the area, and such price is available to all producers who have not otherwise contracted for the sale of their
production.

If an oil and gas property is owned by more than one person, as is the usual case, the purchasing company ordinarily
pays each of the owners of an interest in the property for his
share of the oil and gas purchased, on the basis of division
orders filed by the owners with the purchaser. If the taxpayer's
interest in the property is a net profits interest, or in some instances an oil payment, it is not possible for the purchaser to
make payment directly to the owner of the interest. In such
cases payment will be made to the owner of the interest

---

[60] *Helvering* v. *Bankline Oil Co.*, 303 U.S. 362, 20 A.F.T.R. 782 (1938).

burdened with the net profits interest or the oil payment, and it will be necessary for the owner of that interest to account for such production to the owner of the net profits interest or oil payment. In making payments, the purchasing company deducts from the amounts due the owners the applicable production and severance taxes levied by the state in which the property is located. Since a net amount after deduction of such taxes is remitted to the respective owners, they should account for such taxes by adding them back to the amounts received in order to determine correctly gross income from the property for purposes of computing percentage depletion.[61] Such taxes would then be claimed as a deduction from gross income.

8.13   *Take-or-Pay Contracts.* Present day gas purchase contracts are usually entered into on a long-term basis and frequently provide a schedule of delivery of gas to the purchaser that is designed to exhaust the estimated reserves of the property during the life of the purchase contract. Such contracts usually provide that if the specified scheduled deliveries are not taken by the purchaser in a given period of time, he will pay for such quantities, even though not taken. Such a clause is referred to as a take-or-pay clause. Ordinarily it is provided that if the purchaser does not take the specified minimum quantity of gas in a given period he may offset the payments made for gas not taken under the take-or-pay clause against future deliveries of gas in excess of the specified minimum quantities. The seller of gas under such contracts should treat all amounts received by him as depletable income from the property, even though a portion of the income received in a given taxable period may represent payment for gas to be delivered in the future.

So long as there is a reasonable expectation that gas paid for but not taken in a given taxable year can be recovered from

---

[61] U.S. Treas. Reg. 118, Section 39.23(m)-1(e) and (g).

future production, the purchaser should treat the cost of such gas as a deferred charge to operations. As gas is later taken in excess of the specified minimum quantities, the deferred charge account should be relieved, and the cost so removed from the account should be charged to operations in the year in which excess quantities are taken. In the event that circumstances indicate that payments for gas not taken in a given year cannot be recovered from future production in excess of the minimum specified quantities, it appears that the purchaser should treat payments for gas not delivered as an additional cost of gas delivered in the year in which the payment was made.

The payments made under a take-or-pay clause, to the extent that they do not represent payments for current deliveries, may also be regarded as the sale of a carved-out gas payment by the seller. The tax consequences to both parties would be the same as stated above. The seller would be regarded as having anticipated future income,[62] hence would treat the amounts received as depletable income in the year of receipt. The purchaser would treat the amount paid as consideration for a purchased gas payment, and would claim depletion as deliveries are taken in excess of the specified minimum.

8.14   Income and Deductions Attributable to Carried Interests. Special tax problems arise in determining the income and deductions attributable to each of the parties in a carried interest arrangement. In general, carried interests are created as sharing arrangements, and the tax consequences of the creation of such interests are governed by the general principles discussed in Chapter 7. It was pointed out in Chapter 2, that three different types of carried interest arrangements are recognized, and that the tax consequences attending each type are different. The three classes of carried interest arrangements are named for the taxpayers in three leading carried interest

---

[62] See Chapter 6.

cases and are called (1) the Manahan,[63] (2) the Herndon,[64] and (3) the Abercrombie.[65]

It might be observed that a type of carried interest arrangement can arise by operation of law in some states. For example, if one of the co-owners of the working interest elects not to participate in the drilling of an oil or gas well, or if one of the co-owners cannot be located, the drilling and development of the property may be continued by the other co-owners. One or more of the participating co-owners will advance costs on behalf of the nonparticipating co-owner. In such cases the laws of some states permit the participating co-owners to recover from production, if any, the reasonable cost of drilling and developing the property attributable to the interest of the nonparticipating co-owner. Although no cases have been found specifically covering the tax consequences of such arrangements, it appears that the most practical and equitable result will be achieved if such arrangements are classified as Manahan type carried interests.

8.15   *Manahan.* In the Manahan type of carried interest, A, the grantor, might assign all of his share of the working interest to B, the grantee, subject to a right of reversion in favor of A. The reversionary right entitles A to the reassignment of a specified fraction of the working interest after B has recovered from production designated development and operating costs. Under such an arrangement B may undertake to drill and equip one or more wells, but he may look only to production

---

[63] *Manahan Oil Company,* 8 T.C. 1159 (1947).

[64] *Herndon Drilling Company,* 6 T.C. 628 (1946), acq. on the issue of deductibility of intangibles, 1946-2 C.B. 3, nonacq. on the issue of whether leasehold and oil payment are one or two properties, 1946-2 C.B. 6. Depletion recomputed under cost method, T.C. Memo. Op., Dkt. No. 4193, 1953 P-H T.C. Memo. Dec., Para. 53,092 (1946).

[65] *J. S. Abercrombie Co.,* 7 T.C. 120 (1946), acq., 1949-1 C.B. 1, aff'd, 162 F.(2d) 338, 35 A.F.T.R. 1467 (5th Cir. 1947). *See also Reynolds* v. *McMurray,* 60 F.(2d) 843, 11 A.F.T.R. 840 (10th Cir. 1932), cert. den., 287 U.S. 664; and *Helvering* v. *Armstrong,* 69 F.(2d) 370, 13 A.F.T.R. 695 (9th Cir. 1934), rev'g 25 B.T.A. 928 (1932), nonacq., XII-1 C.B. 14.

from the property for recovery of his costs. If he never recovers his costs from production, A's reversionary interest in the property will never take effect. Inasmuch as the entire working interest has been assigned to B, he is entitled to deduct all intangibles and to capitalize all equipment costs, and he receives and is taxable upon all income from production until he has recovered his costs. After payout, that is, after B has recovered from production an amount equal to the designated costs, the agreed-upon fraction of the working interest will revert to A. Thereafter A and B are co-owners of the working interest, and each will be obligated to pay his specified fraction of equipment costs and intangible development costs subsequently incurred. Each may then deduct the intangibles he pays if he has so elected, because each owns a share of the working interest.

Until payout, the carrying party would capitalize the entire amount of equipment costs and is entitled to the depreciation deduction thereon as if he were the sole owner of the working interest. Upon payout, B re-assigns to A the specified fraction of the working interest, including equipment. Thus, A has an interest in the tangible equipment on the property subsequent to payout, but, since he has no depreciable basis, he is not entitled to a depreciation deduction.[66] B, on the other hand, gives up an interest in depreciable property at payout and shall make some disposition of the depreciable basis attributable to the interest so relinquished. For some time, following the decision of the Supreme Court in the Choate [67] case, the Revenue Service followed the policy that B could amortize the basis of the depreciable equipment that reverts to A over the productive life of the property, and could claim such amortization in addition to percentage depletion. Late in 1953, however, the Revenue Service unofficially reversed its position and

---

[66] G.C.M. 22730, 1941-1 C.B. 214.
[67] *Choate* v. *Commissioner*, 324 U.S. 1, 33 A.F.T.R. 297 (1945).

now contends that the depreciable basis attributable to the interest relinquished must be added to *B*'s depletable basis in the property. Under this rule such basis would thereafter be recovered through depletion charges, and not in addition to depletion.

8.16   *Herndon.* In the Herndon type of carried interest, the grantor assigns a fraction of the working interest together with an oil payment, payable out of his retained fraction of the working interest, equal in amount to the share of development cost attributable to his retained working interest plus operating costs during the period of payout of the oil payment. Thus, *A*, the grantor, may assign to *B* two-thirds of the working interest, together with an oil payment payable out of *A*'s one-third interest, in consideration for which *B* agrees to drill and equip a well. *B* incurs intangible drilling costs of $90,000 and equipment costs of $30,000 in drilling the well. Under the agreement *B* is entitled to receive the entire income from production, two-thirds from his working interest, and one-third from the oil payment, until his receipts from the oil payment equal $40,000 or one-third of the cost of the well, plus the operating expenses attributable to the one-third interest during the period of payout. As in the Manahan type of carried interest, *B* will be taxable on all of the proceeds of production from the property until payout, but, contrary to the result in that case, *B* will be permitted to expense as intangible drilling costs only two-thirds of the intangibles and will be permitted to capitalize as equipment cost only two-thirds of the cost of equipment. The other one-third of each type of cost must be capitalized as the basis of the oil payment. *B* will, therefore, be entitled to deduct $60,000 as intangible drilling costs, capitalize $20,000 as equipment cost, and must capitalize $40,000 as the cost of the oil payment. Since the net income from, and the cost of, the oil payment are equal, his cost depletion will equal 100 per cent of the net income from the oil payment. Under this type of assignment *A*, the carried party, has an interest but no depreciable basis in the equipment because all equipment costs were paid by *B*, the carrying party. As a consequence *A* will at no time be entitled to a deduction for depreciation of equipment on the well drilled under the carried interest arrangement.

In the Manahan and Herndon types of carried interest, the grantor of a nonproducing property carries over to the interest retained any basis that he had in the undeveloped lease. If the lease was partially developed at the time of the assignment, he would carry over to the retained interest any leasehold basis, and it appears that, under the present Revenue Service policy, he would be required to transfer to leasehold cost that part of the unrecovered basis of equipment applicable to the interest transferred. He should continue to depreciate the balance of the equipment cost applicable to his retained and/or reversionary interest, even though during the period of payout he has no income from the property. He is not entitled to the tax benefit of any expenditures made by his assignee.

8.17   *Abercrombie.* In the Abercrombie type of carried interest, the grantor assigns only a fraction of his working interest and gives a lien on his retained interest to secure development advances made on his behalf by the grantee. In this case, *B*, the grantee, is regarded as having made a loan recoverable only from production from the property; and, although he receives the entire proceeds from production, the fraction thereof applicable to *A*'s interest is not income to *B* but is a recovery of the advance. Such amount is, therefore, taxable to *A*, even though he does not actually receive any cash income until after payout. *B*'s costs, to the extent applicable to his own share of the working interest, are treated in the usual manner; to the extent that they are applicable to *A*'s interest, such costs and expenditures represent an account receivable. If production from the property should be insufficient to recover the costs advanced, B would be entitled to a deduction, at the time of abandonment of the property, equal to the unrecovered balance of the account receivable.

In the Abercrombie type of carried interest B, the grantee, is considered to have advanced the development costs for the account of A, the grantor. A is entitled to treat his share of intangible drilling costs in accordance with his option and to capitalize his share of the equipment costs. It appears that A, regardless of whether he reports on the cash or the accrual basis, should deduct intangibles and capitalize equipment costs at the time such costs are paid by the grantee. This question was not considered in the Abercrombie case, but the theory finds support in the McAdams [68] case, which, although it did not involve a carried interest arrangement, did consider the question of the proper time for deduction of intangibles by one co-owner where the other co-owner advances such costs. If in prior years the carried party has had the tax benefit of deductions for which he made no cash outlay, and the property ceases producing before his ratable share of production equals the depreciation claimed and the intangible drilling costs deducted, it appears that the carried party would realize taxable income to the extent that such deductions exceeded his ratable share of production.

Although the economic results of the three types of carried interest arrangements are similar, their tax consequences vary considerably. The variation in consequences is apparently directly attributable to the form of the transaction, so that a taxpayer desiring to achieve a given result can do so by following precisely the prescribed form. If the transaction follows the Manahan form, the Revenue Service has been willing to issue a ruling that the Manahan rule will apply. Presumably, if the transaction follows either of the other two forms, the courts

---

[68] *McAdams* v. *Commissioner*, 198 F.(2d) 54, 42 A.F.T.R. 310 (5th Cir. 1952).

may be expected to follow the other rules, but the Revenue Service has been reluctant to issue rulings to that effect.[69]

8.18   Depreciation. Most of the general rules governing the depreciation deduction are equally applicable to oil and gas properties and other types of property.[70] The depreciation deduction, which is available in addition to depletion, is intended to allow the taxpayer to recover his basis in tangible lease and well equipment. Depletion, on the other hand, is allowed in respect of the taxpayer's investment in a mineral deposit, including intangible drilling and development costs if the taxpayer has elected to capitalize such costs.[71]

Although the adjusted basis for depreciation of oil and gas producing equipment is determined under the same rules as for depreciable assets generally,[72] the depreciable base depends in part upon the taxpayer's election to deduct or to capitalize intangible drilling and development costs.[73] If the taxpayer has elected to deduct such costs, he will also deduct the cost of installation of tangible producing equipment; but if he has elected to capitalize intangibles, that part representing installation costs of tangible producing equipment is added to the depreciable basis of the equipment, and the remainder of the intangible costs is added to the basis for depletion.[74]

---

[69] In the Court of Appeals for the Fifth, Ninth, and Tenth Circuits, the Abercrombie, Armstrong, and McMurray cases cited in n. 65, *supra*, would be strong precedents in favor of a taxpayer claiming Abercrombie treatment.

[70] U.S. Treas. Reg. 118, Section 39.23(m)-18. It should be noted that the depreciation allowance for extractive industries is based on I.R.C. Sections 611 [1939 I.R.C., Section 23(m)] and 167 [1939 I.R.C., Section 23(e)].

[71] *United States* v. *Dakota-Montana Oil Co.*, 288 U.S. 459, 12 A.F.T.R. 18 (1933).

[72] I.R.C., Sections 167(f) and 1011 [1939 I.R.C., Sections 114(a) and 113(b)]. It should be noted that, for periods after January 1, 1952, I.R.C., Section 1016(a)(2)(B) [1939 I.R.C., Section 113(b)(1)(B)(ii)] provides that a taxpayer's basis shall be reduced by the excess of depreciation actually allowed over the amount allowable only to the extent that the excess resulted in a tax benefit. This rule also applies to periods before January 1, 1952, if the taxpayer so elects on or before December 31, 1954, under the provisions of I.R.C., Section 1020 [1939 I.R.C., Section 113(d)].

[73] *See* Chapter 10.

[74] U.S. Treas. Reg. 118, Section 39.23(m)-16(b)(2).

For this purpose the Revenue Service has adopted the policy that the well and tangible producing equipment are complete when the "Christmas tree" is installed. The installation costs up to this point are affected by the option regarding intangibles. Installation costs beyond this point must be capitalized, and become part of the depreciable basis regardless of the taxpayer's election.[75]

Because salt water disposal wells are considered operating facilities, as distinguished from production facilities, the cost of such wells including drilling costs must be capitalized, and are recoverable through depreciation rather than depletion allowances. Such costs do not fall within the option to capitalize or deduct intangible costs incurred in drilling oil and gas wells.[76] On the other hand, water or gas injection wells are considered part of the producing function, and drilling costs incurred in the drilling of such wells are within the option to capitalize or deduct intangibles.[77] Salt water disposal wells may be drilled to serve the dual purpose of injection and disposal. Under such circumstances it appears that the primary purpose of the well would govern the classification of drilling costs.

To be entitled to a depreciation deduction, the taxpayer must have a beneficial interest in the tangible equipment, although he need not hold legal title,[78] and he must have an investment or basis in the equipment.[79] Thus the owner of a royalty, an overriding royalty, a net profits interest, or an oil payment is not entitled to depreciation of equipment, because he has no interest in such equipment. On the other hand, the

[75] Mim. 6754, 1952-1 C.B. 30. The "Christmas tree" is a set of valves to control the flow from a well.

[76] See Mim. 6754, supra, which holds that costs of installing salt water disposal equipment are not within the option.

[77] See also paragraphs 10.12 and 10.13.

[78] Helvering v. F. & R. Lazarus & Co., 308 U.S. 252, 23 A.F.T.R. 778 (1939).

[79] C. A. Happold, T.C. Memo. Op., Dkt. No. 106124, 1942 P-H T.C. Memo. Dec., Para. 42,625 (1942), aff'd on another issue, 141 F.(2d) 199, 32 A.F.T.R. 271 (5th Cir. 1944).

owner of a working interest who assigns an oil payment to an equipment supplier in return for the equipping of a well has an interest in the equipment but has no investment or basis therein, and he is not entitled to a depreciation deduction.[80]

8.19   *Methods of Computation.* Like taxpayers in other industries, oil operators may elect to compute depreciation by any reasonable method having due regard to the operating conditions during the taxable period.[81] With the exception of the declining balance method of depreciation, once a method of computation has been adopted for particular assets, the same method must be used for future years unless permission to change is obtained from the Commissioner of Internal Revenue.[82] The straight-line and unit-of-production methods of computation have in the past been most frequently used, although in some instances a declining balance was permissible.[83] Under the Internal Revenue Code of 1954, with respect to assets acquired after January 1, 1954 and having a useful life of three years or more, the taxpayer may also use a double-rate declining-balance method or the sum-of-the-years-digits method, or any other method consistently applied which does not produce a greater amount of depreciation in the first two-thirds of the useful life of the property than that computed under the double-rate declining-balance method.[84] Any one of these methods can be applied to the various assets of the taxpayer in one of four ways:[85]

1. To all depreciable assets included in one account—a composite account;

2. To the assets segregated into classes according to use, such as all equipment for a certain purpose—classified accounts;

3. To the assets grouped by kind and life—group accounts;

4. To each item separately—item accounts.

---

[80] *See* Chapter 7.
[81] U.S. Treas. Reg. 118, Section 39.23(1)-5(a).
[82] I.T. 3818, 1946-2 C.B. 42; U.S. Treas. Reg. 118, Section 39.41-2(c).
[83] U.S. Treas. Bulletin "F" (Revised January, 1942), U.S. Government Printing Office, Washington, 1948, pp. 4-5.
[84] I.R.C., Section 167.
[85] U.S. Treas. Bulletin "F," *supra,* pp. 6-8.

Classified or group accounts are used most often in oil operations, because they avoid the necessity of keeping detailed and voluminous records of each item and facilitate the recording of transfers. The following comments refer primarily to classified, group, or composite accounts. Normally such accounts are maintained separately for each property unit owned by the taxpayer, because it is necessary to compute depreciation by property units in computing the net income limitation on percentage depletion.

The amount recoverable by depreciation is the basis of the equipment less the estimated salvage value at the end of its useful life.[86] If the straight-line method of computation is used, the amount recoverable is spread in equal annual installments over the useful life of the equipment. If the equipment is not readily movable, so that it has usefulness only on the particular lease on which installed, the depreciation should be based on the useful life of the equipment or on the anticipated life of the mineral deposit, whichever period is shorter. If the equipment is removable, and can be used elsewhere after exhaustion of the mineral deposit where it is first installed, such mineral property should be charged only with the exhaustion of value occurring during use of the equipment on that property. This result might be accomplished by using an estimated life longer than that of the mineral deposit, or by estimating a higher salvage value for the tangible equipment at the anticipated end of its use on the property where it is first installed.

If the unit-of-production method is used, the depreciable sum is divided by the estimated reserves to arrive at a depreciation rate per unit of production. Such rate is multiplied by units produced in a given period to arrive at the depreciation deduction for that period. This method has some advantages because it automatically correlates the depreciation deduction to mineral removal and to income.[87] In theory, the method should be applied only to equipment with a useful life equal

---

[86] U.S. Treas. Reg. 118, Section 39.23(1)-1; U.S. Treas. Bulletin "F," *supra*, p. 2.

[87] *Golconda Oil Co.*, 7 B.T.A. 955 (1927), acq., VII-2 C.B. 15.

to that of the mineral deposit,[88] but in practice it may be applied to all equipment on the property by increasing the salvage value of equipment that is expected to outlive the mineral deposit. Ordinarily, where depreciation is computed on classified or group accounts and by a unit-of-production method, the reserves used in computing depreciation would be the same as those used for computing cost depletion. However, if the property is not fully developed, a smaller reserve figure may be used for the depreciation computation, because such computation should be based on those reserves recoverable with the equipment in use at the time.[89] The record-keeping requirements and the depreciation schedules to be filed with income tax returns are basically similar for oil and for other operations.[90]

8.20 *Transfers and Retirements.* No gain or loss is realized when equipment is transferred from one property of the taxpayer to another property of the same taxpayer.[91] If the taxpayer uses the classified or group accounts method of recording depreciable assets, it is customary to debit and credit the respective asset accounts with the condition value of the item transferred. At the time of the transfer the condition of the item is appraised, and the condition value is generally computed in accordance with the following table:

Class	Condition	Condition Value as Per Cent of Cost
A	New	100
B	Good	75
C	Usable	50
D	Unusable	Scrap

The practice of transferring the condition value of transferred equipment between asset accounts may lead to some

---

[88] *Evangeline Gravel Co., Inc.,* 13 B.T.A. 101 (1928).

[89] *Dulup Oil Company,* B.T.A. Memo. Op., Dkt. No. 94904, 1940 P-H B.T.A. Memo. Dec., Para. 40,412 (1940), rev'd on another issue, 126 F.(2d) 1019, 29 A.F.T.R. 60 (5th Cir. 1942).

[90] Mim. 4170 (Rev.), XV-2 C.B. 148 (1936); U.S. Treas. Bulletin "F," *supra,* pp. 6-9.

[91] U.S. Treas. Reg. 118, Section 39.23(e)-1(b) and (f)-1.

distortion of asset and depreciation reserve accounts, because condition value is usually less than cost. Therefore, if the item transferred is material it is better practice to credit the asset account with the full cost of the item transferred and to charge the related depreciation reserve account with the difference between cost and condition value. However, no distortion of net values occurs, except as between properties, because under either procedure the remaining depreciable basis would be the same.

No loss is recognized upon normal retirement of part of the equipment carried in a classified account or group account of assets, because the depreciation rate established for the group contemplates that some assets may last a shorter or longer time than the average useful life of all the assets in the group. Instead, the cost of the item retired is credited to the asset account and charged, after deduction of salvage, to the depreciation reserve.[92] The salvage value will be charged to an appropriate asset account. In one case,[93] the taxpayer computed depreciation by the unit-of-production method, based on the cost of all the equipment on a lease and on the entire reserves for the lease. The court denied a loss for abandonment of well equipment on one well where other wells on the same lease remained productive, although in some earlier cases [94] such losses were allowed. It would appear that a loss should be allowable under such circumstances if depreciation was computed separately by wells or by items.[95]

In the event that part of tangible equipment is sold or retired for unexpected causes, such as abnormal obsolescence or

---

[92] U.S. Treas. Reg. 118, Section 39.23(e)-3(b).

[93] *Mohawk Petroleum Co.* v. *Commissioner*, 148 F.(2d) 957, 33 A.F.T.R. 1226 (9th Cir. 1945).

[94] *Majestic Oil Corporation*, 42 B.T.A. 659 (1940), nonacq. on this issue, 1940-2 C.B. 12, acq. on other issues, 1940-2 C.B. 5; *Witherspoon Oil Company*, 34 B.T.A. 1130 (1936), appeal dismissed without written opinion (5th Cir. 1939), where it was stated: "In so far as the amounts here claimed represent undepreciated costs of physical assets—other than those held includable in depletable cost . . .—, the petitioner is entitled to deductions upon abandonment of the wells to which they relate. . . ."

[95] U.S. Treas. Reg. 118, Section 39.23(e)-3(d).

casualty, a loss is allowable [96] or gain may be recognized. In computing such gain or loss, the basis of the equipment disposed of is not its cost less a pro rata part of total depreciation previously allowed or allowable, but rather the cost less the depreciation that would have been allowable if the items disposed of had not been depreciated in a group account.[97]

---

[96] U.S. Treas. Reg. 118, Section 39.23(e)-3(c).

[97] *United States Industrial Alcohol Co. (West Virginia)* v. *Helvering*, 137 F.(2d) 511, 31 A.F.T.R. 425 (2nd Cir. 1943), aff'g in part 42 B.T.A. 1323 (1940), acq. on this issue as to result only, 1941-2 C.B. 13, nonacq. on another issue, 1941-2 C.B. 24.

CHAPTER IX

Geological and Geophysical Costs

9.01   Introduction. The purpose and general nature of geological and geophysical expenditures were described briefly in Chapter 1, where it was indicated that such expenditures are usually preliminary to the discovery of oil or gas.

All large oil and gas operators and many medium-sized ones maintain well-staffed and adequately budgeted geological and geophysical departments, the members of which devote their full time to testing oil and gas prospects. Smaller operators may employ independent geological and geophysical firms, on a fee basis, to perform this work for them. Oil operators consider their geological and geophysical costs as ordinary and necessary expenses of conducting their business. For income tax purposes, the question arises whether geological and geophysical expenditures are deductible as ordinary and necessary business expenses under Section 162 of the Internal Revenue Code [1939 I.R.C., Section 23(a)(1)(A)], or whether they must be capitalized as additions to lease costs under Section 263(a) of the Internal Revenue Code [1939 I.R.C., Section 24(a)(2)].[1]

9.02   Development of Present Policy. The petroleum in-

---

[1] *See also* U.S. Treas. Reg. 118, Section 39.24(a)-2.

dustry adopted the practice of expensing geological and geophysical costs long before the first Revenue Act was passed in 1913, and has followed this practice more or less consistently ever since. The industry viewed these expenditures as essential to its normal operations, and hence properly deductible under Section 162 of the Internal Revenue Code in computing taxable income. Prior to 1941 the Revenue Service agreed with the industry that geological and geophysical expenditures were properly deductible from income in the year incurred or paid. In June, 1941, the Revenue Service ruled[2] that if geological and geophysical costs were properly expensed, they must be deducted from the gross income from the property for purposes of computing the limitation on percentage depletion. If such costs were not "directly attributable to a particular producing property, they must be fairly allocated to the several producing properties."[3] In October, 1941, the Revenue Service issued a ruling[4] that superseded the June ruling and held that deductible geological and geophysical expenditures could be allocated among all properties held by a taxpayer, but that if allocated to a producing property, only that portion so allocated would be deductible from the income from that property in computing the limitation on percentage depletion.

Early in 1942, the Commissioner issued instructions to his agents to treat geological and geophysical expenses as capital expenditures when they resulted in the acquisition or retention of properties. Geological and geophysical expenses incurred for the purpose of determining the location of wells to be drilled or of supervising their drilling were to be deducted as lease operating or development expense, provided a proper election had been made under pertinent provisions of the Regulations.[5] Absent from such instructions was any reference

---

[2] G.C.M. 22689, 1941-1 C.B. 225.
[3] G.C.M. 22689, *supra.*
[4] G.C.M. 22956, 1941-2 C.B. 103.
[5] Unpublished Field Procedure Memorandum No. 241, issued by the Revenue Service to its field agents and engineers in 1942.

to the method of allocating costs incurred among leases acquired or retained in the same area. However, a so-called shot-point method was then in use by engineer revenue agents. This method was based on the number of shots made in a seismic survey, or cores made in core drilling surveys, and had the effect of apportioning costs in relation to the amount of work done.

Contemporaneously with the issuance of these field instructions, the Commissioner successfully defended his position requiring capitalization of such costs before the Board of Tax Appeals in the Schermerhorn Oil case.[6] In that case Schermerhorn had hired a geologist to keep in touch with petroleum exploration and development activity, recommend properties for possible acquisition, and perform other related services. The geologist was paid a salary and reimbursed for his expenses, and was given a right to 10 per cent of the net profits after payout from the operation or sale of any properties recommended by him. The Board of Tax Appeals held that the net profits payments to the geologist were a part of the cost of acquiring the properties. The obligation arose when the properties were acquired, but the time of payment was postponed until net profits should be realized. The Board considered the payments similar to commission paid in connection with the purchase of property and to expenditures for surveys and abstracts of title, all of which had been held to be capital expenditures.[7] The Board stated that "the test is whether the expenditures are made in connection with the acquisition or preservation of a capital asset. If so, they are capital expenditures." In 1946, the Tax Court decided the Louisiana Land and Exploration [8] case, in which the petitioner had acquired

---

[6] *Schermerhorn Oil Corporation,* 46 B.T.A. 151 (1942); see discussion of this case in connection with sharing arrangements, paragraph 7.01.

[7] *See Helvering* v. *Winmill,* 305 U.S. 79, 21 A.F.T.R. 962 (1938); *Seletha O. Thompson,* 9 B.T.A. 1342 (1928), acq., VII-2 C.B. 39.

[8] *The Louisiana Land and Exploration Company,* 7 T.C. 507 (1946), acq., 1946-2 C.B. 3.

mineral leases covering two tracts of land, and ten years later had expended $11,361.56 for a geophysical survey of these properties to determine whether subsurface structures in the properties appeared sufficiently favorable to justify drilling for oil and gas. The Tax Court denied the taxpayer's claim for a deduction for this geophysical expense and required that it be capitalized, on the grounds that the expenditure resulted in acquisition or retention of a capital asset.

9.03   Present Revenue Service Position. In April, 1950, the Revenue Service ruled [9] that geological and geophysical expenditures are not deductible as ordinary and necessary business expenses, but are inherently capital in nature and must be added to the cost of property acquired or retained on the basis of data obtained from the exploration project. In accounting for geological and geophysical costs and allocating such costs to specific properties, the first step is to separate them into so-called project costs and area of interest costs.

9.04   *Project Costs.* In the planning stage, the territory over which an exploration program can be conducted advantageously as a single integrated operation is determined and designated a project area. The geographical limits of a project area are outlined after weighing various considerations, namely:

1. Size and topography of area to be explored;
2. Existing information with respect to that area and nearby areas; and
3. Quantity of equipment, men, and money available.

Once the project area has been designated, all costs attributable thereto must be accumulated. The ultimate disposition of such costs depends upon the nature of the work performed and the information obtained.

Ordinarily a reconnaissance survey, which is relatively inexpensive, is first made to locate those portions of the project

---

[9] I.T. 4006, 1950-1 C.B. 48.

area which have the greatest potentiality. All costs in connection therewith are accumulated for the entire project, and then are apportioned equally to each noncontiguous portion of the project area which possesses sufficient mineral-producing potential to merit further exploration. The prudent business man would strive to limit the size of each project to be surveyed. He should bear in mind the definition of a project as a territory over which the exploration program is to be conducted advantageously as a single integrated operation. A single integrated operation implies a series of related steps without break in time or space. A break in time indicates completion of an operation. A break in space prevents correlation of data.

9.05   *Area of Interest Costs.* The noncontiguous portions of the project area selected for further exploration are designated as areas of interest. On each area of interest a detailed survey is conducted, employing such geological and geophysical methods as will obtain subsurface data sufficiently accurate to afford a basis for a decision to acquire or retain properties, or to abandon the entire area as unworthy of development by mine or well. The costs of conducting this type of survey must be charged directly to the particular area of interest covered. These direct costs, plus a portion of the project cost previously apportioned thereto, are then redistributed, on a net acreage basis, to the properties acquired or retained as a result of such survey. Net acreage basis means, for example, that if in a 5,000-acre area of interest, bearing reconnaissance and detailed survey costs of $44,000, 640 acres are acquired in the following tracts:

Tract A, 320 acres: full working interest acquired;
Tract B, 160 acres: undivided ½ working interest acquired;
Tract C, 160 acres: ⅛ overriding royalty acquired.

The total detailed survey costs and the portion of the reconnaissance survey costs are allocated among the properties acquired as follows:

Tract	Gross acres	Fraction of mineral rights obtained			Net acres	Fraction of total	Total area of interest cost	Addition to cost of property acquired
A	320	x	1	=	320	320/440 x	$44,000 =	$32,000
B	160	x	½	=	80	80/440 x	44,000 =	8,000
C	160	x	¼	=	40	40/440 x	44,000 =	4,000
					440			$44,000

Note that in Tract C, the ⅛ overriding royalty is assumed to be equivalent to a ¼ working interest. This relationship has come to be commonly accepted as the relative value of such interests in wildcat property.

If the subsurface data obtained by a detailed survey indicate that the area should be abandoned as unworthy of development, the costs accumulated against the area of interest should be written off as a loss under Section 165 of the Internal Revenue Code [1939 I.R.C., Section 23(e) or 23(f)]. It is recognized that sometimes subsurface data are not convincing in their disclosure. The objective test of what is done about acquisition or retention of leases is important. To maintain that properties are acquired or retained despite poor subsurface data places the burden of proving the negative value of such geological information upon the taxpayer.

At the end of the taxable year a geophysical or geological survey may be incomplete. Since the costs of such surveys are capital in nature, the nonproductive leasehold (or royalty) account will probably reflect an unallocated cost, the disposition of which is deferred until a decision is reached on the results of the survey. The question of how much time may elapse between the time the survey is completed and the time a decision is reached on the merits of the properties is unsettled. If a charge is deferred over the end of a taxable year, although the survey was completed before the year ended, and it is then charged off because no properties were acquired or retained, the taxpayer may be required to offer evidence that the time lapse was justified.

9.06   An Alternative Position. Although the petroleum industry has contested every effort of the Revenue Service to require capitalization of geological and geophysical costs, it appears that such exploration costs over a limited and confined area are properly capital in nature. It has been the contention of the Revenue Service that such expenditures are part of the cost of acquiring oil in the ground, the goal of every oil producer. This theory may be questioned on the grounds that geological and geophysical costs are incurred for the purpose of evaluating every acre of territory surveyed, in which case the costs should be apportioned on the basis of the entire acreage surveyed. Under this evaluation test, such costs would be apportioned to areas of disinterest as well as areas of interest by applying an allocation factor, the denominator of which is the total acreage surveyed and the numerator of which is the acreage constituting the area of interest or area of disinterest. If a taxpayer adopted a consistent accounting practice in the allocation of exploration expenditures on the basis of the evaluation test, his position might well be accepted by the courts on the grounds that the method is an accepted accounting method consistently applied by the taxpayer.

CHAPTER X

Intangible Drilling and Development Costs

10.01   Introduction. It has been indicated in previous chapters that the owner of operating rights in an oil or gas property has the burden of developing the property, and that in the course of developing the property by drilling oil or gas wells he incurs costs that are segregated between intangible drilling and development costs and equipment costs. It has also been stated that under certain circumstances the taxpayer had the option of expensing or capitalizing the intangible drilling and development costs. It is the purpose of this chapter to consider the nature of this election as well as to consider in some detail the nature of intangible costs. For convenience intangible drilling and development costs will be referred to as intangibles.

10.02   *History of the Election.* Until 1954 no specific statutory authority existed for the election to deduct intangibles. However, the Revenue Acts of 1918[1] and 1921[2] indicate by implication that Congress may have considered intangibles to be deductible by providing: "In case of . . . oil and gas wells . . . , a reasonable allowance for depletion . . . , according to the peculiar conditions in each case, based upon cost including cost of development not otherwise deducted. . . ." Subsequent acts did not contain similar provisions. However, congressional recognition of the right to deduct intangibles is contained in the excess profits tax laws enacted in 1940[3] and in 1950,[4] where intangible costs were specified as one of the classes of deductions that may have been abnormal in the base period.

The election was first made available by administrative ruling in connection with the Revenue Act of 1916,[5] and it has been available in modified form ever since.[6] As might be expected in the case of a regulation that did not have specific statutory authority, there has been a considerable amount of litigation over the validity of the ruling. The attack was first made under the Revenue Act of 1918 and was founded upon the argument that the expenditure was capital in nature and that the Commissioner had no authority to determine arbitrarily, by regulation or otherwise, that a purely capital item could be treated as a business expense.[7] The Board of Tax Appeals did not rule on the validity of the regulation because the question was not properly at issue.

In 1931 the question came before the District Court for the

---

[1] Revenue Act of 1918, Section 214(a)(10).

[2] Revenue Act of 1921, Section 214(a)(10).

[3] Excess Profits Tax Act of 1940 as amended March, 1941, Section 711(b)(1)(I). This section was I.R.C., Section 711(b)(1)(I) when it was repealed by the Revenue Act of 1945, Section 122(a).

[4] 1939 I.R.C., Section 433(b)(9)(B).

[5] U.S. Treas. Reg. 33, Article 170.

[6] For example, *see* U.S. Treas. Reg. 118, Section 39.23(m)-16(a)(1) and (b)(1).

[7] *Old Farmers Oil Company*, 12 B.T.A. 203 (1928), acq., VII-2 C.B. 30 (1928).

Western District of Kentucky, and the Court concluded that, although it felt that intangibles might more properly be classified as a capital expenditure, the point was sufficiently debatable to justify the Commissioner's action in devising a regulation to govern the situation.[8] The Court recognized that the continued administrative acceptance, and the congressional sanction implied by reenactment of the statute without specific provision overthrowing the regulation, gave the regulation the force and effect of law. In 1933, the Court of Appeals for the Tenth Circuit reached a similar conclusion, citing Supreme Court decisions in which the treatment of intangibles had been considered and no question raised as to the validity of the regulation.[9]

It was not until 1945 that a contrary view appeared in the courts, when the Court of Appeals for the Fifth Circuit held, in the F.H.E. Oil case,[10] that the regulations granting the election in respect of intangibles were invalid. The Court reasoned that the nature of the expenditure was capital, and that such an allowance was contrary to Section 24(a)(2) of the 1939 Internal Revenue Code [1954 I.R.C., Section 263], which prohibits a deduction for any amounts paid for permanent improvements or betterments made to increase the value of property. The Court thought that no specific authority could be inferred from the depletion provisions of Section 23(m) of the 1939 Internal Revenue Code [1954 I.R.C., Section 611], since they expressly provided for the recoupment of depletable cost by a method other than by charge to expense, and that

---

[8] *Sterling Oil and Gas Company* v. *Lucas*, 51 F.(2d) 413, 10 A.F.T.R. 255 (W.D. Ky. 1931), aff'd on another issue, 62 F.(2d) 951, 12 A.F.T.R. 90 (6th Cir. 1933).

[9] *Ramsey* v. *Commissioner*, 66 F.(2d) 316, 12 A.F.T.R. 1000 (10th Cir. 1933) cert. den., 290 U.S. 673. The Court cited the following cases: *United States* v. *Dakota-Montana Oil Company*, 288 U.S. 459, 12 A.F.T.R. 18 (1933); *Murphy Oil Company* v. *Burnet*, 287 U.S. 299, 11 A.F.T.R. 1095 (1932).

[10] *F.H.E. Oil Company* v. *Commissioner*, 147 F.(2d) 1002, 33 A.F.T.R. 785 (5th Cir. 1945), reh. den., 149 F.(2d) 238, 33 A.F.T.R. 1263 (5th Cir. 1945), second reh. den., 150 F.(2d) 857, 34 A.F.T.R. 112 (5th Cir., 1945), aff'g 3 T.C. 13 (1934), nonacq., 1944 C.B. 37.

congressional acquiescence in the regulation could not be presumed by the mere failure to correct, by statute, a regulation promulgated by the Treasury Department, where there was no statutory authority for the regulation.

Since the industry had long accepted the right to make such an election as provided in the regulations, it is not surprising that this decision was followed by a request for rehearing of the case,[11] in which thirty briefs were filed by counsel for other oil producers as *amici curiae*. The Court, in denying the request for rehearing, stated that it would reach the same conclusion apart from the validity of the regulation, relegating to dicta the portion of its opinion dealing with the validity of the regulation. The industry was sufficiently concerned, however, to obtain a concurrent resolution from the Seventy-ninth Congress[12] recognizing the validity of Section 29.23(m)(16) of Regulations 111 and corresponding provisions of prior regulations. In the concurrent resolution, express reference was made to Section 711(b)(1) of the 1939 Internal Revenue Code, enacted in 1940, to indicate previous congressional recognition of the regulations. In denying a second request for rehearing,[13] the Court indicated that a congressional resolution was entitled to respectful consideration by the courts but did not have the force of law, since it was not an act of Congress approved by the president or passed over his veto.

Because of this decision there was some uncertainty about the right to deduct intangibles, although the Revenue Service continued to follow the regulation and allowed the deduction, if properly claimed. This policy was impliedly sanctioned by Congress, because the Excess Profits Tax Act of 1950 gave recognition to the practice of expensing intangibles. In addition, in providing in 1951 for the deduction of development

---

[11] *F.H.E. Oil Company* v. *Commissioner, supra.*

[12] H. Con. Res. 50, Concurrent Resolution of July 21, 1945, Seventy-ninth Congress, First Session, 1945 C.B. 545, 1945 P-H, Para. 70,512 and 70,651.

[13] *F.H.E. Oil Company* v. *Commissioner, supra.*

costs of mines other than oil and gas wells,[14] both the House Ways and Means [15] and the Senate Finance [16] Committee reports clearly stated that a similar provision for oil and gas wells was unnecessary because optional deduction of intangibles was already permitted. In 1954 the question was laid to rest by express statutory direction [17] to prescribe regulations granting the option. Although this provision is effective only for taxable years beginning after December 31, 1953 and ending after August 16, 1954,[18] it may be assumed that the question will not again arise for earlier years.

10.03   *Rules in Effect Prior to January 1, 1943.* Any discussion of intangibles must distinguish between the rules in effect for taxable years beginning prior to January 1, 1943, and years beginning after December 31, 1942. Rulings and court decisions must be closely scrutinized to determine whether the tax year involved was in the earlier or later period. Because of the substantial change in the administrative rules taking effect in the later period, an opportunity to make new elections was afforded each taxpayer for the first taxable year within the later period in which he incurred intangible costs.[19] An understanding of the difference in the two periods will enable the reader to recognize the significance of any opinion of a court or administrative body considering a taxable year in the earlier period. For that reason it has been thought desirable to discuss the two major differences that mark the change in treatment of intangibles.

Perhaps the *obligation well doctrine* is worthy of first con-

---

[14] 1939 I.R.C., Section 23(cc) [1954 I.R.C., Section 616].

[15] House of Representatives Report No. 586, Eighty-second Congress, First Session (June 18, 1951), 1951-2 C.B. 357 at 379.

[16] Senate Report No. 781, Eighty-second Congress, First Session (September 18, 1951), 1951-2 C.B., 458 at 489.

[17] I.R.C., Section 263(c).

[18] I.R.C., Section 7851.

[19] T.D. 5276, 1943 C.B. 151, amended U.S. Treas. Reg. 103 by adding Section 19.23(m)-16(b), applicable to taxable years beginning after December 31, 1942.

sideration. In the earlier period, whenever drilling of a well was undertaken in consideration for the assignment of operating or royalty rights in a property, the entire cost of drilling the well was capitalized as an acquisition cost necessary to perfect title in the assignee.[20] The doctrine was extended to apply to acquisition of operating rights that would terminate in a short period unless drilling was begun.[21] This treatment was justified on the basis that drilling cost was incurred to acquire a property interest and, like all acquisition costs, should be capitalized. The present rule recognizes that drilling costs applicable to the driller's operating rights constitute intangibles subject to the election, but those applicable to operating rights owned by another are not subject to the election.

The *turnkey well doctrine* was another peculiarity of the rule in effect prior to January 1, 1943. A turnkey well may be defined as one in which drilling and equipping of a well is undertaken by a drilling contractor who is to turn over to the operator a completed, operating well. It is similar to construction of a home under a contract where the contractor is to erect the house and turn the key over to the owner upon completion. If the contract contemplated a completed and equipped well, the entire cost had to be capitalized; if the contract contemplated completion of the hole only and not installation of the equipment, the expenditure was considered for intangibles and the costs were governed by the taxpayer's election. This thin line of distinction was dependent in some cases upon whether the contract was considered divisible. Once this rule was established it became easy to circumvent it, and taxpayers were in a position to control their deductions by the nature of their contracts. The current definition, as expressly stated in the regulations,[22] includes as intangibles subject to the election "cost to operators of any drilling or

[20] *Hardesty v. Commissioner,* 127 F.(2d) 843, 29 A.F.T.R. 420 (5th Cir. 1942); *Hunt v. Commissioner,* 135 F.(2d) 697, 31 A.F.T.R. 49 (5th Cir. 1943).
[21] *F.H.E. Oil Company v. Commissioner, supra.*
[22] U.S. Treas. Reg. 118, Section 39.23(m)-16(a)(1).

development work . . . done for them by contractors under any form of contract, including turnkey contracts."

10.04   Election to Expense or Capitalize. Any taxpayer who owns the operating rights in an oil or gas property and who incurs intangible costs must elect to expense or to capitalize such costs. If he elects to capitalize intangibles, he is granted a second election to capitalize or charge to expense the portion of intangibles attributable to dry or nonproductive wells. The election to expense must be made by the taxpayer for his first taxable year beginning after December 31, 1942, in which intangibles are incurred; once made, the election is binding on the taxpayer for all subsequent years.[23] If the taxpayer elects to capitalize intangibles, that election must also be made in the first year in which such costs are paid or incurred, but he need not exercise his election in respect of the cost of non-productive wells until the first year in which a dry hole is drilled. If a taxpayer elects to capitalize intangibles and further elects to deduct the cost of dry holes, the deduction for dry-hole costs is allowed as a loss in the year the dry hole is completed and abandoned.[24] If the taxpayer elects to expense intangibles, such costs may not also be included in the basis of the property.[25]

10.05   *Who May Elect.* Only the owner of the operating rights in a property has the responsibility of developing the property and is accorded the privilege of treating intangibles as a deduction under this election. It makes no difference whether the operating rights are held by a fee owner, or under a lease or any other form of contract granting working or operating rights. Nor does it matter whether the intangible

---

[23] U.S. Treas. Reg. 111, Section 29.23(m)-16(b); *See also* U.S. Treas. Reg. 118, Section 39.23(m)-16(d).

[24] U.S. Treas. Reg. 118, Section 39.23(m)-16(b)(4); cf. *Great Western Petroleum Corporation*, 1 T.C. 624 (1943).

[25] *Ramsey* v. *Commissioner, supra; Fort Ring Oil and Gas Company,* 34 B.T.A. 307 (1934); *Continental Oil Company* v. *Jones,* 177 F.(2d) 508, 38 A.F.T.R. 815 (10th Cir. 1949), cert. den., 339 U.S. 931.

costs are incurred prior or subsequent to the formal grant or assignment to the taxpayer of operating rights.[26]

Each taxpayer, no matter how closely related he may be to another taxpayer, is entitled to a separate election. Thus, a partnership, as to partnership properties, and its partners, as to their individual properties, are each entitled to a separate election.[27] Trusts as separate taxpayers are entitled to an election apart from any election made by the beneficiaries. Each corporation that is a member of a consolidated group is entitled to make an election without regard to that of another member of the same group.[28] The acquisition by one corporation of all the assets of another through a nontaxable reorganization [29] or the transfer of assets from one corporation to a related corporation [30] in no way controls the election of the transferee. Similarly, a subsidiary corporation is entitled to a separate election, even though all of its assets were acquired from its parent.[31] In the case of co-owners of an oil and gas property, if the arrangement does not represent a partnership [32] or an association taxable as a corporation,[33] each of the co-owners makes his own election.

10.06 *Drilling for an Interest in the Property.* The rules stated above are subject to the limitation, provided in the regulations,[34] that in any case where the taxpayer undertakes drilling or development for the grant or assignment of a fraction of the operating rights, only that part of his costs, otherwise classifiable as intangibles, that is attributable to the fractional interest acquired is within the option. To the extent

---

[26] U.S. Treas. Reg. 118, Section 39.23(m)-16(a).

[27] I.R.C., Section 703(b); *Bentex Oil Corporation,* 20 T.C. 565 (1953), appeal pending to 5th Cir.; Rev. Rul. 54-42, I.R.B. No. 5, p. 7 (February 1, 1954).

[28] I.T. 3763, 1945 C.B. 113.

[29] I.T. 1661, II-1 C.B. 116 (1923).

[30] I.T. 3763, *supra.*

[31] I.T. 3763, *supra.*

[32] *See* Chapter 13.

[33] *See* Chapter 14.

[34] U.S. Treas. Reg. 118, Section 39.23(m)-16(a)(1).

that such intangibles are allocable to fractions of the operating rights held by others they must, together with a similar proportion of equipment costs, be capitalized as the cost of the interest acquired. For example, if A contracts to drill a well on B's undeveloped property in exchange for two-thirds of the working interest therein, he will be entitled to deduct only two-thirds of the costs of drilling that are attributable to his share of the working interest. The costs attributable to the one-third interest retained by B must be capitalized by A as cost of acquisition of his interest in the lease. If A agreed not only to drill but also to equip the well, then one-third of his equipment costs, attributable to B's one-third working interest, would be capitalized also as cost of acquisition of his interest in the lease. If the lease was partially developed prior to the assignment, the capitalized cost would be allocated between leasehold and equipment in proportion to their respective fair market values before the drilling or equipping of the obligation well. On the other hand, if A agrees to drill a well on B's property in exchange for a nonoperating interest, such as an oil payment or an overriding royalty, A will be entitled to no intangibles deduction, since he does not own or acquire any part of the operating rights in the property; he would be required to capitalize all expenditures as cost of the nonoperating interest acquired.

The section of the regulations granting the option to expense intangibles uses the word "undertaken," and because of the interpretation placed on the word in at least one case, it is necessary to consider its meaning in some detail. In the Platt case [35] the taxpayer acquired an interest in a lease on which a well was drilled to 11,200 feet. As part of the consideration for the assignee's payments to him, the assignor agreed to drill the well an additional 1,500 feet. At a later date the taxpayer paid an addional sum, for which he did not receive any

---

[35] *Sidney Platt,* 18 T.C. 1229 (1952), aff'd 207 F.(2d) 697, — A.F.T.R. —, 1953 P-H, Para. 72,736 (7th Cir. October 26, 1953).

additional interest, but the assignor pledged to use such money in deepening the well. The last payment had been deducted by the taxpayer, and the Revenue Service had not questioned the item. However, the taxpayer also sought to deduct the entire expenditure for his interest on the grounds that it was intangible drilling costs, and it does not appear that the amount paid exceeded the taxpayer's proportionate cost of drilling to the 12,700 foot level. The courts denied the deduction of any part of this amount, on the ground that the taxpayer had not undertaken the drilling of the well. It pointed out that the assignor was the operator of the property and that it was he who had undertaken its development.

It is not entirely clear whether in reaching this conclusion the courts considered the well undertaken by the assignor because it had been started before the assignee acquired his interest or because the assignor was primarily responsible for the drilling. In either case, it is submitted that either meaning of the term is without significance from a tax or an economic standpoint. More appropriately, the term might refer to the assumption of the financial burden of development before development costs have been incurred. If this test were applied, it is clear that no portion of the taxpayer's costs applicable to the leasehold or the first 11,200 feet, which had been drilled prior to the assignment, would qualify as intangibles, because the costs had been incurred prior to the time the taxpayer acquired his interest. He could not, as to those costs, undertake the development but could only assume or satisfy another's financial obligations. As to the cost of drilling the additional 1,500 feet contemplated in the original assignments, the taxpayer did not undertake the primary obligation of the costs, but he did agree to pay such costs by providing funds to the assignor to be used for the purpose. As to these costs he should be considered to have undertaken the development, because he assumed the financial responsibility therefor before the costs had been incurred. Based on the theories expressed in Chapter 7, it appears that the courts might have made an allocation of the original cost between acquisition and drilling costs in proportion to the value of each. However, the case does not disclose that this issue was argued or that evidence of such values was submitted.

It might appear that the concern over the meaning of a word is academic, but the consequence from a tax standpoint can be very material. For example, if *A* assigns to *B* all of the working interest in a lease, subject to a retained overriding royalty, in exchange for *B*'s promise to drill a well that cost *B* $100,000, *B* would be entitled to deduct the $100,000 as intangible drilling costs. However, the same economic result would be achieved if *B* paid *A* $100,000, which *A* pledged to, and did, use in drilling a well. The tax result under the theory of the Platt case would be entirely different, because under this theory *B* would be required to capitalize the entire expenditure as the cost of his interest in the lease. *A* would have no income or deduction, because his drilling costs exactly equalled *B*'s contribution. The significant fact from an economic and tax standpoint is not whether *A* or *B* contracts for the drilling of the well, but rather who agrees to assume financial responsibility for the development costs which are to be incurred.

10.07   *Manner of Election.* The taxpayer is required by the regulations to make a clear election; in the absence thereof, the taxpayer will be deemed to have elected to capitalize intangible costs, and such costs will be recoverable through depletion or depreciation.[36] If the taxpayer deducts such expenses on his tax return, he has made an election to expense; and where a taxpayer expenses a portion of the intangibles and through error capitalizes a portion thereof, it has been held that he

---

[36] U.S. Treas. Reg. 111, Section 29.23(m)-16(b)(4); *See also* U.S. Treas. Reg. 118, Section 39.23(m)-16(d).

has elected to expense all intangibles.[37] The election is made upon the return and not upon a taxpayer's books. An amended return filed after the original due date will not serve to change an election,[38] but a binding election is not made by a tentative return.[39] The election to expense intangibles cannot be made on a delinquent return.[40] If the taxpayer desires to expense intangibles, discretion dictates that he include in his return an express statement to the effect that he elects to deduct intangible drilling and development costs in accordance with the option granted by Regulations 118, Section 39.23(m)-16(a)(1). It might be noted in this connection that the deduction of dry-hole costs on the taxpayer's return is not a clear statement of election to deduct intangibles. The ambiguity arises from the fact that a taxpayer may expense the costs of dry holes, whether he has elected to expense or to capitalize intangibles on productive wells.

10.08   *Time of Election.* The taxpayer must make his election to expense or to capitalize intangibles in his first taxable year beginning after December 31, 1942, in which he incurs such costs. Once the election is made it is binding on the taxpayer for all properties owned by him for all subsequent years.[41] It will be apparent that the proper time for making the election is closely related to the proper time for claiming the deduction for intangibles, and this subject will be discussed further in paragraph 10.10.

10.09   *Recovery of Costs if Capitalized.* If the taxpayer

[37] *Commissioner* v. *Sklar Oil Corporation,* 134 F.(2d) 221, 30 A.F.T.R. 1105 (5th Cir. 1943).

[38] *Commissioner* v. *Titus Oil and Investment Company,* 132 F.(2d) 969, 30 A.F.T.R. 716 (10th Cir. 1943), rev'g 42 B.T.A. 1134 (1940), nonacq., 1942-1 C.B. 30; *Burford Oil Company* v. *Commissioner,* 153 F.(2d) 745, 34 A.F.T.R. 1055 (5th Cir. 1946).

[39] *Haggar Company* v. *Helvering,* 308 U.S. 389, 23 A.F.T.R. 794 (1940).

[40] *See Joe Degnan,* 47 B.T.A. 899 (1942), aff'd, 136 F.(2d) 891, 31 A.F.T.R. 234 (9th Cir. 1943), cert. den., 320 U.S. 778.

[41] U.S. Treas. Reg. 111, Section 29.23(m)-16(b)(4); *See also* U.S. Treas. Reg. 118, Section 39.23(m)-16(d).

elects to capitalize intangibles, the regulations require that expenditures for items not represented by physical property—such as expenditures for clearing ground, draining, road making, surveying, geological work, excavating, grading, and the drilling, shooting, and cleaning of wells—be capitalized and recovered through depletion.[42] Expenditures represented by physical properties, including wages, fuel, repairs, hauling, supplies, and so on, used in the installation of casing and equipment when intangibles are capitalized, are to be recovered through depreciation.[43] If the owner of the property engages an independent drilling contractor to drill and equip a well, and the owner has elected to capitalize intangibles, the total payments to the contractor must be allocated on an equitable basis between the two classes of drilling costs discussed above and recovered, respectively, through depletion and depreciation.[44]

Only rarely would it be to the taxpayer's advantage to elect to capitalize intangibles. Because of the allowance of percentage depletion, as discussed in Chapter 11, without regard to income tax basis of the property interest, the taxpayer is allowed depletion even if he has no depletable basis. As a consequence, he generally will gain nothing by capitalizing his intangibles as part of his depletable investment.

10.10   Time for Claiming Deduction. Under the general rules, if a taxpayer has properly elected to deduct intangibles, the time for the deduction is the taxable year in which such costs are incurred, by an accrual-basis taxpayer, or in which such costs are paid, by a cash-basis taxpayer. A taxpayer reporting on the accrual basis who drills his own well must de-

---

[42] U.S. Treas. Reg. 118, Section 39.23(m)-16(b)(1). Although capitalized intangible drilling and development costs are not depreciable, it has been held that they could be amortized where the wells were certified as emergency facilities, *Arkansas-Oklahoma Gas Co.* v. *Commissioner*, 201 F.(2d) 98, 43 A.F.T.R. 120 (8th Cir. 1953).

[43] U.S. Treas. Reg. 118, Section 39.23(m)-16(b)(2).

[44] U.S. Treas. Reg. 118, Section 39.23(m)-16(b)(3).

duct expenses incurred during a given year, even though at the end of that year a well is not completed.[45] The rule would be the same for an accrual-basis taxpayer who contracts the well to an independent contractor on a footage or day basis, if his liability accrues as the footage is drilled or as the days pass. However, if the liability does not accrue until the contractor has reached a specified depth, no deduction for intangibles will be permitted until the well reaches the specified depth. A payment in advance of drilling is not deductible by either a cash- or accrual-basis taxpayer except to the extent that the drilling has been completed.[46] The situation is analogous to prepaid insurance, which is deductible only over the period covered by the policy.[47] If a cash-basis taxpayer receives a loan, the proceeds being applied as payment for intangibles, his deduction should be taken when the proceeds are so applied.[48]

The rules regarding the proper time for deduction of intangibles have an important effect upon the proper time for making the election to claim such deductions. The election must be made in the first year in which the taxpayer incurs,

[45] *Great Western Petroleum Corporation, supra.*

[46] Rev. Rul. 170, 1953-2 C.B. 141.

[47] *Commissioner v. Boylston Market Association,* 131 F.(2d) 966, 30 A.F.T.R. 512 (1st Cir. 1942); *Higginbotham-Bailey-Logan Company,* 8 B.T.A. 566 (1927), acq. and nonacq. on other issues, VII-1 C.B. 14, 38.

[48] *See McAdams* v. *Commissioner,* 198 F.(2d) 54, 42 A.F.T.R. 310 (5th Cir. 1952) where the taxpayer and his brother-in-law were co-owners of a lease and the brother-in-law paid the drilling costs to a drilling contractor during 1940 and 1941. The taxpayer reimbursed his brother-in-law in 1944 and 1945 for his pro rata share. The Court held that the money advanced by the brother-in-law constituted a loan to the taxpayer, even though there was no agreement to make a loan. The Court reasoned that the loaned funds were applied in satisfaction of the taxpayer's share of intangibles and that he should have claimed the deduction in 1940 and 1941 when his brother-in-law paid the funds for the drilling of the wells. It is difficult to draw a general principle from this case because the Court did not explain the basis upon which it found a constructive loan. If the Court was influenced by the relationship of the parties, or by the length of time before reimbursement, the case is of limited application. If, on the other hand, the Court was holding that a disbursement by an agent to a third party is a payment by the principal, the case is of widespread application, and if generally applied could alter extensively the method of accounting for income by all cash-basis taxpayers in the oil and gas industry.

pays, or constructively pays such costs. If a co-owner of a working interest attaches a statement that he elects to deduct intangibles to his return in the first year in which an oil or gas well is started, even though he has not been billed, he protects his right to a deduction in the event that a later determination is made that some part or all of the cost should have been deducted on the return for that year.

10.11   Definition of Intangible Drilling Costs. The regulations define intangibles as any cost incurred which in itself has no salvage value and which is "incident to and necessary for the drilling of wells and the preparation of wells for the production of oil and gas." These expenditures expressly include "labor, fuel, repairs, hauling, supplies, etc." that are used:

(i) in the drilling, shooting and cleaning of wells;

(ii) in such clearing of ground, draining, road making, surveying, and geological works as are necessary in preparation for the drilling of wells; and

(iii) in the construction of such derricks, tanks, pipelines, and other physical structures as are necessary for the drilling of wells and the preparation of wells for the production of oil or gas.[49]

This definition includes the cost of installation of tangible equipment placed in the well itself although the equipment is to be capitalized and depreciated. Expressly excluded from classification as intangibles are expenditures, including installation charges, incurred in connection with equipment, facilities, or structures that are not incident to or necessary for the drilling of oil or gas wells, such as structures for storing and treating oil or gas.[50] Items which are expense items by their very nature are not included within the option, but must be expensed in every case. Such items include expenditures for the operation of the wells and of other facilities on the property for the production of oil or gas.[51] It is important to dis-

---

[49] U.S. Treas. Reg. 118, Section 39.23(m)-16(a)(1).
[50] U.S. Treas. Reg. 118, Section 39.23(m)-16(c)(1).
[51] U.S. Treas. Reg. 118, Section 39.23(m)-16(c)(2).

tinguish carefully the two types of installation costs referred to above, since one is deducted as intangible cost and the other is capitalized and recovered through depreciation. In general, the cost of installing equipment necessary for the drilling of wells and for the preparation of wells for production is regarded as intangibles, if the taxpayer has elected to expense intangibles. The Revenue Service regards the well as complete when the casing and a "Christmas tree" have been installed. The cost of installing the equipment to this point, which equipment would include casing, tubing, "Christmas tree," and other well facilities, is considered to be intangible. If, however, the taxpayer has elected to capitalize intangibles, such costs become part of the equipment costs and are to be recovered through depreciation. The Revenue Service considers pumping equipment, flow lines, separators, storage tanks, treating equipment, salt water disposal equipment, and so on, as production facilities, and costs incurred in their installation must be capitalized as equipment costs.[52]

The Revenue Service has ruled specifically that the cost of casing cemented in a well is to be capitalized and depreciated, not charged off as intangibles.[53] To justify its conclusion that casing cemented in the well is not intangible, the Revenue Service points out that casing is property of a character which ordinarily has a salvage value, and it is immaterial that it may have no useful life in any other than its original location. The cost of installing the casing and cementing it in place is properly classified as an intangible cost.

10.12 *Water and Gas Injection Wells.* Water injection and gas injection are now well recognized as secondary recovery methods. Wells which have stopped producing may begin anew upon the injection of gas or water into the sand. One injection well may cause several oil or gas wells to produce

---

[52] Mim. 6754, 1952-1 C.B. 30.
[53] Mim. 6754, *supra.*

again or to produce more. The costs of injection wells are costs incurred in "the preparation of [oil] wells for production," [54] and it should follow that the cost of such wells is subject to the option regarding intangibles.

10.13 *Salt Water Disposal Wells.* Frequently salt water encroaches upon and ultimately takes over the oil sand. During the period of increasing encroachment, some disposition must be made of the salt water that is found in each barrel of liquid produced. The nature of salt water is such that it is harmful to almost everything it touches, and the safest disposition of it is to put it back into the ground. Wells are drilled for that purpose, and such costs must be capitalized because they are related to operation, not to the drilling of an oil or gas well or preparing it for production. [55] Wells may be drilled that serve a dual purpose, water injection and salt water disposal. If the principal purpose is repressuring rather than disposal, the intangible cost should be subject to the option.

10.14 *Redrilling or Workover Costs.* After a well has begun to produce, it may tend to sand up when the flow of oil or constant pumping pulls sand into the tubing. It then becomes necessary to shut the well down for workover. In this process it may be necessary to pull out the tubing, thoroughly wash out the inside of the casing with mud, and cause explosives to be set off at the bottom of the well to dislodge the accumulated silt and sand. These costs are operating in nature and should be expensed, but some courts have treated them as intangibles subject to the election. [56] The cost of deepening a well is a cost of preparing for production, and is treated as intangible cost.

---

[54] *Page Oil Company*, 41 B.T.A. 952 (1940), nonacq., 1940-2 C.B. 13, aff'd, on other issues, 129 F.(2d) 748, 29 A.F.T.R. 971 (2nd Cir. 1942).

[55] Mim. 6754, *supra.*

[56] *Consolidated Mutual Oil Company*, 2 B.T.A. 1067 (1925); *Monrovia Oil Company*, 28 B.T.A. 335 (1933), aff'd on another issue, 83 F.(2d) 417, 17 A.F.T.R. 978 (9th Cir. 1936).

CHAPTER XI

Depletion

INTRODUCTION

11.01   The Depletion Concept. The removal of a mineral from its natural reservoir diminishes the quantity remaining in the reservoir until eventually the supply is exhausted. The exhaustion of supply of a wasting asset is called physical depletion. As the supply of the mineral diminishes, the value of the mineral deposit also undergoes a gradual reduction, which is known as economic depletion. To illustrate, let us assume that the taxpayer acquired for $1,000,000 a productive lease, exclusive of equipment, which has a reservoir of oil estimated at 1,000,000 barrels. During the first year of operation the well produces 100,000 barrels of oil. The property has suffered physical depletion of 100,000 barrels of oil, or one-tenth of the total reservoir, and the taxpayer's capital investment has been reduced in value by $100,000, or one-tenth of its total cost. This reduction in value is referred to as economic depletion.

Although physical and economic depletion depends upon the units produced, the federal income tax concept makes depletion depend not upon units produced but upon the income derived from that production. In other words, depletion, for federal tax purposes, depends not upon production of a mineral but upon its sale.[1] Since the depletion allowance is dependent upon sale of the mineral, no depletion is allowable for minerals consumed in the operation of the property.[2] For the same reason, no depletion deduction is allowable for minerals destroyed before sale;[3] however, if the taxpayer has a cost basis in the mineral deposit, and if the loss is due to a clearly identifiable event,[4] such as a fire, it would appear that a loss deduction should be claimed.[5]

---

[1] U.S. Treas. Reg. 118, Section 39.23(m)-2 and 4.

[2] *The Roundup Coal Mining Company*, 20 T.C. 388 (1953), acq. and non-acq. on other issues, I.R.B. No. 10 p. 5 (March 8, 1954).

[3] *Pioneer Cooperage Co.* v. *Commissioner*, 53 F.(2d) 43, 10 A.F.T.R. 593 (8th Cir. 1931), cert. den., 284 U.S. 686; I.T. 2053, III-2 C.B. 107 (1924).

[4] I.R.C., Section 165 (a) and (c) [1939 I.R.C., Section 23(e) and (f)]; U.S. Treas. Reg. 118, Section 39.23(e)-1(c).

[5] By analogy from *Oregon Mesabi Corporation*, 39 B.T.A. 1033 (1939), acq., 1944 C.B. 22, appeal dismissed on stipulation of parties, 109 F.(2d) 1014, 24 A.F.T.R. 458 (9th Cir. 1940), which dealt with fire, insect, and fungus damage to timber, a depletable resource. A loss could be claimed only for that part

11.02 **Depletion for Tax Purposes.** Only the owner of an economic interest in a property is entitled to depletion on the income derived from production and sale of the oil or gas from that property.[6] The various types of property interests in oil or gas were described in Chapter 2, which also contains a definition of economic interest. It was pointed out in that chapter that the owners of mineral interests, royalties, working interests, overriding royalties, net profits interests, or production payments were all owners of economic interests in the minerals. The owner of each such property is entitled to depletion for federal tax purposes.

The Internal Revenue Code provides two methods of computing the depletion allowance: cost depletion[7] and percentage depletion.[8] Cost depletion provides for a deduction for the taxpayer's basis in the mineral property in relation to the production and sale of minerals therefrom. Percentage depletion, on the other hand, is a statutory concept which provides for a deduction equal to 27½ per cent of the gross income from the property but not to exceed 50 per cent of the net income from the property. The taxpayer is not given an election to compute his depletion one way or the other, but is required to compute depletion both ways and claim the larger of the two sums.[9] Allowable depletion, which is the higher of cost or percentage depletion, serves to reduce the taxpayer's basis in the mineral property.[10] Allowable depletion is not

---

of the destroyed oil and gas which corresponds to the taxpayer's proportionate interest. The amount of the loss would be computed by the formula:

$$\text{Adjusted basis} \times \frac{\text{Units destroyed}}{\text{Reserves before destruction (including units destroyed)}}.$$

I.R.C., Section 1016(a)(1) [1939 I.R.C., Section 113(b)(1)(A)] requires reduction of the basis by the amount of the loss.

[6] *Palmer* v. *Bender*, 287 U.S. 551, 11 A.F.T.R. 1106 (1933); *Anderson* v. *Helvering*, 310 U.S. 404, 24 A.F.T.R. 967 (1940).

[7] I.R.C., Sections 611-12 [1939 I.R.C., Sections 23(m) and 114(b)(1)].

[8] I.R.C., Sections 611 and 613 [1939 I.R.C., Sections 23(m) and 114(b)(3)].

[9] I.R.C., Section 613 [1939 I.R.C., Section 114(b)(3)]; *Murphy Oil Co.* v. *Burnet*, 287 U.S. 299, 11 A.F.T.R. 1095 (1932).

[10] I.R.C., Section 1016(a)(2) [1939 I.R.C., Section 113(b)(1)(B)]. In

restricted to the recovery of the taxpayer's basis, however; although cost depletion will be zero after the taxpayer's basis has been fully recovered, he may continue to claim percentage depletion based on income from the property.[11]

It should be observed that cost depletion for income tax purposes may be entirely different from cost depletion for accounting purposes. For accounting purposes the depletion is computed, and the depletable base reduced, only on a cost basis; however, for income tax purposes, depletable basis must be reduced by the higher of cost or percentage depletion, and the depletable basis would be reduced by percentage depletion when it exceeds cost depletion. In computing depletion for a subsequent year, therefore, the income tax basis would be lower than the book basis of the property, and the unit cost depletion would be lower for tax purposes than for accounting purposes. Thus in any case where percentage depletion has been claimed in respect of a given property, book cost and tax cost depletion will not thereafter be the same.

American National Realty Company, 47 B.T.A. 653 (1942), aff'd on another issue, 136 F.(2d) 486, 31 A.F.T.R. 189 (5th Cir. 1943), a corporation acquired certain land in fee (surface and minerals) and allocated the entire basis to the surface. The corporation leased the minerals, receiving a bonus upon which it claimed and was allowed percentage depletion. When the corporation subsequently sold the property (both surface and minerals), the Tax Court required it to reduce its basis in the surface by the amount of depletion previously claimed, indicating, by way of dicta, that the result might be otherwise if the mineral rights had been retained.

For taxable years prior to the taxable year 1932, the basis is reduced only by the amount that would have been allowable as cost depletion; i.e., for such years any excess of percentage or discovery over cost depletion did not reduce the taxpayer's basis. I.R.C., Section 1016(a)(2)(B) [1939 I.R.C., Section 113 (b)(1)(B)(ii)] provides, for periods after January 1, 1952, that a taxpayer's basis shall be reduced by the excess of depletion actually allowed over the amount allowable only to the extent that the excess resulted in a tax benefit. This rule also applies to periods before January 1, 1952, if the taxpayer so elects on or before December 31, 1954, under the provisions of I.R.C., Section 1020 [1939 I.R.C., Section 113(d)].

[11] I.T. 2327, VI-1 C.B. 18 (1927); *Louisiana Iron & Supply Company, Inc.,* 44 B.T.A. 1244 (1941), acq., 1941-2 C.B. 8.

COST DEPLETION

11.03   General Rule. Fundamentally, cost depletion for tax purposes relates the recovery of the taxpayer's investment to the proportion that the current unit sales of mineral products bears to the total anticipated unit sales of products from the property. The formula to be used in computing cost depletion for tax purposes, as prescribed by the regulations,[12] may be stated as $B\left(\dfrac{S}{U+S}\right)$, where

B = Basis (adjusted) of property at end of period;
U = Units remaining at the end of period;
S = Units sold during period.

This formula contemplates that the factors used relate only to the interest of the taxpayer in the property. Three points about this formula are noteworthy. First, the basis of the property used in the formula is the basis of the property at the end of the taxable year, adjusted for prior years' depletion but not for the current year's depletion. By using the tax basis of the property at the end of the year, provision is automatically made for additions to such basis during the taxable year. Second, by using the units remaining at the end of the period, adjustment is automatically allowed for revised estimates of the reserves. If, for example, operations of the current year disclosed additional reserves not previously known, such increase in reserves would be reflected in the computation of current depletion. Third, current depletion is based on the units sold and not the units produced during the period. As stated above, tax depletion is dependent upon sales rather than production, although the units produced and the units sold may be substantially equal, because of the relatively small storage capacity on most leases. The regulations provide that

---

[12] U.S. Treas. Reg. 118, Section 39.23(m)-2.

units are considered sold in the year in which the proceeds of their sale are taxable under the taxpayer's accounting method, thus emphasizing the relation of depletion and income.[13]

An alternative method of computing cost depletion for tax purposes is prescribed for "a natural gas well where the annual production is not metered and is not capable of being estimated with reasonable accuracy." [14] Rarely do circumstances exist which warrant the use of the formula prescribed, but for the sake of completeness it may be stated as $B\left(\dfrac{D}{ED}\right)$, where

B = Basis (adjusted) of property at end of period;

D = Decline in closed or rock pressure during taxable year;

ED = Expected total decline in closed or rock pressure for period from taxable year to economic limit of production.

In Chapter 6 it was explained that the Revenue Service views the sale of a carved-out oil payment as a present sale of oil to be produced in the future, and the proceeds of such a sale as depletable income. If the income from the property in a given year includes such proceeds, the units sold in the cost depletion computation for that year should include the estimated number of units necessary to satisfy the oil payment. As oil is actually produced and delivered to the owner of the oil payment, or its proceeds paid to him, such income is excluded from the income of the seller, and the units represented thereby must also be excluded from the units sold by him. The units remaining at the end of the period, which would otherwise correspond to the gross reserves applicable to the interest of the seller of the oil payment, are reduced by the estimated number of units necessary to satisfy the unpaid balance of the oil payment. This procedure automatically reflects not only

---

[13] U.S. Treas. Reg. 118, Section 39.23(m)-2(b).
[14] U.S. Treas. Reg. 118, Section 39.23(m)-2(e).

revised estimates of total reserves, but also fluctuations in the price of oil,[15] if the oil payment is measured in terms of dollars rather than units of production.

11.04 Oil Payments. Although the regulations contemplate a computation of cost depletion based upon units sold and total units to be sold, that method of computation would not be appropriate in a case where the taxpayer's interest in the oil property is an oil payment limited in dollars rather than in units of production. If the taxpayer's oil payment entitles him to a certain number of units of production, he can use the general formula in determining his cost depletion. However, if the oil payment entitles the taxpayer to a certain number of

---

[15] To illustrate the operation of the adjustments described in this paragraph, assume that of the oil under a productive tract, *F* is entitled to a royalty of 1/8 and *L* owns the entire working interest. The price of oil during the year is $2.00 a barrel. At the beginning of the year *L* sells to *Y* for $190,000 an oil payment of $210,000 payable out of 2/8 of 7/8. During the year 128,000 barrels are sold for $256,000, of which *F* receives $32,000 (1/8 of 8/8), *L* receives $168,000 (6/8 of 7/8), and *Y* receives $56,000 (2/8 of 7/8). Total reserves at the end of the year are 2,464,000 barrels. *L*'s depletable basis is $240,000. His cost depletion is computed as follows:

(a) Units sold:		
Sold from production (6/8 of 7/8 of 128,000 bbls.)	84,000 bbls.	
Sold in advance ($210,000/$2.00 per bbl.)	105,000 bbls.	
Total units sold by *L*	189,000 bbls.	
(b) Units remaining at end of period:		
Total units	2,464,000 bbls.	
L's continuing share (7/8 of 8/8)		2,156,000 bbls.
Less units required by oil payment:		
Initial amount of oil payment	$210,000	
Satisfied during the year	56,000	
Remaining balance	$154,000	
Barrel equivalent at $2.00 a bbl.		77,000 bbls.
Units remaining for *L*		2,079,000 bbls.

(c) Cost depletion: $\$240{,}000 \times \dfrac{189{,}000}{2{,}079{,}000 + 189{,}000} = \$20{,}000.00$

If the price of oil had been raised to $2.50 a barrel by the end of the year, *L* would have reduced his reserves by only 61,600 barrels ($154,000/$2.50 a barrel) instead of 77,000 barrels on account of the unpaid balance of the oil payment.

dollars, the courts have recognized that depletion may properly be computed by relating the dollars realized in the current taxable year to the total dollars to be realized from the oil payment.[16] The formula for this computation might be stated as $B\left(\dfrac{S}{F}\right)$, where

B = Basis (adjusted) of property at end of period;

F = Face amount of oil payment, unpaid at beginning of period;

S = Amount of proceeds from oil payment production for period.

This formula may not produce a satisfactory result where the oil payment is equal to a stated sum plus an additional sum equivalent to interest determined periodically on the unrecovered balance of the stated sum. In other words, the face amount of such an oil payment is uncertain because of the interest factor in the computation. It would be possible, however, to use the preceding formula if the unpaid face amount is increased by the estimated interest to be paid based on the anticipated payout of the oil payment.[17] Another formula, probably the one most frequently used by taxpayers, might be described as the decline in stated sum (principal amount) of oil payment method. By this formula, cost depletion is equal to $B\left(\dfrac{S\text{-}S_1}{S}\right)$, where

B = Basis (adjusted) of oil payment at end of period;

S = Principal amount of oil payment at beginning of taxable period;

---

[16] *John Vaccaro*, T.C. Memo. Op., Dkt. No. 111858, 1943 P-H T.C. Memo. Dec., Para. 43,433 (1943), appeal dismissed without written opinion on stipulation of parties, Dkt. No. 11080, 33 A.F.T.R. 1672 (5th Cir. 1944).

[17] *Herndon Drilling Company*, T.C. Memo. Op., Dkt. No. 4193, 1953 P-H T.C. Memo. Dec., Para. 53,092 (1946), recomputing deficiency according to decision in 6 T.C. 628 (1946), acq. and nonacq. on other issues, 1946-2 C.B. 3, 6.

S_1 = Principal amount of oil payment at end of taxable period.

Both of the above formulas are based on the assumption that the oil payment will pay out in full. If the oil payment is not expected to pay out, it is in the nature of an overriding royalty and the general formula for computation of cost depletion set forth in paragraph 11.03 should be used.

11.05 Bonus. Although it is common practice to claim percentage depletion on lease bonuses, this practice is not necessarily correct. The taxpayer is required to claim the higher of cost or percentage depletion, and cost depletion on a lease bonus is sometimes higher than percentage depletion.[18] In theory, the lease bonus is an advance royalty that represents part of the grantor's share of the income from units to be sold in the future.[19] Because the units to be sold cannot readily be estimated, it is necessary to use dollar equivalents in computing cost depletion on a lease bonus. The Revenue Service has adopted the formula[20] that cost depletion equals $B\left(\dfrac{A}{A+R}\right)$, where

B = Adjusted basis of the depletable property immediately before the lease or sublease;

A = Advance royalty or bonus;

R = Royalties expected to be received in the future.

Two problems arise in applying this formula: First, there can be no cost depletion without a depletable basis. The basis is

---

[18] *Murphy Oil Co.* v. *Burnet, supra.*

[19] *Herring* v. *Commissioner*, 293 U.S. 322, 14 A.F.T.R. 717 (1934).

[20] U.S. Treas. Reg. 118, Section 39.23(m)-10(a). A formula based on present values such as

$$\text{Basis} \times \frac{\text{Advance Royalty}}{\text{Advance Royalty} + \text{Market Value of Retained Royalty}}$$

might be easier to apply than the Revenue Service formula. However, the Service will probably not accept such a formula. *See* I.T. 2361, VI-1 C.B. 73 (1927). Any attack upon the Revenue Service formula would have to be based upon its being unreasonable under the circumstances of a particular case.

usually not difficult to compute and prove in the case of a sublessor. However, when a lease is granted by a fee owner who acquired the surface and the minerals together for a lump-sum price, such price must be allocated between surface and minerals in relation to their respective values, considering, along with any other evidence of values, the intended use of the property when it was acquired.[21] The taxpayer has the burden of proving the basis allocable to the minerals.[22] He may be helped by evidence created at the time of the acquisition, such as book entries. If the principal value of the land was in the surface when it was acquired, little or no cost can be allocated to the mineral content.[23] The second problem is that it is difficult to estimate the royalties to be received in the future, and even more difficult to prove that the estimate is reasonable, particularly in unproven or wildcat areas. If the taxpayer fails to carry the burden of proof, he may be limited to percentage depletion.[24]

Even for wildcat areas, the Revenue Service does not accept an estimate of zero for royalties expected to be received, although under the Murphy case [25] it would appear that the taxpayer should claim 100 per cent cost depletion if the bonus is less than the basis of the property and it cannot reasonably be assumed that the bonus plus expected royalties will exceed the basis. The Commissioner in that case computed cost depletion as being equal to 100 per cent of the bonus received, because the regulations then in effect so required.[26] At the time the case came to trial the regulations had been changed [27]

[21] *Plow Realty Company of Texas,* 4 T.C. 600 (1945), acq., 1945 C.B. 6; *Perkins v. Thomas,* 86 F.(2d) 954, 18 A.F.T.R. 699 (5th Cir. 1936) aff'd on another issue, 301 U.S. 655, 19 A.F.T.R. 538 (1937).

[22] G.C.M. 14448, XIV-1 C.B. 98 (1935).

[23] *Plow Realty Company of Texas, supra.*

[24] *F.-K. Land Co.* v. *Commissioner,* 90 F.(2d) 484, 19 A.F.T.R. 862 (9th Cir. 1937).

[25] *Murphy Oil Co.* v. *Burnet, supra.*

[26] U.S. Treas. Reg. 45, Article 215(a).

[27] T.D. 3938, V-2 C.B. 117 (1926) amended U.S. Treas. Reg. 45, Article 215; U.S. Treas. Reg. 62, Article 215; and U.S. Treas. Reg. 65, Article 216, relating

to read substantially as they do today, and the Supreme Court
felt constrained to consider them as so amended. The Court
observed that the Commissioner had made no determination
of expected royalties from the leased property, but stated that
it was not necessary for him to do so unless there was some
reason to assume that the total of the bonus and of the expected royalties would exceed the taxpayer's investment in the
property. The Court stated that where no estimates of reserves
can be made with reasonable accuracy the Commissioner cannot determine that the sum of the bonus and royalties expected
to be received would exceed the capital investment and, in such
a case, the whole of the bonus would be treated as a return of
capital. It would appear, under the authority of this case, that
where a taxpayer has an investment or basis in the property
equal to or in excess of the bonus received, and where there is
no reasonable basis to assume that the expected royalties plus
the bonus will exceed such investment, the amount of such
bonus should be treated as a recovery of all or a portion of his
capital investment in the property.

11.06   Net Profits Interest. The computation of cost depletion of a net profits interest is exceedingly difficult, because it
is necessary to estimate the total expected future receipts from
the net profits interest. The formula for cost depletion may be
stated as $B\left(\dfrac{S}{U+S}\right)$, where

  $B =$ Basis (adjusted) of net profits interest at the end of the
taxable period;

  $U =$ Total expected future receipts from the net profits
interest at the end of the taxable period;

  $S =$ Receipts from the net profits interest during the taxable
period.

---

to cost depletion on a lease bonus to read substantially as they do today. The
present regulations are U.S. Treas. Reg. 118, Section 39.23(m)-10(a).

This formula will, of course, give effect to any change in estimated reserves, operating conditions, or prices during the taxable period, by using the estimated future receipts at the end of the taxable period.

PERCENTAGE DEPLETION

11.07   Introduction. The statutory provision governing the allowance of percentage depletion in the case of oil and gas wells reads as follows:

In the case of . . . [oil and gas] wells . . . the allowance for depletion under section 611 [1939 I.R.C., Section 23(m)] shall be . . . [27½ percent] of the gross income from the property excluding from such gross income an amount equal to any rents or royalties paid or incurred by the taxpayer in respect of the property. Such allowance shall not exceed 50 percent of the taxpayer's taxable income from the property (computed without allowance for depletion). In no case shall the allowance for depletion under section 611 be less than it would be if computed without reference to this section.[28]

The terminology used in this statutory provision has been amplified by regulations, rulings, and court decisions. Such key phrases as *gross income, the property, during the taxable year, excluding from such gross income an amount equal to any rents or royalties paid or incurred*, and *net income*, have meanings peculiar to the mineral extraction business.

11.08   Gross Income. The regulations define gross income as "the amount for which the taxpayer sells the oil and gas in the immediate vicinity of the well." [29] If the oil and gas are not sold in the immediate vicinity of the well, "the gross income from the property shall be assumed to be equivalent to the representative market or field price (as of the date of sale) of the oil and gas before conversion or transportation." [30] Con-

---

[28] I.R.C., Section 613 [1939 I.R.C., Section 114(b)(3)].
[29] U.S. Treas. Reg. 118, Section 39.23(m)-1(e)(1).
[30] U.S. Treas. Reg. 118, Section 39.23(m)-1(e)(1).

version here refers to any process of manufacturing by which the crude product of the well is converted into a refined or semirefined product. Transportation refers to the carrying of the product of the well away from the immediate vicinity of the lease, usually to a point at which there are refining or marketing facilities.

The determination of gross income where the product is not sold in the immediate vicinity of the well is not difficult if there is a current posted market or field price. However, the posted market or field price is frequently based, not on the product as it comes from the well and in the immediate vicinity of the well, but on the product transported to a marketing point or converted. In such cases the taxpayer must adjust the posted price at the marketing point to determine the price of the untransported and unrefined product. In some cases the cost of transporting the crude product to the point of sale has been deducted from the sales price to determine the representative market price at the well location.[31] A similar adjustment may be made with respect to conversion costs where appropriate.

11.09 *Sale of Oil Property Distinguished.* Proceeds from the sale of an oil property, as distinguished from proceeds from sale of the product of an oil or gas well, are not included in gross income from the property.[32] The distinction between

---

[31] *James P. Evans, Sr.,* 11 T.C. 726 (1948); *See also Consumers Natural Gas Co. v. Commissioner,* 78 F.(2d) 161, 16 A.F.T.R. 335 (2d Cir. 1935), cert. den., 296 U.S. 634 where the taxpayer, who produced and transported the product, was forced to allocate a reasonable portion of income as well as deductions to the transportation, thus reducing the gross income from the property.

[32] *Anderson v. Helvering, supra; Majestic Oil Corporation,* 42 B.T.A. 659 (1940), acq. and nonacq. on other issues, 1940-2 C.B. 5, 12; *Ortiz Oil Company,* 37 B.T.A. 656 (1938), acq. and nonacq. on other issues, 1938-2 C.B. 24, 54, aff'd., 102 F.(2d) 508, 22 A.F.T.R. 908 (5th Cir. 1939), cert. den., 308 U.S. 566. The present position of the Revenue Service with respect to the Majestic and Ortiz cases, which involved carved-out oil payments, is explained in Chapter 6. Inasmuch as these cases held the sale of a carved-out oil payment to be the sale of a property interest instead of an anticipation of income, they may be considered as authority for the proposition that the sale of an oil property is not included in gross income from the property for purposes of computing percentage depletion.

sales, subleases, and anticipation of income has been discussed in preceding chapters. If a transaction is properly classifiable as a sale of an oil property, there is no depletion problem, inasmuch as the proceeds of sale do not constitute depletable income. On the other hand, in a leasing or subleasing transaction, the cash consideration received does not constitute proceeds from sale of the property, but is treated as a lease bonus that may properly be included in the gross income from the property for computing depletion.[33]

The anticipation of income doctrine treats the sale of a carved-out oil payment as a present realization of future production,[34] and under this theory any cash consideration for such an assignment would be treated as gross income from the property subject to depletion. It was pointed out in Chapter 6 that the validity of this rule is subject to some question. If the position of the Revenue Service in this regard is ultimately sustained, the proceeds from the sale of a carved-out oil payment will constitute depletable gross income from the property. On the other hand, if that position is overruled by the courts, such consideration will represent proceeds from the sale of an oil or gas property and could not be included in gross income for the purpose of computing percentage depletion.[35]

11.10   *Conversion before Sale.* It was indicated above that gross income from the property does not include any income derived from the conversion or refining of the products of the well. It is difficult, however, to distinguish a normal separation process necessary to put the product in a marketable condition in the vicinity of the well, which is considered a production process, from a conversion or refining process. Frequently the product of an oil and gas well will be run through a gravity separator located on the lease. Such separators remove the water from the oil and permit some separation of the so-called

[33] *Herring v. Commissioner, supra.*
[34] G.C.M. 24849, 1946-1 C.B. 66 and I.T. 4003, 1950-1 C.B. 10.
[35] *Majestic Oil Corporation, supra; Ortiz Oil Company, supra.*

lighter and heavier hydrocarbons. The Revenue Service has recognized [36] that the gravity-type separator is an instrument of production and not a refining process, and therefore the proceeds of sale of the separated products need not be adjusted to determine the sales price of the products in the vicinity of the well. Some maintain that a separator, no matter how large or expensive, is an instrument of production and not a refining process, so long as its purpose is merely to break down the component parts of the raw product in the reservoir. If the raw product is treated by the addition of any extraneous material, the process must be considered a manufacturing or refining process.

When the processes performed by the lease or field equipment are more extensive than simple separation, such as is sometimes the case in natural gasoline plants, casinghead gas plants, and some cycling operations, it is possible that the operation of the plant involves both producing and manufacturing phases. If so, the income attributable to the manufacturing operation cannot be included in gross income for purposes of computing percentage depletion, and it becomes necessary to separate the proceeds of sale of plant products between depletable and nondepletable income. In relatively rare instances there may be a current posted price for the products of the well before they have been run through the plant; if so, that portion of the proceeds of sale of plant products would probably represent the depletable income. More commonly, however, it is necessary to find some other means of determining the income from production and the income from manufacturing.

There are very few court decisions concerning this question, and those that have been made are not of great assistance. For example, in one such case [37] the reservoir of natural gas con-

---

[36] See reference to arguments of counsel in *Brea Canon Oil Co.* v. *Commissioner*, 77 F.(2d) 67, 15 A.F.T.R. 1335 (9th Cir. 1935), cert. den., 296 U.S. 604.

[37] *Edward J. Hudson*, 11 T.C. 1042 (1948), nonacq. on this issue, 1949-1

tained 95 per cent lighter elements known as methane and ethane and 5 per cent heavier elements known as propanes, butanes, pentanes, and so on, all existing in a natural state. Although the court regarded the process of separation as a severance of natural resources and not a manufacturing process, it was not called upon to make an allocation between production and refining, or even to decide whether any income should be allocated to refining, because the parties had stipulated that a portion of the income was not depletable.[38] In another case, the extraction of casinghead gasoline from wet gas, a mixture of liquids with dry gas, was held to be principally a manufacturing process.[39] In the absence of a showing of the market value of the wet gas at the well head, the court treated 60 per cent of the proceeds of sale of plant products as the value attributable to the manufacturing process. The balance of the proceeds was treated as income from severance of minerals, which was subject to depletion.

In practice, the allocation of the gross proceeds from the sale of plant products between the producing and refining processes is dependent upon the facts of each case and may be the subject of considerable discussion with the Revenue Service. Where it is determined that a plant processing the product is engaged in both producing and refining operations, and there is no other or better evidence of the portion of the proceeds attributable to the severance and sale of minerals, the Revenue Service may make the allocation by reducing the proceeds of sale of plant products by the sum of (1) the costs of operation, including depreciation, attributable to the refining process, and (2) an amount representing a fair return on the plant invest-

---

C.B. 5, acq. on another issue, 1949-1 C.B. 2, aff'd, 183 F.(2d) 180, 39 A.F.T.R. 646 (5th Cir. 1950).

[38] See Roger S. Randolph, *Problems of the Oil and Gas Industry: Depletion Problems Including Those Arising from the Hudson and Abercrombie Decisions*, New York University Ninth Annual Institute on Federal Taxation (New York: Matthew Bender & Company, 1951), p. 497, n. 20.

[39] *Brea Canon Oil Co.* v. *Commissioner, supra.*

ment attributable to the refining process. The balance of the proceeds is considered to represent the income from severance and sale of minerals. If some products are sold at an intermediate stage of processing, but after the refining processes have started, this formula will be applied only to the value of the products at that intermediate stage. Any increase in value of products arising from processing after that stage will be considered manufacturing income.

This formula is much simpler of statement than it is of application. It is frequently difficult to determine the point in the processing at which refining operations begin, and, when that determination has been made, difficult accounting problems may arise in ascertaining the plant investment attributable to the refining operation. What constitutes a fair return on the investment in the refining process is the subject of much conjecture, but the Revenue Service has in certain instances insisted on an annual return equal to 20 per cent of the total investment.[40] In setting the rate of return, consideration should certainly be given to risk involved, since that is usually the principal factor in determining the rate of return on money invested in any type of property.

11.11   The Property. The property unit for purposes of computing depletion is considered in detail in Chapter 12. It might be noted, however, that each separate property is a separate depletable unit. A separate computation of gross and net income is required for each such unit so that percentage depletion may be determined by properties. Similarly, cost depletion must be computed for each separate property unit so the taxpayer may deduct, and reduce his basis by, the higher of cost or percentage depletion.

It should also be noted that the property, for depletion purposes, must be some kind of economic interest in an oil or gas property. If the rights owned by the taxpayer do not constitute

---

[40] *See* Roger S. Randolph, *supra,* p. 496, n. 16.

an economic interest, he is not entitled to depletion in respect of income received from the property.[41] For example, if the owner of a casinghead gasoline plant has no economic interest in the property from which the wet gas is produced, he is not entitled to depletion, even though his share of income may be a percentage of the proceeds from the sale of the plant products.[42] On the other hand, the owner of an economic interest from which the wet gas is produced is entitled to depletion, even though gross income may be computed as an allocable fraction of the proceeds received from the disposition of the products of the plant.[43] Nothing would prevent the acquisition of an economic interest in a property by the owner of a recycling or other processing plant,[44] yet the mere sharing of the finished products is not conclusive evidence of an economic interest.[45]

11.12   During the Taxable Year. Depletion is to be computed in relation to the income from production sold during a given taxable period. Production alone does not create any income, although, as a practical matter, when the oil is delivered to a common carrier for the account of a producer it is treated as a sale, since accountability to the royalty owner has then been established. The accounting method employed by a taxpayer is important in determining when gross income is realized. If the taxpayer is on a cash basis, the general rule is followed, and only when he receives payment for his share of production does he realize gross income. An accrual-basis taxpayer has gross income when he sells the production and not when payment is received. Where ownership of the property is in dispute, and the proceeds from production are impounded pending final determination of ownership through litigation,

[41] *Anderson v. Helvering, supra.*
[42] *Helvering v. Bankline Oil Co.,* 303 U.S. 362, 20 A.F.T.R. 782 (1938).
[43] *Brea Canon Oil Co. v. Commissioner, supra.*
[44] *Edward J. Hudson, supra.*
[45] *Helvering v. Bankline Oil Co., supra.*

the general rules apply: unless they actually receive a portion of the impounded funds by posting a bond, both the cash- and the accrual-basis taxpayers postpone reporting income until the dispute is settled.[46]

11.13   *Stored Oil or Gas.* On some occasions a lease owner will produce oil or gas, pay the royalty owner, and transport the oil or gas to another location for storage. The reservoir selected for storage may be surface tanks or, frequently in the case of gas, underground sands of exhausted oil and gas fields. Storage of oil or gas usually occurs in anticipation of a rising price structure, peak seasonal demand, or a further processing, or it may occur because of a lack of marketing facilities. The integrated oil company, which may produce oil in Texas and refine it in New Jersey, using intermediate points for storage, has had this problem for many years. It is customary to record a sale of the oil when it leaves the property and account to the royalty owners at that time for their share. By reflecting the shipment as a sale of oil or gas at the posted field price or existing contract price, accounting for the product through pipeline and storage facilities is greatly simplified. Both oil and gas suffer quantity losses from transportation and storage operations. Market fluctuations during the time interval between production and sale are inevitable. These problems are all relegated to the category of inventory questions, once the policy of treating the transportation from the property as though a sale had been made is adopted and consistently applied. Depletion can then be computed, since the income is determinable for each property.

This reporting procedure makes it possible to compute depletion when the product is shipped, but it does not require the realization of income until the oil or gas is sold. If the taxpayer elects to use the lower of cost or market method of

---

[46] *North American Oil Consolidated* v. *Burnet,* 286 U.S. 417, 11 A.F.T.R. 16 (1932).

valuing inventories and reduces the closing inventory to actual cost—that is, the price paid for purchased products plus cost of producing oil or gas from its own leases—income will not be realized until the product is sold. The result is that oil or gas is treated as sold for purposes of computing depletion but not for reporting income. The Revenue Service has permitted the taxpayer to follow such a policy on a consistent basis.

The practice of handling depletion on stored gas and oil in the manner set forth above is, in a sense, inconsistent with the principle that depletion follows income, but where the practice is consistently followed, no distortion of income will occur. The practical impossibility of computing depletion in other ways is apparent when it is realized that the gas or oil placed in a given storage facility is usually produced from many separate and distinct properties, and will usually include both purchased and produced gas or oil. The problem of allocating the actual sales proceeds back to the many properties is nearly insurmountable. In addition, losses from transportation and storage of inventory and price fluctuations will directly affect the depletion computation. A policy of storing production for a number of years would tend to distort operating income unless the cost of production is deferred until income attributable thereto is realized. With all these factors before him, a taxpayer would do well to weigh the disadvantages before arbitrarily deferring the depletion deduction to the time of sale.

11.14 Excluding Rents and Royalties. Depletion for tax purposes is available to each holder of an economic interest in a property from which the production emanates, and it follows that the holder of the leasehold interest must, to avoid duplication of depletion deductions, exclude from his income any royalties paid the owner of an economic interest. The courts have so interpreted the depletion provisions from their inception, although there was no specific provision to this effect in

the earlier income tax acts.[47] In 1932, however, statutory recognition was given to this practice by expressly requiring that
"an amount equal to any rents or royalties paid or incurred by
the taxpayer" must be excluded from gross income.[48] The
meaning of the term "rents" in this clause has not yet been
clearly defined. In one case, payments based on production of
coal, which were in addition to royalties and were to compensate the lessor for the use of his plant and equipment, were
held to be rents and had to be excluded.[49] This rule will probably be applied by the Revenue Service whenever so-called
rents are measured by production.

Since a lease bonus is considered an advance royalty and
therefore depletable by the lessor, it follows that the lessee
must, in each taxable year, exclude a proportionate part of the
bonus from gross income before computing percentage depletion of 27½ per cent of gross income.[50] If this adjustment were
not made, a depletion deduction would, in effect, have been
obtained by both the lessor and the lessee on the same income.[51] This exclusion, however, is only for the purpose of
computing depletion based on gross income. No part of the
bonus is excluded in computing the net income from the property, nor in computing taxable income.[52] The amount to be
excluded is determined by a formula [53] similar to the cost
depletion formula. The bonus exclusion for any period equals

$$L\left(\frac{S}{U+S}\right), \text{ where}$$

---

[47] *Helvering* v. *Twin Bell Oil Syndicate*, 293 U.S. 312, 14 A.F.T.R. 712
(1934).
[48] I.R.C., Section 613 [1939 I.R.C., Section 114(b)(3)].
[49] *Leechburg Mining Company*, 15 T.C. 22 (1950).
[50] U.S. Treas. Reg. 118, Section 39.23(m)-1(e)(5).
[51] *Quintana Petroleum Co.* v. *Commissioner*, 143 F.(2d) 588, 32 A.F.T.R.
1031 (5th Cir. 1944); *Sunray Oil Co.* v. *Commissioner*, 147 F.(2d) 962, 33
A.F.T.R. 763 (10th Cir. 1945), cert. den., 325 U.S. 861.
[52] *Sunray Oil Co.* v. *Commissioner, supra.*
[53] U.S. Treas. Reg. 118, Section 39.23(m)-1(e)(5).

L = Amount of lease bonus not already excluded in prior years;

S = Units sold during the period;

U = Units remaining at the end of the period.

The rule regarding exclusion of the bonus may also be applicable to certain minimum royalty payments. For discussion of this subject see paragraph 8.07.

11.15   Net Income. The regulations define net income as the "gross income from the property . . . less the allowable deductions attributable to the mineral property upon which the depletion is claimed . . . including overhead and operating expenses, development costs properly charged to expense . . . , depreciation, taxes, losses sustained, etc., but excluding any allowance for depletion." [54] In certain instances the gross and net income from a property may be the same amount, as in the case of a net profits interest. The owner of the net profits interest treats as depletable gross income only the net amounts received by him,[55] and such amounts will ordinarily represent both gross and net income from the property.

Where a taxpayer is engaged in several different activities, one of which is oil and gas production, the regulations provide that ". . . deductions for depreciation, taxes, general expenses, and overhead, which cannot be directly attributed to any specific activity, shall be fairly apportioned between (1) the mineral extraction . . . and (2) the additional activities, taking into account the ratio which the operating expenses directly attributable to the mineral extraction . . . bear to the operating expenses directly attributable to the additional activities. If more than one mineral property is involved, the deductions apportioned to the mineral extraction . . . shall, in turn, be

---

[54] U.S. Treas. Reg. 118, Section 39.23(m)-1(g).

[55] *Commissioner* v. *Felix Oil Co.,* 144 F.(2d) 276, 32 A.F.T.R. 1186 (9th Cir. 1944); *See also Helvering* v. *Mountain Producers Corporation,* 303 U.S. 376, 20 A.F.T.R. 789 (1938).

fairly apportioned to the several properties, taking into account their relative production." [56]

11.16   *Allowable Deductions.* As the definition indicates, not every allowable deduction is attributable to the property. Allowable deductions are listed in various sections of the Internal Revenue Code and the term may be assumed to be all-inclusive. On the other hand, the Internal Revenue Code lists certain items which are not deductible, and effectively excludes those items from the depletion computation. Reference should be made to Section 266 [1939 I.R.C., Section 24(a)(7)], by which the Commissioner is authorized to issue regulations prescribing treatment of taxes and carrying charges as capital items upon proper election by the taxpayer. Of course, if a taxpayer elects to capitalize, he is not required to treat the item as a deduction in computing depletion.[57] Since delay rentals are carrying charges on unimproved and unproductive real property, they may be capitalized or deducted at the taxpayer's election, with permission to make a new election each year on each property.[58] It should be noted that credits against income and credits against tax provided for in various sections of the Internal Revenue Code are not deductions. Hence, no deduction is required for the personal exemption or dependency credit, nor should a foreign income tax claimed as a credit against tax be treated as a deduction for depletion purposes. Charitable contributions have been held to be inapplicable to the business of mineral extraction.[59]

The following items, among others, have been held deductible, directly or indirectly, in computing net income from the property for purposes of the percentage depletion limitation:

---

[56] U.S. Treas. Reg. 118, Section 39.23(m)-1(g).
[57] U.S. Treas. Reg. 118, Section 39.24(a)-6(a).
[58] *See* paragraph 8.05.
[59] *F.H.E. Oil Company,* 3 T.C. 13 (1944), nonacq. on this issue, 1944 C.B. 37, aff'd on other issues, 147 F.(2d) 1002, 33 A.F.T.R. 785 (5th Cir. 1945), reh. den., 149 F.(2d) 238, 33 A.F.T.R. 1263 (5th Cir. 1945), second reh. den., 150 F.(2d) 857, 34 A.F.T.R. 112 (5th Cir. 1945).

1. Intangible drilling and development costs, if the taxpayer has elected to deduct them in computing taxable income.[60]

2. Interest paid during the taxable year on federal income tax deficiencies for prior years, where taxpayer's only activity was production of oil and gas.[61]

3. Interest on bonds, bond discount, and expense amortization.[62]

4. Bad debts, dues, assessments, attorneys' fees, capital stock taxes, and interest on borrowed money for development.[63]

5. Interest paid on money borrowed to purchase a producing oil and gas property.[64]

6. Damage claims of employees who had been injured in prior years while working on the taxpayer's mineral property.[65]

7. Income taxes paid to the State of Oklahoma must be deducted in arriving at the net income from the property, where such state tax was based wholly on income derived from such property.[66] A similar result was reached regarding

    (a) Wisconsin real estate taxes;

    (b) Wisconsin personal property taxes;

    (c) Wisconsin income tax;

    (d) Ohio franchise tax and miscellaneous taxes;

    (e) Federal and state social security and unemployment compensation taxes; and

    (f) Federal capital stock tax.[67]

---

[60] *Helvering* v. *Wilshire Oil Co., Inc.*, 308 U.S. 90, 23 A.F.T.R. 743 (1939), reh. den., 308 U.S. 638, 23 A.F.T.R. 787 (1939).

[61] *Holly Development Company*, 44 B.T.A. 51 (1941), appeal dismissed on stipulation of parties, 127 F.(2d) 293, 29 A.F.T.R. 262 (9th Cir. 1942).

[62] *Sheridan-Wyoming Coal Co., Inc.* v. *Helvering*, 125 F.(2d) 42, 28 A.F.T.R. 908 (C.A.D.C. 1942).

[63] *Lumaghi Coal Co.* v. *Helvering*, 124 F.(2d) 645, 28 A.F.T.R. 847 (8th Cir. 1942); *See also Mirabel Quicksilver Company*, 41 B.T.A. 401 (1940).

[64] *St. Marys Oil & Gas Company*, 42 B.T.A. 270 (1940).

[65] *Montreal Mining Company*, 41 B.T.A. 399 (1940).

[66] *Grison Oil Corporation*, 42 B.T.A. 1117 (1940).

[67] *Montreal Mining Company*, 2 T.C. 688 (1943), acq. and nonacq. on other issues, 1944 C.B. 20, 45, aff'd on this issue on stipulation of parties, Dkt. No. 9889, 33 A.F.T.R. 1660 (6th Cir. 1944).

Foreign income taxes claimed as a deduction were also held partly attributable to oil-producing properties in computing net income from the properties for percentage depletion purposes.[68]

8. Depreciation on lease equipment.[69]

9. Back wages paid by the taxpayer under a National Labor Relations Board settlement.[70]

10. Officers' salaries, interest expense, and office expenses.[71]

11.17 *Attributable to the Property.* Even if an item is determined to be an allowable deduction, it must also be attributable to the producing properties before the depletion computation is affected. It is recognized that some deductions are directly attributable to the producing property, and the determination of these amounts is simply an accounting matter. On the other hand, expenses will be incurred which are applicable to the producing operation and also to other activities conducted by the taxpayer, and such expenses must be allocated to the properties. Such general or overhead expenses must first be apportioned between the producing operations and the other activities carried on by the taxpayer, and the part attributable to the producing operation must be fairly allocated among the producing properties if the taxpayer has more than one.[72]

11.18 *Allocation Among Activities.* It is clear that a taxpayer who is engaged in oil and gas operations, as well as

---

[68] *Kern Oil Company, Ltd.,* 9 T.C. 1204 (1947).

[69] U.S. Treas. Reg. 118, Section 39.23(m)-1(g); *See also Commissioner* v. *Crews,* 108 F.(2d) 712, 24 A.F.T.R. 87 (10th Cir. 1939), rev'g and remanding on another issue, 37 B.T.A. 387 (1938), acq. and nonacq. on other issues, 1938-1 C.B. 7, 39.

[70] *Rialto Mining Corporation,* T.C. Memo. Op., Dkt. No. 6978, 1946 P-H T.C. Memo. Dec., Para. 46,148 (1946).

[71] *Rocky Mountain Oil Company,* 36 B.T.A. 365 (1937), acq. and nonacq. on other issues, 1937-2 C.B. 24, 50, appeal dismissed without written opinion *(Nolle Prosse)* (5th Cir. 1938). The issue decided in this case, that intangibles were not deductible in determining net income from the property, was later overruled by the Supreme Court in *Helvering* v. *Wilshire Oil Co., Inc., supra.*

[72] U.S. Treas. Reg. 118, Section 39.23(m)-1(g).

farming or ranching and possibly some kind of manufacturing operation, is conducting three unrelated activities, each of which should bear its fair share of the overhead or general operating expenses. The regulations cited above require an allocation of such overhead expenses among the different activities on the basis of the operating expenses directly applicable to each. The overhead incurred or allocated to the oil operations is not necessarily all applicable to the oil producing operation, and it is only that overhead applicable to the producing operation that is a factor in computing the depletion deduction. For example, deductions attributable to the acquisition, retention, or forfeiture of nonproducing properties are not attributable to the producing operation. Similarly, transportation or processing costs should not be attributed to the producing operation.[73] In this instance also, the allocation among the various activities involved in the oil operation should, under the regulations, be made in proportion to the operating expenses directly incurred in the furtherance of each activity.

The requirement of the regulations that direct expense ratios be used in making the overhead allocation among various business activities should not be regarded as setting an invariable rule. The Tax Court has held that the regulation does not prevent an allocation on any reasonable basis, and found, in the case of a coal mining company which also had other activities, that 15 per cent of the power purchased, 25 per cent of superintendent's salary, 15 per cent of depletion-mine timbers, 90 per cent of building repairs, 20 per cent of officers' salaries, and 36.6 per cent of state franchise tax should be allocated to activities other than mining.[74] It appears, therefore, that the primary test to be applied to any basis of allocation is one of reasonableness and consistency.

---

[73] G.C.M. 22956, 1941-2 C.B. 103.

[74] *Tennessee Consolidated Coal Company*, 15 T.C. 424 (1950), acq. on this and other issues, 1951-2 C.B. 4, nonacq. on another issue, 1951-2 C.B. 6, appeal dismissed on stipulation of parties (6th Cir. 1952 and 1953).

11.19 *Allocation Among Properties.* All costs properly at-tributable to the mineral extraction or production activity must then "be fairly apportioned to the several properties, taking into account their relative production." [75] Relative production may be measured in terms of dollars as well as units, and is customarily based on the gross income from the respective properties. It might be noted that, if the taxpayer owns both working interests and nonoperating interests, allocation among all properties in proportion to gross income would probably not constitute a reasonable method of allocation, because non-operating interests require less administrative effort per dollar of gross income than working interests. They do, however, re-quire some administrative effort and should bear a reasonable share of the overhead expense. In this case also, as in the case of allocation between various business activities, the test of the method of allocation is primarily one of reasonableness and consistency.

11.20 *Without Allowance for Depletion.* Net income, for computation of the limit on percentage depletion, is to be computed without regard to the allowance for depletion.[76] This provision might appear inconsistent when it is considered that if intangibles are capitalized, such costs are to be recov-ered through depletion, whereas if the intangibles are expensed under the option granted the taxpayer by the regulations, they must be deducted from gross income in computing net income from the property.[77] This apparent inconsistency does not seem to have troubled the courts.

11.21 **Restoration of Depletion.** If a lessor has received a lease bonus upon granting a lease and has reported it as in-come, claiming depletion thereon, he has followed the theory that he has received an advance royalty related to future

---

[75] U.S. Treas. Reg. 118, Section 39.23(m)-1(g).
[76] I.R.C., Section 613 [1939 I.R.C., Section 114(b)(3)].
[77] *Helvering* v. *Wilshire Oil Co., Inc., supra.*

production from the property.[78] When the lessor claims depletion on the bonus, he is required to reduce the basis, if any, of
his retained interest by the amount of the depletion.[79] If the
lease is subsequently terminated without any production, the
lessor is required to restore his basis, if any, in the property and
to report as income, in the year the lease is terminated by the
lessee, the depletion previously claimed.[80] The regulations require depletion to be restored even though the parties enter
into a new lease after the old lease has terminated and depletion would be allowable upon any bonus paid for the new lease.
These rules are applicable whether the lessor has claimed cost
or percentage depletion [81] and are also applicable under certain circumstances to minimum royalty payments.[82] It is immaterial that the taxpayer may not have derived any tax benefit
from the depletion deduction or may pay a greater tax upon
restoration of the depletion to income than the saving from its
deduction.[83] Where the retained interest has been given to
another person, it has been held that the lessor-donor must
restore all of the depletion if after the date of the gift the lease
is terminated without production.[84]

The restoration of depletion rule does not apply if there has
been any production income from the property, no matter how
small.[85] Depletion need not be restored unless the lessee has
completely abandoned the lease. Abandonment of a portion of
a lease is not conclusive evidence that there will be no produc-

---

[78] *Herring v. Commissioner, supra.*

[79] I.R.C., Section 1016(a)(2) [1939 I.R.C., Section 113(b)(1)(B)].

[80] U.S. Treas. Reg. 118, Section 39.23(m)-10(c).

[81] *Louisiana Delta Hardwood Lumber Co., Inc.,* 12 T.C. 576 (1949), aff'd,
183 F.(2d) 189, 39 A.F.T.R. 648 (5th Cir. 1950).

[82] *Douglas v. Commissioner,* 322 U.S. 275, 32 A.F.T.R. 358 (1944).

[83] *Douglas v. Commissioner, supra.*

[84] *Mary F. Waggoner,* 47 B.T.A. 699 (1942), acq., 1945 C.B. 7, appeal dismissed on motion of Commissioner, Dkt. No. 10652, 32 A.F.T.R. 1754 (5th
Cir. 1943).

[85] *Dolores Crabb,* 41 B.T.A. 686 (1940), acq., 1940-2 C.B. 2, remanded on
other issues, 121 F.(2d) 1015, 27 A.F.T.R. 780 (5th Cir. 1941). Upon remand
other issues were decided in 47 B.T.A. 916 (1942), aff'd, 136 F.(2d) 501, 31
A.F.T.R. 197 (5th Cir. 1943). *See also* G.C.M. 14448, XIV-1 C.B. 98 (1935).

tion; thus no depletion need be restored at that time.[86] If the term of a lease is extended by the parties prior to its expiration, there need be no restoration.[87] There can be no restoration of income in the absence of a termination of the lease, even though the interest retained upon granting the lease is transferred by death of the owner,[88] by an estate in final distribution of its corpus to its sole beneficiary,[89] by an individual who makes a gift of an undivided fraction of his mineral rights,[90] or by a corporation for a consideration.[91]

DEPLETION IN THE INCOME TAX RETURN

11.22   Information Requirements. The regulations [92] set forth in some detail the information to be filed with the tax return whenever a taxpayer is claiming a depletion deduction. The Revenue Service has provided "Form O" to be used in submitting such information. However, Form O consists of four pages, and if the taxpayer has many properties, submission of a separate form for each property would increase considerably the bulk of the tax return and the burden of its preparation. Therefore, it has become customary for taxpayers to submit schedules summarizing the most essential information required by the regulations and by Form O, and to maintain the rest of the information in their files where it is available for examination by Revenue Agents. This procedure has in the past been accepted by the Revenue Service, and it

---

[86] *Driscoll* v. *Commissioner,* 147 F.(2d) 493, 33 A.F.T.R. 704 (5th Cir. 1945); *Houston Farms Development Co.* v. *Commissioner,* 194 F.(2d) 520, 41 A.F.T.R. 725 (5th Cir. 1952), rev'g 15 T.C. 321 (1950).

[87] *Houston Farms Development Co.* v. *Commissioner, supra.*

[88] *Estate of Emma Louise G. Seeligson,* 1 T.C. 736 (1943), acq., 1944 C.B. 25, aff'd, 141 F.(2d) 358, 34 A.F.T.R. 390 (5th Cir. 1944).

[89] *Estate of Robert Driscoll,* T.C. Memo. Op., Dkt. No. 112199, 1943 P-H T.C. Memo. Dec., Para. 43,312 (1943), appeal dismissed on motion of Commissioner, Dkt. No. 10910, 34 A.F.T.R. 1629 (5th Cir. 1944).

[90] *Mary F. Waggoner, supra.*

[91] *American National Realty Company, supra.*

[92] U.S. Treas. Reg. 118, Section 39.23(m)-12 and 13.

Figure 5
XYZ OIL COMPANY
Corporation Income Tax Return
Calendar Year 1953

Statement of Taxable Income

	Per books	Tax adjustments	Taxable income	ALLOCATION BETWEEN OPERATIONS			
				Oil and gas operations	Drilling* operations	Other operations	Overhead
Income:							
Contract drilling income	$ 3,850,000.00		3,850,000.00		3,850,000.00		
Oil and gas sales	1,519,684.00		1,519,684.00	1,519,684.00			
Royalty income	2,100.00		2,100.00			2,100.00	
Interest	24,000.00		24,000.00				24,000.00
Capital gains	149,000.00		149,000.00			149,000.00	
Dividends	3,000.00		3,000.00			3,000.00	
Other income	12,000.00		12,000.00			12,000.00	
Gross income	5,559,784.00	—	5,559,784.00	1,519,684.00	3,850,000.00	166,100.00	24,000.00
Expenses:							
Contract drilling expense	3,010,000.00		3,010,000.00		3,010,000.00		
Oil and gas production expense	212,864.00		212,864.00	212,864.00			
Intangible drilling and development cost:							
Producing wells	—	85,750.00†	85,750.00	85,750.00			
Dry holes:							
On producing properties	17,000.00		17,000.00	17,000.00			
On nonproducing properties	15,000.00		15,000.00			15,000.00	
Delay rentals	880.00		880.00			880.00	
Depreciation	392,335.00		392,335.00	45,335.00	310,000.00		37,000.00
Compensation of officers	139,000.00		139,000.00				139,000.00
Office salaries and wages	199,000.00		199,000.00				199,000.00
Rent	21,000.00		21,000.00				21,000.00
Taxes	109,009.00		109,009.00	102,889.00		120.00	6,000.00
Interest	26,500.00		26,500.00				26,500.00
Subtotal before allocation of overhead	4,142,588.00	85,750.00	4,228,338.00	463,838.00 (12.21%)	3,320,000.00 (87.37%)	16,000.00 (.42%)	428,500.00

Expenses, Continued:

Proration of overhead on basis of direct expense before depletion				49,389.45	353,411.65	1,698.90	(404,500.00)
Charitable contributions	1,500.00		1,500.00			1,500.00	
Depletion:							
Amortization of intangible drilling and development costs—per books	185,077.22						
Depletion of other depletable costs—per books	171,774.28						
Allowable depletion for income tax return—see Figure 6		18,301.83‡	375,153.33	374,572.83	—	580.50	—
Total deductions	4,500,939.50	104,051.83	4,604,991.33	887,800.28	3,673,411.65	19,779.40	24,000.00
Net income	$ 1,058,844.50	(104,051.83)	954,792.67	631,883.72	176,588.35	146,320.60	—

* This column is not necessary for the income tax return but is often used in departmental allocation for accounting purposes.
† Intangible drilling and development costs capitalized on books, deductible for income tax purposes.
‡ Difference between depletion allowable on federal income tax return and sum of depletion and amortization of intangible drilling and development costs per books.

may be presumed that it will continue to be acceptable. It should be observed, however, that the administrative acceptance of summary schedules does not relieve the taxpayer of the burden of having all the required information available upon request by the Revenue Service.

In the past, returns have proved acceptable if accompanied by the following summary information:

1. Summary of income, expense, and percentage depletion by properties.

2. Computation of cost depletion by properties.

3. Computation of depreciation by properties.

4. Possibly, a schedule showing the computation of overhead and its allocation between various activities.

This information need not be presented in any prescribed form. Except for the computation of depreciation, Figures 5 through 7 illustrate how the data might be presented.

11.23   Illustrative Examples. Figures 5 through 7 are largely self-explanatory, but the following comments will aid the reader in understanding the treatment of certain items:

1. The taxpayer has elected to deduct intangible drilling and development costs (see Chapter 10).

2. In Figure 5, interest income is treated as a credit to overhead on the theory that the interest income is an offset to interest expense. If the interest expense were less than the interest income, the credit to overhead would be limited to the amount of the expense.

3. In Figures 5 and 6, intangible drilling and development costs are segregated between those resulting in productive wells and those resulting in dry holes. This breakdown is for accounting purposes and is not necessary on the return of a taxpayer who has elected to deduct intangible costs. Such a taxpayer deducts all intangible drilling and development costs, regardless of the outcome of the drilling.

Figure 6

XYZ OIL COMPANY

Corporation Income Tax Return
For Calendar Year 1953

Allowable Depletion

Leases	Gross income	DEDUCTIONS Production expense	Intangible drilling and development expense	Dry holes expense	Depreciation expense	Taxes expense	Other deductions	Overhead°	Total deductions before depletion	Net income before depletion	DEPLETION 27½% of gross income	50% of net income	Cost depletion (See Figure 7)	Allowable depletion	Net income after depletion
Texas:															
Lease #1	$ 370,157.00	25,741.32	—	—	5,618.00	17,027.35	—	12,030.03	60,416.70	309,740.30	101,793.18	154,870.15	56,617.45	101,793.18	207,947.12
Lease #2	147,035.00	66,233.88	—	—	9,487.00	6,765.00	—	4,778.61	87,264.49	59,770.51	40,434.63	29,885.26	27,995.46	29,885.26	29,885.25
Lease #3	267,305.00	21,985.08	—	—	4,456.00	12,296.29	—	8,687.36	47,424.73	219,880.27	73,508.88	109,940.14	17,203.45	73,508.88	146,371.39
Total Texas	784,497.00	113,960.28	—	—	19,561.00	36,088.64	—	25,496.00	195,105.92	589,391.08	215,736.69	294,695.55	101,816.36	205,187.32	384,203.76
Louisiana:															
Lease #4	109,652.00	32,502.88	85,750.00	—	9,157.00	10,636.07	—	3,563.67	141,609.62	(31,957.62)	30,154.30	(15,978.81)	7,862.28	7,862.28	(39,819.90)
Lease #5	529,265.00	28,706.08	—	—	10,955.00	51,339.00	—	17,201.01	108,201.09	421,063.91	145,547.88	210,531.96	—	145,547.88	275,516.03
Total Louisiana	638,917.00	61,208.96	85,750.00	—	20,112.00	61,975.07	—	20,764.68	249,810.71	389,106.29	175,702.18	194,553.15	7,862.28	153,410.16	235,696.13
New Mexico:															
Lease #6	96,270.00	37,694.76	—	17,000.00	5,662.00	4,825.29	—	3,128.77	68,310.82	27,959.18	26,474.25	13,979.59	15,975.35	15,975.35	11,983.83
Total New Mexico	96,270.00	37,694.76	—	17,000.00	5,662.00	4,825.29	—	3,128.77	68,310.82	27,959.18	26,474.25	13,979.59	15,975.35	15,975.35	11,983.83
Total leases	$ 1,519,684.00	212,864.00	85,750.00	17,000.00	45,335.00	102,889.00	—	49,389.45°	513,227.45	1,006,456.55	417,913.12	503,228.29	125,653.99	374,572.83	631,883.72
Royalties															
Texas:															
Royalty A	120.00	—	—	—	—	10.00	—	—	10.00	110.00	33.00	55.00	36.00	36.00	74.00
Royalty B	1,240.00	—	—	—	—	70.00	—	—	70.00	1,170.00	341.00	585.00	—	341.00	829.00
Royalty C	740.00	—	—	—	—	40.00	—	—	40.00	700.00	203.50	350.00	—	203.50	496.50
Total royalties	$ 2,100.00	—	—	—	—	120.00	—	—	120.00	1,980.00	577.50	990.00	36.00	580.50	1,399.50
											Total allowable depletion			$ 375,153.33	

° Allocated to leases on basis of gross income.

Figure 7

XYZ OIL COMPANY

Corporation Income Tax Return
For Calendar Year 1953

Cost Depletion

Leases	Date acquired	INVESTMENT				DEPLETION RESERVE				OIL RESERVES (BARRELS)			Unit rate	Production 1953 barrels	Cost depletion	Allowable depletion (see Figure 6)	Depletion reserve 12–31–53
		Balance 1–1–53	Additions	Reductions	Balance 12–31–53	Balance 1–1–53	Adjustments	Adjusted reserve	Depletable sum	Balance 1–1–53	Adjustments	Total for period					
Texas:																	
Lease #1	1–18–50	$ 425,710.00	21,686.00	——	447,396.00	231,396.00	——	231,396.00	216,000.00	565,253.00	——	565,253.00	.382130	148,162.80	56,617.45	101,793.18	333,189.18
Lease #2	2–2–51	278,020.00	890.00	——	278,910.00	48,050.00	——	48,050.00	230,860.00	460,000.00	25,000.00°	485,000.00	.476000	58,814.00	27,995.46	29,885.26	77,935.26
Lease #3	10–31–50	212,179.00	——	(5,304.48)†	206,874.52	137,975.00	(3,449.38)†	134,525.62	72,348.90	392,550.00	(4,910.00)†	387,640.00	.186639	92,175.00	17,203.45	73,508.88	206,874.52 ‖
Total Texas		915,909.00	22,576.00	(5,304.48)	933,180.52	417,421.00	(3,449.38)	413,971.62	519,208.90						101,816.36	205,187.32	617,998.96
Louisiana:																	
Lease #4	6–1–51	70,190.00	7,286.00	——	77,476.00	52,020.00	——	52,020.00	25,456.00	80,450.00	45,000.00‡	125,450.00	.202917	38,746.30	7,862.28	7,862.28	59,882.28
Lease #5	1–14–49	715,097.00	——	——	715,097.00	715,097.00	——	715,097.00	——	——	——	——	——	193,160.50	——	145,547.88	715,097.00 ‖
Total Louisiana		785,287.00	7,286.00	——	792,573.00	767,117.00	——	767,117.00	25,456.00						7,862.28	153,410.16	774,979.28
New Mexico:																	
Lease #6	12–29–49	270,216.00	——	——	270,216.00	198,330.00	——	198,330.00	71,886.00	197,290.00	(24,070.00)§	173,220.00	.414998	38,495.00	15,975.35	15,975.35	214,305.35
Total New Mexico		270,216.00	——	——	270,216.00	198,330.00	——	198,330.00	71,886.00						15,975.35	15,975.35	214,305.35
Total leases		$ 1,971,412.00	29,862.00	(5,304.48)	1,995,969.52	1,382,868.00	(3,449.38)	1,379,418.62	616,550.90						125,653.99	374,572.83	1,607,283.59
Royalties																	
Texas:																	
Royalty A	1–27–50	1,250.00	——	——	1,250.00	275.00	——	275.00	975.00	1,600.00	(300.00)°	1,300.00	.750000	48.00	36.00	36.00	311.00
Royalty B	3–15–48	875.00	——	——	875.00	875.00	——	875.00	——	——	——	——	——	476.90	——	341.00	875.00
Royalty C	3–17–48	500.00	——	——	500.00	500.00	——	500.00	——	——	——	——	——	290.20	——	203.50	500.00
Total royalties		$ 2,625.00	——	——	2,625.00	1,650.00	——	1,650.00	975.00						36.00	580.50	1,686.00
														Total allowable depletion		$ 375,153.33	

° Adjustment based on new geological study.
† To record sale of overriding royalty interest.
‡ Reserve added by additional development.
§ Reserves reduced because of dry hole drilled this year.
‖ Does not crossfoot; allowable depletion exceeds depletable sum.

4. In Figure 5, depletion per books is shown as two items, "amortization of intangible drilling and development costs" and "depletion of other depletable costs." Most larger firms and many smaller ones capitalize the intangible costs of productive wells on their books, even though they deduct them for tax purposes. Such costs are frequently shown in a separate account and charged off separately from other depletable costs, though the charge-off or amortization is computed in a similar manner to depletion. It should be noted that after the first year of operation, book depletion of leasehold costs will be different from cost depletion for tax purposes because they are computed on different bases. Book depletion disregards percentage depletion entirely, while cost depletion for tax purposes is computed on the cost less prior cost or percentage depletion, whichever was higher in each prior year, as explained in paragraph 11.02.

5. In Figure 6, no overhead was allocated to royalty income. Some small portion of the overhead should normally be borne by royalty income, but in the example, the amount allocable is insignificant.

CHAPTER XII

The Property Unit

12.01   Introduction. At various places in preceding chapters the term "property" was used as though the term were readily understandable. On the contrary, and despite a statutory definition, the unit described thereby is not easily identifiable. It has been indicated that in the field of oil and gas income taxation the term is significant in connection with the following matters:

1. Geological and geophysical costs that are capitalized must ultimately be allocated to a property unit, or aggregation of properties, and become an element of cost of the depletable interest therein.[1]

2. If the taxpayer has elected to capitalize intangible drilling and development costs, such costs, to the extent that they are not represented by physical property, must be added to the depletable basis of the property.[2]

---

[1] I.T. 4006, 1950-1 C.B. 48.
[2] *United States* v. *Dakota Montana Oil Co.,* 288 U.S. 459, 12 A.F.T.R. 18 (1933); U.S. Treas. Reg. 118, Section 39.23(m)-16(b).

3. Depletion must be computed separately for each property or aggregation of properties.[3]

4. In the event of a sale or exchange of a mineral property, gain or loss must be computed separately for each property or aggregation of properties.[4]

5. Under certain conditions a mineral property may become worthless or be abandoned and a loss may be claimed under Section 165 of the Internal Revenue Code, but no loss may be claimed because of the worthlessness or abandonment of part of a property unit.[5]

Although the term "property" has been used in the field of oil and gas tax law for many years, the word was not defined in the Internal Revenue Code until 1954, and the definition then adopted leaves many questions to be answered regarding the determination of the property unit in the oil and gas industry.

12.02   Definition of Property. Section 614(a) of the Internal Revenue Code states:

For the purpose of computing the depletion allowance in the case of mines, wells, and other natural deposits, the term "property" means each separate interest owned by the taxpayer in each mineral deposit in each separate tract or parcel of land.

This statutory definition is a composite based on prior regulations and administrative rulings issued at a time when there was no statutory definition. In adopting such a composite definition it must be assumed that Congress intended to adopt most of the rules previously applied by the Revenue Service.

It is apparent that this definition places emphasis upon separateness, whether of interest, deposit, or tract or parcel of land. The Revenue Service has long viewed each interest owned by a taxpayer as a separate property unless the taxpayer

---

[3] I.R.C., Sections 612-13 [1939 I.R.C., Section 114(b)(1) and 114(b)(3)].
[4] I.R.C., Sections 1011 and 1016 [1939 I.R.C., Section 113(b) and 113 (b)(1)].
[5] *Frank Lyons,* 10 T.C. 634 (1948).

acquired the same kind of interest, at the same time, from the same assignor, in tracts or parcels of land which are geographically contiguous. If any one of these four tests is not met, the taxpayer is considered to have acquired separate property interests.

Because the statutory definition follows so closely the prior regulations and rulings, the rulings and decisions issued prior to the adoption of the statutory provision in 1954 will be very significant in its interpretation. It will be found, however, that some of the prior decisions did not follow the regulations and rulings. It is perhaps significant in this connection that in those cases where the courts have seen fit to vary from the Revenue Service rulings, they have not held the regulations or rulings invalid, but have found them inapplicable to the circumstances of the case before them. As a consequence, decisions of the courts that appear to be at variance with the regulations and rulings must be carefully considered to determine whether they establish a different principle of law or, which is more likely, whether they hold the application of the Revenue Service rules in the particular facts would produce an unreasonable result. Some of the problems that were created by such decisions in the past have been laid at rest, not only by a statutory definition of the term "property," but also by the provisions permitting aggregation of certain types of property interest. These provisions are discussed later in this chapter.

12.03   *Separate Interest.* The taxpayer's interest may refer to the kind of interest that he holds in a mineral property, such as fee simple, working interest (operating rights), royalty or overriding royalty, oil payments, and possibly a carried interest. Frequently, the taxpayer's interest in a property refers to his fractional share of the production. The Revenue Service took the position, in a ruling in 1941, that the acquisition of different kinds of interest, even though acquired simultaneously, and from the same grantor, resulted in the acquisition of separate property interests.[6] However, in a 1946 case the Revenue Service argued that the simultaneous acquisition from one grantor of a working interest and an oil payment in the same property resulted in the creation of only a single property unit.[7] The Tax Court did not sustain this contention, but held that the two interests were to be regarded as separate properties,[8] with the comment that a working interest and an oil payment are "inherently separate and different in character," the former being "an outright ownership in fee of an undivided part of the leasehold estate," and the latter being "less than a fee title interest in the remaining part of the leasehold."

Despite the decision in this case, the Revenue Service unofficially takes the position that the simultaneous acquisition, or retention, of two kinds of interest in a single tract or parcel of land creates only one property interest. Thus, although the ruling described in the preceding paragraph has not been modified, the Revenue Service would probably argue that the simultaneous acquisition from the same grantor by a grantee of a share of the working interest and an oil payment in the same tract would result in only a single property. Also if the owner of a working interest assigns the property and retains an overriding royalty and an oil payment, it is probable that the Revenue Service would regard the two retained interests as a single property. One consequence of such a view would be that the subsequent assignment of the oil payment, retaining either the working interest or the override, would be treated by the Revenue Service as an anticipation of future income. If two different kinds of interest are acquired at different times the Revenue Service would treat such interests as separate properties. This view was sustained in a case where the taxpayer acquired two-thirds of the fee royalty after he owned the working interest, and the Court held that the taxpayer had two sep-

---

[6] G.C.M. 22332, 1941-1 C.B. 228.

[7] Herndon Drilling Company, 6 T.C. 628 (1946), nonacq. on this point, 1946-2 C.B. 6.

[8] Herndon Drilling Company, supra.

arate properties.[9] The statutory definition of the property unit does not appear to affect this problem.

If the taxpayer's interest refers to his share of the proceeds from production, the Revenue Service holds that he acquires as many separate properties as there are conveyances to him,[10] even though some represent reconveyances of oil payments previously carved out by him.[11] Thus, the Revenue Service would hold that the acquisition of a one-half working interest in one conveyance and a one-fourth working interest in a separate conveyance from a different assignor would create two properties in the same lease. Although this result is contrary to a decision of the Board of Tax Appeals rendered under prior law,[12] it may be assumed that the position would be sustained under the new statutory provisions. The question is of less significance because of the taxpayer's right, subject to proper election, to aggregate certain types of property interests.

12.04   *Separate Tract or Parcel.* The taxpayer's interest in the property may also refer to the area covered by that property. The Revenue Service holds that separate interests exist in each of two or more areas of land that are separated geographically,[13] even though such interests are of the same kind and were acquired simultaneously from the same grantor. The Revenue Service also contends that separate properties are owned by a taxpayer in two tracts or parcels of land that are connected geographically but are acquired from different grantors or at different times.[14] This view was sustained by the Tax Court, in an oil and gas case where the taxpayer obtained, in a single conveyance, a lease of four lots, two of which were contiguous and two of which touched only at a corner.[15] The Court held that the two contiguous lots constituted a single

---

[9] Badger Oil Co. v. Commissioner, 118 F. (2d) 791 26 A.F.T.R. 910 (5th Cir. 1941).

[10] G.C.M. 22106, 1941-1 C.B. 245. However, see paragraphs 12.05 and 12.07 relating to the right to aggregate certain interests.

[11] G.C.M. 24094, 1944 C.B. 250.

[12] William H. Cree, 47 B.T.A. 868 (1942), nonacq. 1943 C.B. 29.

[13] G.C.M. 22106, *supra.*

[14] Example VI, G.C.M. 22106, *supra.*

[15] *Berkshire Oil Company,* 9 T.C. 903 (1947), acq., 1948-1 C.B. 1.

property, whereas those which had only a common corner were separate properties. The principle that properties must be contiguous to constitute a single tract or parcel of land appears to be realistic from an economic standpoint, particularly in the oil and gas business, because ordinarily each such separate tract may be developed and operated as a separate unit. Frequently it will be necessary to do so because of the difference in ownership of interests in each tract. This problem is also affected to some extent by the statutory provision dealing with aggregation of property interests.

12.05   Aggregation of Operating Interests. Effective for taxable years beginning after December 31, 1953 and ending after August 16, 1954 the law [16] provides that if a taxpayer owns two or more separate operating interests which constitute part or all of an operating unit, it may elect to form an aggregation of any two or more of such interests and treat such aggregation as a single property, and to treat all such interests in the operating unit not aggregated as separate properties. As long as the operating interests are part of the same operating unit such interests may be aggregated, regardless of whether they are included in a single tract or parcel of land or whether they are included in contiguous tracts or parcels of land. The taxpayer may not elect to form more than one aggregation in any one operating unit. An operating mineral interest is defined as one in respect of which the costs of production of the mineral are required to be taken into account by the taxpayer in determining the net income limitation on percentage depletion, or would be so required if the well were in the production stage.

These statutory provisions probably were adopted in recognition of two decisions, one affecting the mining of sand and gravel,[17] and the other affecting the mining of coal,[18] in which the courts refused to follow a regulation holding that each

[16] I.R.C., Section 614(b).

[17] *Gifford-Hill & Company, Inc.*, 11 T.C. 802 (1949), nonacq. on this issue, 1949-1 C.B. 5, acq. on another issue, 1949-1 C.B. 2, aff'd, 180 F.(2d) 655, 39 A.F.T.R. 60 (5th Cir. 1950).

[18] *The Black Mountain Corporation*, 5 T.C. 1117 (1945), nonacq., 1946-2 C.B. 6.

separate acquisition in a tract or parcel of land constituted a separate property interest. It is perhaps significant in this connection that it is not economically sound to attempt to mine sand and gravel or coal within the confines of a single tract or parcel of land, unless such tract happens to be coextensive with the area of the deposit. On the other hand, in the oil and gas industry it is customary to develop properties in relatively small tracts or parcels of land, depending upon the well-spacing requirements imposed by the various state regulatory authorities. Since operating units tend to follow specific geographical boundaries in the oil industry, it appears that the right to aggregate operating interests will be of less significance in the oil industry than it may be in other extractive industries.

In the oil industry, this section will certainly permit an aggregation in a case where the taxpayer acquires a fraction of a working interest in a lease and acquires another fraction of a working interest in the same lease at another time or from a different grantor. It will also continue the option, given a taxpayer by prior regulations,[19] to combine or aggregate two or more separate mineral deposits on the same tract or parcel of land. Beyond this point, the question of aggregation will depend upon the application of the term "operating unit" in the oil industry.

The Senate Finance Commitee Report [20] indicates that the term "operating unit" contemplates an aggregation only of interests that may conveniently and economically be operated together as a single working unit. The report also indicates that interests that are geographically widespread may not be considered parts of the same operating unit merely because the products of the interests are processed at the same treatment plant or because one set of accounting records is maintained by the taxpayer. Because of the recentness of this statutory provision, it is difficult to forecast accurately the application

---

[19] U. S. Treas. Reg. 118, Section 39.23(m)-1(i).
[20] Senate Report No. 1622, Eighty-third Congress, Second Session (June 18, 1954), p. 334.

of the term in the oil and gas industry. Some precedent for other extractive industries is found in the two decisions mentioned above, but there is serious question as to whether these decisions would be applicable to the oil or gas industry. It may be anticipated that later rulings and decisions will clarify this question.

12.06 *Time and Effect of Election.* The taxpayer must exercise his election to aggregate property interests in the first taxable year beginning after December 31, 1953, or in the first taxable year in which any expenditure for exploration, development, or operation in respect of the operating mineral interest is made by the taxpayer after acquisition of such interest, whichever year is later. For the purpose of this section the acquisition of an option to acquire an operating mineral interest does not constitute the acquisition of the interest. The election must be made not later than the time for filing the return for the taxable year above specified. The election once made is binding for all subsequent taxable years, unless the consent of the Commissioner is obtained to any different treatment of the interest in respect of which the election is made. The Report of the Senate Finance Committee [21] indicates that a change in tax consequences of the election would not warrant a change, but that a change in the operating unit so that part of the aggregation is no longer included would make appropriate the Commissioner's consent to a new election.

The election to aggregate separate properties is effective for all purposes of the income tax provisions of the Internal Revenue Code. Thus, if a taxpayer elects to aggregate certain properties, he must compute both cost and percentage depletion, and gain or loss on sale or exchange, in respect of the aggregation. If only a portion of an aggregation is sold or otherwise disposed of, the adjusted basis of the aggregation must be reasonably apportioned to determine the adjusted basis of the part disposed of. If a part of the aggregation becomes worthless, the taxpayer, presumably, would not be permitted to

---

[21] *Ibid.* p. 335.

claim a deduction for the loss, even though the part that becomes worthless was a separate property prior to the election to aggregate.[22]

12.07 Aggregation of Nonoperating Interests. A taxpayer is also given the right to aggregate two or more separate non-operating mineral interests in a single tract or parcel of land, or in two or more contiguous tracts, on a showing of undue hardship.[23] Undue hardship is not defined, but the report of the Senate Finance Committee indicates that it is not intended to include mere tax disadvantage to the taxpayer. Nonoperating mineral interests are defined to include those which do not constitute operating mineral interests as defined in Section 614(b)(3).

12.08 Creation of More Than One Property from a Single Property. The Revenue Service recognizes and adheres to the principle that the taxpayer effects a separation of property interests in any type of assignment, whether the interest assigned is different in kind, share, or area.[24] Thus, the owner of the working interest in a 640-acre lease could assign an oil payment carved out of that working interest. He has created in the hands of the assignee a new property, and, even if he reacquires the carved-out oil payment at a subsequent date, he would be considered as having two separate properties in the lease.[25] Similarly, if he assigns one-half of his working interest, retaining an overriding royalty, he is considered as having two properties: (1) his retained share of the working interest, and (2) his retained overriding royalty. If he subsequently reacquires the assigned working interest, he would be considered as having three properties,[26] although he could elect to aggregate the two operating interests. The taxpayer could assign the entire working interest in the north 320 acres of his tract, thereby creating two property rights. Upon subsequent acquisition of the assigned working interest, he would be considered

---

[22] See discussion in paragraphs 8.09-8.11.
[23] I.R.C., Section 614(c).   [25] G.C.M. 24094, *supra.*
[24] G.C.M. 22106, *supra.*   [26] G.C.M. 24094, *supra.*

as having two property rights.[27] Whether he could aggregate the two working interests would depend upon whether they constituted parts of the same operating unit.

The rule of separation by geographical area finds support in the Jewel Mining case,[28] where it was held that a separate tract was created by the sublease of a geographical portion of a leasehold. The Court held that the sublessor should not be allowed to combine the income from the retained royalty with the operating income from the portion of the lease that was not subleased. In the Mascot Oil case [29] a different type of geographical separation was involved. Here the lessor subleased a portion of his property consisting of all sands below a depth of 1,600 feet, and the Court permitted the taxpayer to treat the royalty income from the subleased portion and the operating income from the leased portion as if from one property. The Court gave no consideration to the regulations that might appear to give the taxpayer an election in such a case, but viewed the situation from the standpoint of the lessee-sublessor, whose obligations to the lessor were not relieved by the fact that he had subleased the lower sands to another person. It is probable that a different conclusion would have been reached by the Court if this case had been decided under the 1954 Internal Revenue Code.

---

[27] *J. T. Sneed, Jr.*, 40 B.T.A. 1136 (1939), aff'd, 119 F.(2d) 767, 27 A.F.T.R. 188 (5th Cir. 1941), cert. den., 314 U.S. 686.

[28] *Helvering* v. *Jewel Mining Co.*, 126 F.(2d) 1011, 29 A.F.T.R. 53 (8th Cir. 1942).

[29] *Mascot Oil Company*, 29 B.T.A. 652 (1933), appeal dismissed on stipulation of parties, 75 F.(2d) 1009, 15 A.F.T.R. 361 (9th Cir. 1935).

CHAPTER XIII

Joint Operation–Co-Ownership Versus Partnership

INTRODUCTION

13.01   Definition of Joint Operation. Because of the heavy investment and high risks involved in the development and

204

operation of oil and gas properties, it is common for several taxpayers to join together in a single enterprise. When co-owners of the working interest in a lease desire to develop and operate the lease, some type of agreement becomes necessary in order to define their rights and obligations. In such case, the co-owners have started a joint operation or co-ownership, and the agreement entered into between them is usually called a joint operating agreement. One of the co-owners is usually designated as the operator, and the others are termed non-operators. Ordinarily, revenues from the joint operation will be paid by the pipeline company directly to each co-owner according to his participating interest, although occasionally the operator alone will be designated to receive the proceeds, and will in turn account for such proceeds to the nonoperators. The operator is charged with the managerial responsibility for the operation, and also with the duty of paying bills and keeping records. The operator will ordinarily bill the nonoperators monthly for expenses incurred in the joint operation.

13.02   Tax Significance of Form of Organization. A joint operation of an oil or gas property may be conducted under any one of the following forms of business organization: co-ownership, joint venture, partnership, trust, or corporation. Each form may be attended by different tax consequences in relation to the selection of the taxable year, certain elections available to owners or operators of oil and gas properties, and the distribution of income and deductions between the owners. In determining the form of organization, it will be found that the principal test is whether a separate entity has been created that acts as principal in the development and operation of the property, or whether there is no separate entity, in which event the operator of the property is acting merely as agent for the owners.

13.03   *Taxable Year.* If the association of persons takes a form which causes it to be considered as an entity for tax purposes, such entity other than a partnership is entitled to adopt a taxable year that may or may not correspond with a taxable year of the owners of the enterprise. Any partnership that adopts a taxable year beginning after April 1, 1954, may not adopt a taxable year other than that of all its principal partners unless it establishes a business purpose therefor.[1] The entity reports income and deductions on the basis of the fiscal year so adopted. Assuming that the entity is not a corporation or a trust, each owner would include in his return for a given taxable year his share of income or loss of the enterprise for its fiscal year, which ended within the owner's taxable year. If, on the other hand, the enterprise is not considered to be a separate entity, then each co-owner reports, as part of his income or loss, his share of the income or loss of the enterprise for the period ended with the owner's taxable year.

13.04   *Elections.* In the oil and gas business certain elections are available to a taxpayer. It will be found that the term taxpayer refers, not necessarily to one who pays taxes, but rather to an entity which is considered to be separate and distinct from the owners thereof. Thus, if the form of organization is such that a separate entity is considered to exist, that entity must elect whether to capitalize or expense intangible drilling costs.[2] Such election, when properly made by the entity, is binding as to the entity, and the owners thereof are not entitled to a separate election as to property owned by the entity. By the same token, the entity is not bound by any individual elections made by the owners thereof.

13.05   *Allocation of Income and Deductions Among Owners.* In general, it will be found that most forms of joint operating arrangements contemplate or require that each participant share income or expense in direct proportion to the participant's interest in the property operated. However, in a

---

[1] I.R.C., Section 706(b)(1), Section 771(b)(1).
[2] I.R.C., Section 703(b). *See* Chapter 10, *supra.*

partnership, it is well recognized that the participants may make varying contributions to the enterprise and share the net income therefrom in a way that is not necessarily related to their capital contributions.

CO-OWNERSHIP VERSUS PARTNERSHIP

13.06   General. Because of the differences in tax consequence described above, it is necessary to distinguish the attributes of those forms of joint effort which result in a separate entity. When the association of taxpayers takes the form of a corporation or a trust, it is clear that a separate entity acting as principal has been created. The attributes of such organizations are well known, and require no further consideration in this chapter. Neither will consideration be given to associations that are regarded for tax purposes as taxable as corporations, because such classification is a potential hazard that may confront any noncorporate form of organization under circumstances that are discussed in Chapter 14.

Unincorporated oil and gas operations, not carried on by a trustee, may be conducted in the form of a co-ownership, a joint venture, a partnership, or a limited partnership. A joint venture, a limited partnership, and a general partnership all fall within the general provisions of the Code relating to partnerships, and each is considered a separate entity that acts as principal for its own account, not as agent for its owners. In the co-ownership, however, a separate entity is not created, and the operator acts as agent of the other co-owners. Fundamentally, therefore, the purpose of this chapter is to establish the distinguishing characteristics between co-ownership and partnership.

Before making these distinctions, however, reference should be made to certain elections available to taxpayers regarding the form of business organization. For example, Section 1361 of the Internal Revenue Code makes it possible for certain unincorporated business enterprises to be taxed as corporations. In this case also, the election must be made by all of the owners, certain qualifying requirements must be met, and the election is irrevocable unless there is a change in ownership of more than 20 per cent. Excluding income that would constitute personal holding company income as defined in Section 543, and the deductions attributable thereto, the income would be taxable to the enterprise at corporate tax rates, and not to the owners unless distributed to them.

Section 761(a) of the Internal Revenue Code grants an option to the members of an unincorporated organization for taxable years beginning after December 31, 1954 to exclude such organization from the application of the partnership tax rules contained in Subchapter K of the Code. The election must be made by all of the members of the organization and is available only if the organization is availed of:

(1) for investment purposes only and not for the active conduct of a business, or

(2) for the joint production, extraction or use of property, but not for the purpose of selling services or property produced or extracted,

if the income of the members of the organization may be adequately determined without the computation of partnership taxable income.

13.07   Title to Property. One characteristic of co-ownership that appears to distinguish it from a partnership is the fact that under a co-ownership, title to the property is ordinarily retained in the names of the participants individually. In a partnership, on the other hand, title to property used by the partnership is normally placed in the name of the partnership, or in the name of one of the partners, or in the name of a nominee, on behalf of the partnership. Although the Revenue Service does not attach great significance to the question of title, the courts appear to consider title important.[3] In the

---

[3] In *Bentex Oil Corporation*, 20 T.C. 565 (1953), appeal pending to 5th Cir., the Court disregarded the resting place of title to property. Three co-

Appleby [4] case the Court was considering whether a tenancy in common, which is the usual form of co-ownership in the oil business, should be treated as a partnership. Although this case did not involve oil and gas property, the Court held that tenancy in common was an estate so old and so well known that it was almost inconceivable that it should fall in the statutory class of partnerships by reason of any general terms contained in the Internal Revenue Code. The Court observed that it had never known a tenancy in common to be regarded as a unit, and stated that, if it were to be held a statutory partnership, the term would be so expanded in scope as to raise a question as to the classification of marital communities and tenancies by the entirety. Similarly, in the Gilford [5] case the Court held that co-owners of improved realty who appointed a common agent to maintain and manage store and apartment buildings were not to be considered partners in the absence of a showing of an intention on their part to become partners. The Court went on to say that the appointment of a common

---

owners of a lease had, pursuant to a ruling of the Revenue Service, filed a partnership-information return of income, designating the operation on the return as a joint venture. On that return a deduction had been claimed for intangible drilling costs. The taxpayer, who was one of the co-owners, had elected to capitalize intangible drilling costs on his individual return. In examining the taxpayer's returns the Commissioner at first disallowed the loss of the co-ownership to the extent that it was attributable to intangible drilling costs which were expensed. The disallowance was based on the grounds that the co-owners were not partners. After protest by the taxpayer, the entire loss was allowed on the basis that the operation of the lease constituted a partnership. In the case before the Court the taxpayer was arguing that its previous position was incorrect, that the co-ownership did not constitute a partnership, and that the intangible costs incurred should have been capitalized. The Court, without stating a reason for its conclusion, made a finding of fact that the operation of the lease constituted a joint venture or partnership. Unless the Court decided the issue on some grounds of equitable estoppel, or on the grounds that the filing of the partnership-information return designating the operation as a joint venture was a conclusive indication of the intention of the parties to form a joint venture, the decision appears questionable.

[4] *Estate of Edgar S. Appleby*, 41 B.T.A. 18 (1940), nonacq. on this issue, 1940-2 C.B. 9, aff'd on another issue, 123 F.(2d) 700, 28 A.F.T.R. 396 (2nd Cir. 1941).

[5] *Almy Gilford*, T.C. Memo. Op., Dkt. No. 29641, 1952 P-H T.C. Memo. Dec., Para. 52,049 (1952), aff'd, 201 F.(2d) 735, 43 A.F.T.R. 221, (2nd Cir. February 5, 1953).

agent was not a manifestation of an intent to create such a partnership, and each of the co-owners was regarded as being individually engaged in the trade or business. Despite the holdings of the courts in such cases, the Revenue Service has never seen fit to consider the resting place of title as an important factor in determination of the partnership relation.[6]

13.08   *Principal–Agency.* The importance of the title test is perhaps indicated by the decisions of the courts regarding the rights to income and deductions as between principal and agent. In the Oliver Iron Mining [7] case it was clearly held that when one person operates a property as agent for another, the latter being the owner of the property, the owner is taxable on all income and entitled to claim all deductions in respect of the property. Although it was not directly in point in that case, the Court commented that the result would be no different when a property is operated by one person on behalf of another, if the operator is also owner of an interest in the property. The Court stated that each owner would be required to report his proportionate share of the gross income and deductions from the property. The appointment of a common agent by a group of co-owners does not change the result.[8]

13.09   **Joint Profit Objective.** The Revenue Service has now taken the position that the most important single test to be applied in determining whether the organization is a co-ownership or a partnership is the presence of a joint profit objective.[9] If there is a joint profit objective, the Revenue Service will probably hold that the association of individuals is either a partnership or an association taxable as a corpora-

---

[6] Neither does the Revenue Service regard title as an important test in determining whether an association is taxable as a corporation. *See* paragraph 14.13.

[7] *Oliver Iron Mining Co., Successor,* 10 T.C. 908 (1948), appeal dismissed without written opinion *(Nolle Prosse)* (2nd Cir. 1949).

[8] *Almy Gilford, supra.*

[9] I.T. 3930, 1948-2 C.B. 126, as modified by I.T. 3933, 1948-2 C.B. 130. I.R.C., Section 761(a). The same test is applied in determining whether an organization is an association taxable as a corporation. *See* paragraph 14.13.

tion, depending upon which of the two forms the organization more nearly resembles. The Revenue Service has ruled that, when the parties to the agreement associate themselves only in the operation of the property and not in the sale of the product from the property, they do not have a joint profit objective. In other words, if the parties to the agreement reserve the right to take the product from the property in kind and dispose of it themselves, or if they delegate the right of disposal for a limited period of time and the right is terminable at will, they have reserved to themselves individually the income producing features of the operation and, therefore, do not have a joint profit objective.

13.10   *Development of Revenue Service Position.* The Revenue Service has not always taken this position. In 1934 it ruled [10] that co-owners of a jointly operated lease were partners. Obviously, that ruling disregarded both the question of title to property and the joint profit objective in determining the existence of partnership status. It followed, if such an association of individuals constituted a partnership, that the partnership was entitled to make the elections as to the taxable year and as to the capitalization or expensing of intangible drilling costs. About the same time the Revenue Service ruled [11] that in the case of co-ownership of oil and gas leases, it would be a sufficient compliance with the requirements of its previous ruling as to the filing of information returns if the operator of the co-owned property prepared and filed a modified partnership return, on the partnership return of information, showing only the owners' respective shares of revenues and expenditures.

The views expressed in these rulings remained in effect until 1948, when the Revenue Service issued a ruling [12] dealing

---

[10] I.T. 2749, XIII-1 C.B. 99 (1934). This ruling was later modified by I.T. 3930, *supra.*

[11] I.T. 2785, XIII-1 C.B. 96 (1934). This ruling was later modified by I.T. 3930, *supra.*

[12] I.T. 3930, *supra.*

with the problem of associations taxable as corporations. It was in this ruling that the concept of the joint profit objective was introduced. Although this ruling did not specifically deal with the partnership problem, it did modify the prior partnership rulings in that the Revenue Service recognized that the lack of a joint profit objective not only would prevent an association from being taxable as a corporation, but also implied that a co-ownership would not be classified as a partnership.

13.11   *Information Returns.* The status of the ruling [13] which requires the filing of modified partnership returns by co-owners of oil and gas leases is at present uncertain. As a practical matter, such an information return is of little benefit to the Revenue Service and its field agents in the examination of returns of the co-owners, inasmuch as such co-owners may have different taxable years and different elections as to intangibles. In view of these facts, it is not difficult to understand that the industry practice regarding the filing of such returns varies widely. Some operators file a full partnership return, even though they may be operating as co-owners, whereas others file a modified partnership return. The majority probably file no return at all. In any case where it appears desirable to avoid classification as a partnership, or to avoid being estopped from denying that a partnership exists, it seems undesirable to file either a partnership return or a modified partnership return. Since no other form is provided for the purpose, the operator might discharge whatever responsibility he has for information reporting by sending a letter containing the designated information to the Revenue Service.

13.12   **Summary.** The co-ownership arrangement may be distinguished from a partnership in that the co-ownership has no joint profit objective, as defined by the Revenue Service,

---

[13] I.T. 2785, *supra.*

and in that title to the property is retained in each of the co-owners. On the other hand, a joint profit objective is one of the essential characteristics of the partnership form of organization, and it is customary for title to rest in the entity itself. Since a joint operation conducted by co-owners does not result in the creation of a separate entity for tax purposes, the operator acts not as principal but as agent of the co-owners, each of whom would report as income and expense the receipts and expenditures during his own taxable year, without regard to any fiscal accounting period which might be adopted for joint operating purposes. A partner, of course, will report as income from the partnership the amount thereof for the taxable year ending within his taxable year.[14] Each of the co-owners may exercise his own election regarding intangibles, delay rentals, and so on, because he, as principal, is not bound by elections of his agent and has not authorized his agent to make such election for him; in the partnership form of organization, however, the partnership exercises such elections. As to the allocation of income and deductions, co-owners are restricted to their fractional interest in the property. On the other hand, in the partnership, income and expenses may be allocated, within certain limits that will be discussed below, in different proportions, if the partners so agree.

ALLOCATION OF INCOME AND DEDUCTIONS AMONG PARTNERS

13.13   General Principles. It is a well-established rule that no gain or loss is recognized by a taxpayer as a result of the formation of a partnership. This rule is applicable regardless of the nature of the capital contributed to the partnership, if any, and without regard to the respective shares of the partners in relation to the capital contributed. For example, A may contribute property, B may contribute services, and C may

---

[14] I.R.C., Section 706(a) [1939 I.R.C., Section 188].

contribute cash to a partnership and agree that profits shall be shared equally. Regardless of the relative values of the contributions, and regardless of the share of income to which each partner becomes entitled, the formation of the partnership is nontaxable. Assuming the partnership to be bona fide, there appears to be no reason why the profit-sharing formula should be restricted in any sense.

13.14 *Guaranteed Salaries.* The partnership agreement may provide guaranteed payments to members of a partnership for services or for the use of capital. Prior to the 1954 Internal Revenue Code these guaranteed payments were considered merely factors in a formula for dividing the partnership profit. Section 707(c) of the Internal Revenue Code now provides that, to the extent the payments are determined without regard to partnership income, such salaries and interest represent allowable deductions to the partnership for tax purposes. The amount of such payment shall not be considered a distributive share of partnership profit; however, such amount shall be included in the partner's gross income at the same time, as a distributive share of the partnership income.

13.15 *Indemnification Against Loss.* An agreement by which one partner indemnifies the other partners against loss in a particular undertaking has been considered by the courts. The Court of Appeals for the Third Circuit held that such losses were indemnity losses of the indemnifying partner, and were not losses of the partnership.[15] The Revenue Service has also recognized agreements in which some partners are excluded entirely from sharing losses.[16]

13.16 *Formula for Determination of Net Income.* Generally, it appears that the partners may agree to divide the net profit or loss of a partnership in any manner that they desire.

---

[15] *Lederer* v. *Parrish*, 16 F.(2d) 928, 6 A.F.T.R. 6476 (3rd Cir. 1927).
[16] I.T. 1849, II-2 C.B. 6 (1923).

A partnership agreement has been recognized where certain partners were temporarily excluded from sharing in profits. The Revenue Service ruled that an ordinary partnership could exist even though the profit sharing arrangement provided for one partner to receive all income and bear all losses until he recovered his investment.[17] Section 704(a) of the Internal Revenue Code provides the general rule that a partner's distributive share of partnership income, gains, losses, deductions, or credits, is to be determined by the partnership agreement. Where the partnership agreement does not provide specifically for the manner of sharing one or more of these items, Section 704(b) of the Internal Revenue Code provides that a partner's distributive share of such items shall be determined in accordance with the profit or loss ratios prescribed in the partnership agreement.

13.17   Application to Oil Industry. The partnership form of operation is not often used in the oil and gas industry, probably because of the hazards of unlimited personal liability. A partnership offers some advantages in the oil industry which might, to a considerable extent, compensate for the unlimited liability. For example, A might contribute an undeveloped lease and B contribute cash to a partnership, with an agreement that profits and losses are to be shared equally, except that for the first taxable period of the partnership operation A shall be indemnified against losses from operation or development of the property. The partnership could then proceed to drill a test well on the property scheduling completion immediately prior to the close of its first taxable year. The loss for that year would be represented by the amount of the intangible development costs plus any operating expenses for the period. Because of the loss-indemnity provision, all of such loss would be charged to B and would be deductible on his individual income tax return as a loss from partnership operations.

---

[17] Rev. Rul. 54-84, I.R.B. No. 11, p. 16 (March 15, 1954).

The benefits derived from the partnership in this case are apparent when it is considered that if *B* had drilled a well for part of the working interest in the lease, he would have been permitted to deduct only the portion of the intangible drilling and development costs applicable to the working interest acquired.[18]

13.18   *Alternative to Sharing Arrangement.* Various types of sharing arrangements and their tax consequences were discussed in some detail in Chapter 7. Consideration of the rules stated above will make it apparent that the economic and tax results of the sharing arrangements described in that chapter could be effected with equal benefit through the formation of a partnership.

13.19   **Limited Partnership.** Limited partnerships are sometimes used in an effort to circumvent the unlimited liability that attends partnership operation. The statutory provisions in a number of states require that there be at least one general partner who is subject to unlimited liability. In some cases the state laws provide that, if the limited partners have any part in the management or operation of the enterprise, they become liable as general partners. A limited partnership form of organization under the statutes of some states bears such a close resemblance to a corporation that it is sometimes treated as an association taxable as a corporation.[19]

CONCLUSION

13.20   **General.** In order to protect the individual elections of the participants in a joint operation, it is necessary that the parties maintain a status of co-ownership. However, there is a degree of flexibility in partnership operation which might make such protection less important. In fact, it may well follow that

---

[18] U.S. Treas. Reg. 118, Section 39.23(m)-16(a). *See also* paragraph 10.05.
[19] *See* Chapter 14.

the complexities of some oil and gas transactions are more clearly reflected in the profit-sharing provisions of a partnership agreement. Caution, however, must be exercised to prevent the partnership from becoming an association taxable as a corporation, the attributes of which are discussed in the chapter that follows.

CHAPTER XIV

Associations Taxable as Corporations

STATEMENT OF PROBLEM

14.01   General. The Internal Revenue Code provides that certain associations of persons in a common effort, but not in corporate form, may so resemble a corporation as to become taxable as one.[1] If such is the case, any income from the joint effort will be subject to the corporate income tax before dis-

---

[1] I.R.C., Section 7701(a)(3) [1939 I.R.C., Section 3797(a)(3)]; *See also* U.S. Treas. Reg. 118, Section 39.3797-1.

tribution to the participants as well as a tax on the participants upon distribution received by them. This rule, which may be applicable to any type of business, poses some difficult questions in the oil and gas industry. The financial burdens and risks involved in development of oil and gas properties are so great that it is frequently necessary for the owner of a property to spread the burdens and risks among a group of people. It is desirable to do so in such a way that the resulting joint effort will not be classified as an association taxable as a corporation. The words "joint effort" are particularly significant in this connection, because the owners of nonoperating interests are not considered to be a part of the joint effort. The owner of the working interest can carve out and assign any type of nonoperating interest to raise funds for development without creating an association taxable as a corporation. However, when two or more persons own fractions of the working interest, there is some risk that their joint effort may result in an association taxable as a corporation.

The Revenue Service has adopted a rule (described in paragraphs 14.13 and 14.14) that is intended, and presumably will operate, to prevent the joint operation of oil and gas leases from being classed as associations taxable as corporations. It is believed, however, that this rule is unduly restrictive, and that it is possible to avoid such classification even though that rule is not followed, either intentionally or through inadvertence. As a consequence, a considerable part of this chapter is devoted to the development of the general rules applicable in determining whether a joint effort is an association taxable as a corporation.

TESTS OF ASSOCIATION

14.02   General. The Internal Revenue Code states that the term "corporation" includes what are commonly known as corporations, and in addition associations, joint stock companies, and insurance companies.[2] The regulations define an association as any organization, not otherwise properly classified as a trust, estate, or partnership, created for the transaction of designated affairs or the attainment of some object, having, like a corporation, continuity of existence regardless of changes in ownership, and the affairs of which are conducted by a management acting in a representative capacity.[3]

Although the provisions of the law and regulations are concise, they do not embody precise tests, and as a result there has been a considerable amount of litigation concerning the question. Since the association provisions are applicable to all types of businesses, the tests developed are of general application and are not confined to any particular industry. As a consequence, the discussion of such tests which follows will be of general application, and the specific application of the test to the oil and gas industry will be covered later in this chapter.

A review of the decided cases on the subject indicates that the courts regard the co-existence of three elements as necessary to a finding that an association of persons, not in corporate form, should nevertheless be taxable as a corporation. These elements are:

1. Two or more persons must be associated together in a joint undertaking;

2. The purpose of the joint undertaking must be to carry on a business for profit; and

3. The organization must have a substantial resemblance to a corporation.

All three of these elements must be present. If any one is lacking, the joint undertaking will not be classed as an association taxable as a corporation. Before applying these tests to the oil and gas industry, however, it is desirable that their significance be considered in some detail so that they will be clearly understood.

---

[2] I.R.C., Section 7701(a)(3) [1939 I.R.C., Section 3797(a)(3)].
[3] U.S. Treas. Reg. 118, Section 39.3797-2.

14.03   **Associates.** In order to have an association, it is necessary that two or more persons take part in the undertaking. Person is used in a sense which includes individuals, corporations, partnerships, trusts, and so on.[4] If only one person is involved, or if several are involved but there is no joint action, no association will be found. The requirement that more than one person be engaged in the undertaking is indicated by a Tax Court decision [5] in which it was held that a sole proprietorship, and not an association, existed where the sole owner of a corporation carried on the business after revocation of the corporate charter. Although the operation of a business after expiration of the corporate charter ordinarily creates an association taxable as a corporation, the Court held that the general rule was not applicable in these circumstances because there were no associates.

The same principle is illustrated by the Lewis case,[6] in which the grantor of a trust assigned a tract of land to a trustee who was empowered to collect and distribute to the grantor the funds received from disposition of portions of the land. Sales of the land were handled by an exclusive real estate agent. The trustee paid the prearranged commission to the agent and the remainder of the proceeds to the grantor. The court held that there were no associates, that the relationship between the parties was one of agency, and that there was therefore no association taxable as a corporation.

Even though two or more persons are involved in the arrangement, the combination must be voluntary and with the intent of conducting a joint effort in order to constitute an association taxable as a corporation. This principle has been applied in a number of cases involving trusts. In one case the

---

[4] I.R.C., Section 7701(a)(1) [1939 I.R.C., Section 3797(a)(1)].

[5] *Knoxville Truck Sales and Service, Inc.*, 10 T.C. 616 (1948), acq., 1948-2 C.B. 3; *See also Coast Carton Co.*, 10 T.C. 894 (1948), nonacq., 1948-2 C.B. 5, appeal dismissed without written opinion, Dkt. No. 11221 (9th Cir. 1948).

[6] *A. A. Lewis and Co.* v. *Commissioner*, 301 U.S. 385, 19 A.F.T.R. 486 (1937).

Court stated that in the ordinary trust the beneficiaries are in no real sense associated in the conduct of the trust affairs and do not become an association simply because there are two or more beneficiaries.[7] The Court observed that the associates test is not ordinarily supplied by the existence of the trust, but that the features supplied by the trust may fulfill the test of resemblance to a corporation. A similar test was advanced in the Morrissey case,[8] in which the Supreme Court observed that the beneficiaries of a trust do not ordinarily plan a common effort or enter into a combination for the conduct of a business enterprise. In both of these cases, however, it was held that the organizations were associations taxable as corporations, in part because there was such a voluntary association.

In another case where a trust was not formed or continued by voluntary action of the beneficiaries (two of the beneficiaries did not know of the trust for six months), it was stated that there was no conclusive evidence that it was a business venture or that the trustee had engaged in business for livelihood, and the Court held the trust was not taxable as a corporation. The case stated that the presence of corporate attributes is evidence, but not a conclusive test, of an association taxable as a corporation, since an association implies associates and doing business. This trust was substantial in amount, having property consisting of corporate stocks, bonds, and notes, bank deposits, controlling stock in a corporation, and loans to several companies. The trust property was held by the trustee for benefit of the four children who held transferable shares or trust certificates which were, in fact, never transferred. The purpose of the trust was to convert the trust property and make distribution to the beneficiaries. The Court held that association implies entering into a joint enterprise, and that there was no joint enterprise in this case because

---

[7] *Kilgallon* v. *Commissioner*, 96 F.(2d) 337, 21 A.F.T.R. 110 (7th Cir. 1938), cert. den., 305 U.S. 622.

[8] *Morrissey* v. *Commissioner*, 296 U.S. 344, 16 A.F.T.R. 1274 (1935).

the trust was not formed by voluntary act of the benefici-aries.[9]

On the other hand, where the grantors of the trust are also the beneficiaries, and they are using the trust as a means of pooling their common interests to conduct a joint business enterprise for their own profit, the trust is not an ordinary trust, but is merely an instrumentality used by the associates to promote a business venture. Under such circumstances, the trust would be an association taxable as a corporation.[10]

14.04   Business Conducted for Profit. Even if two or more persons have associated themselves in a joint effort and in a form that has a substantial resemblance to a corporation, there is no association taxable as a corporation unless such joint effort amounts to the conduct of a business for profit. The con-duct of a business for profit has two facets, both of which must be present, although they do not always appear together. It is conceivable that profits may be derived that are not from the conduct of a business, and, conversely, that a business may be conducted without a profit objective.

14.05   *Profit Derived Not from Conduct of Business.* Income may be derived from investments, such as royalty interests, that require no particular management decisions; the income or profit so derived is not considered to be income from the conduct of a business. The applicable regulations distinguish between the trust that is created for the purpose of protecting or conserving property and the trust arrangement under which the trustee is required to hold and manage the property with a view to income or profit.[11] It appears, therefore, that the dis-tinguishing characteristic between the two types of trusts is the

---

[9] *United States* v. *Davidson*, 115 F.(2d) 799, 25 A.F.T.R. 1073 (6th Cir. 1940).

[10] *Edward Leszczynski*, 29 B.T.A. 551 (1933); *Kilgallon* v. *Commissioner, supra.*

[11] U.S. Treas. Reg. 118, Section 39.3797-3.

presence or absence of management directed at producing income or profit.[12]

In appraising the extent of the management authority, it is necessary to consider the rule that the purposes of the trust and the extent of management authority will not be considered more narrow than that which is formally set forth in the trust instrument.[13] On the other hand, if the activities of the trustee ostensibly exceed those authorized in the creating instrument, such activities may be assumed to be within the purpose of the trust. The fact that the trustee does not exercise the powers granted will not be considered in appraising the extent of management authority.

14.06   *Conduct of Business without Profit Objective.* Although the conduct of a business without a profit objective is relatively rare, examples may be found in groups which are formed to furnish services or supply products to members of the group. In one such case three corporations purchased a power plant and operated it exclusively for their mutual benefit, through a committee composed of one representative from each corporation. The joint operation was held not to be an association taxable as a corporation, because it did not meet several of the tests stated above, but the Court emphasized the fact that profit was not the objective of the co-operative arrangement.[14]

14.07   **Corporate Resemblance.** In addition to the two tests stated and discussed above, the organization must have a substantial resemblance to a corporation. The Supreme Court has stated that there are five essential characteristics, all, or a majority, of which must be present if the organization is to

---

[12] *Royalty Participation Trust,* 20 T.C. 466 (1953), acq., I.R.B. 1953-23, 1.
[13] *Helvering v. Coleman–Gilbert Associates,* 296 U.S. 369, 16 A.F.T.R. 1270 (1935); *See also* U.S. Treas. Reg. 118, Section 39.3797-3.
[14] *Cooperative Power Plant,* 41 B.T.A. 1143 (1940), acq., 1940-2 C.B. 2; *See also Cooperative Insurance,* 41 B.T.A. 1151 (1940), acq., 1940-2 C.B. 2.

have a substantial resemblance to a corporation.[15] These characteristics are:

1. Title to property is held by the organization.
2. There is centralized management authority.
3. Continuity of the enterprise is not affected by death of an individual owner.
4. Continuity of the enterprise is not affected by a transfer of beneficial interest.
5. Personal liability of the participants is limited.

The Revenue Service probably will not concede that all five of the above characteristics must be present to cause an organization to have a substantial resemblance to a corporation. However, substantial resemblance certainly would require that a majority of such features be present in order to distinguish the organization from a noncorporate operation.

14.08 *Title to Property.* Title to property owned by a corporation will rest in the corporation whether held in the corporate name or held in the name of nominees for the benefit of the corporation. It appears that the vesting of title in the business entity is very important, if not essential, to a holding that the entity is an association taxable as a corporation. When a noncorporate business arrangement takes the form of a trust, title to any property owned by the organization usually rests in the trustee. Thus, in a number of cases where the tax status of a trust has been under question, considerable importance was attached by the courts to the fact that title to the property was vested in the trustee. In one case a syndicate was controlled by a trustee who was authorized to lease, sell, and manage petroleum properties, and the trust provisions permitted the transfer of beneficial interests and the continuance of the organization for 25 years except by vote of two-thirds of the beneficiaries. The Court held the trust or syndicate to be an

---

[15] *Morrissey v. Commissioner, supra.*

association taxable as a corporation. However, where the same trust was dissolved and the beneficiaries conveyed their interests to an agent who managed the properties and leases and sold parts thereof, the income received by the agent was not income of an association taxable as a corporation.[16]

A "multiple trust" might be defined as a creature of a single trust instrument in which several trust estates under the management of a single trustee are established. Each trust estate holds title to an undivided interest in a property. The purpose of the grantor is usually to bestow benevolence on several members of his family. The leading multiple trust case[17] involved the conveyance of property by a father and four children to a trust in which the father and two sons were trustees. The Court, in holding that the trusts did not constitute an association taxable as a corporation, distinguished the Morrissey case and related cases because they dealt with a single trust by means of which several owners of property had combined title and management of their property in the one trust, with substantially the results that would have been attained by conveying it to a corporation for purely business purposes. The Court stated that so long as each owner keeps his interest separate, and for the use of his own chosen beneficiaries, with no compulsory co-operation with the others, corporate resemblance is lacking, and that several individuals, each of whom owns an undivided interest in property, may co-operate voluntarily in its management, and may hire the same agent to manage the property without becoming an association taxable as a corporation.

In at least two cases title was not vested in the entities, yet each entity was held taxable as an association. In the first case[18] the entity was a joint stock company, which in any

---

[16] *Helm and Smith Syndicate* v. *Commissioner*, 136 F.(2d) 440, 31 A.F.T.R. 177 (9th Cir. 1943).

[17] *McKean* v. *Scofield*, 108 F.(2d) 764, 24 A.F.T.R. 98 (5th Cir. 1940).

[18] In *Burk-Waggoner Oil Association* v. *Hopkins*, 269 U.S. 110, 5 A.F.T.R. 5663 (1925), the taxpayer was a joint stock company operating as a Massachu-

event would appear to be subject to corporate taxes because of specific provisions of the Internal Revenue Code. The second case [19] is distinguishable on the basis of its unusual fact situation and does not necessarily lessen the importance of the vesting of title in the entity as a basic test of association status.

Cotenants in mining partnerships retain legal title in themselves individually, and their operations have in several cases been held not to constitute associations taxable as corporations, partly on the basis of such retention of title.[20] In effect, the courts have recognized that the mining partnership, the usual joint operation vehicle in the oil and gas industry, is a cotenancy with title resting in the owners rather than in the entity. The same observation is not necessarily applicable to a general partnership, a limited partnership, or a joint venture. In these instances the courts apparently follow the entity theory of

setts Trust in Texas, the laws of which did not permit such an entity to hold title to property. Title was not held in the name of the certificate holders but in the name of the trustees, who could be considered as holding title for the benefit of the organization. Since Section 7701(a)(3) [1939 I.R.C., Section 3797(a)(3)] of the Internal Revenue Code specifically provides for the taxation of joint stock companies as corporations, such an entity is taxable even though the state law prohibits the holding of title by the organization.

[19] In *Fortney Oil Company*, B.T.A. Memo. Op., Dkt. No. 97440, 1940 P-H B.T.A. Memo. Dec., Para. 40,032 (1940), rev'd, 125 F.(2d) 995, 28 A.F.T.R. 1207 (6th Cir. 1942), a corporation assigned to a number of individuals fractional undivided interests in about two-thirds of its interest in a leasehold. The Court of Appeals for the Sixth Circuit reversed the decision of the Board of Tax Appeals and held the enterprise taxable as a corporation. The Court pointed to the substantial corporate resemblance of the association. The corporation retained complete managerial power over the property, and the individuals had no right to participate in management at any time. If any individual elected not to pay his share of the cost of drilling a particular well, his rights in the property underlying such well reverted to the corporation. There was centralized management, continuity of existence, operation for a joint profit, transferability of interests, and an attempt to limit personal liability. Under these circumstances the Court concluded that the organization was taxable as an association, even though *under state law* such an organization was not a legal entity but a tenancy in common, and did not hold title to property. This case appears distinguishable by reason of the fact that absolute management control was retained by the grantor and that the grantor retained a type of reversionary interest in the property conveyed.

[20] *C. A. Everts, Jamison Lease Syndicate*, 38 B.T.A. 1039 (1938); *Rector and Davidson v. Commissioner*, 111 F.(2d) 332, 24 A.F.T.R. 919 (5th Cir. 1940), cert. den., 311 U.S. 672; *Commissioner v. Horseshoe Lease Syndicate*, 110 F.(2d) 748, 24 A.F.T.R. 775 (5th Cir. 1940), cert. den., 311 U.S. 666.

partnership insofar as ownership of property is concerned, and it appears that under the entity theory title to property is considered to be vested in the joint venture or partnership.

14.09   *Centralized Management.* It is characteristic of the corporate form of organization that the owners vest management powers in a few persons, thereby achieving a centralized management of corporate affairs. This characteristic is also found in almost every type of business organization. It is usual for co-owners to designate one of their members as an operator of the property. Managing partners are the rule rather than the exception in partnership operations. In the case of a limited partnership the statutes frequently require that a general partner be the managing partner. Ordinarily in the trust form of organization the trustee has an implied or an express right and duty to manage the properties which constitute the corpus of the trust. Because centralized management is characteristic of so many forms of business organization, it is apparent that this test or qualification by itself would not cause a group of associates to be treated as an association taxable as a corporation.

14.10   *Continuity of Enterprise.* Another characteristic of a corporation is that the existence of the entity continues regardless of the continued existence of the participants. Thus there is no effect upon the existence of a corporation if one of its stockholders, who is an individual, should die or if another stockholder, which is a corporation, should discontinue its existence. The corporate existence is not related to, nor dependent upon, a continued identity of the participants in the corporate enterprise. On the other hand, a partnership may be dissolved by the death of one of the partners, and, ordinarily, a limited partnership lasts only so long as the general partner or the general partners continue to live. In the case of a trust, the continued existence of the trust is not affected by the death of one of the beneficiaries; similarly, a mining partnership, which is in effect a cotenancy, continues regardless of the survival of the individual members thereof. This characteristic of the existence of a corporation, like that of centralized management, is found in a number of types of business organizations and is not conclusive as to the existence of an association taxable as a corporation. However, it should be noted that in any case where the normal operation of a particular form of business organization, such as a partnership, does not contemplate a continued existence in the event of the death of one of the participants, the Revenue Service may look with question upon provisions for continuity of the organization.

14.11   *Transferability of Interest.* The shares of stock in a corporation are transferable, and transfer of such shares between various persons has no effect upon the continuity of existence of the corporation. Other forms of business organization do not ordinarily possess this characteristic, although co-owners of undivided interests in property may ordinarily transfer such interests without effect on the type of organization which is operating the property. Hence, although transferability of interest is not conclusive [21] as to the existence of a corporation, the fact that it occurs very rarely in other types of business organization raises some question as to the possibility of corporate status if interests are freely transferable.

14.12   *Limitation of Liability.* One of the fundamental economic purposes fulfilled by the corporation is limitation of liability of the participants in the enterprise. It is this factor which permits the aggregation of large sums of capital contributed by a large number of individuals, each of whom makes a contribution to the total pool of capital. On the other hand, limitation of liability is not characteristic of other types of business organization, except in the case of limited partner-

---

[21] *C. A. Everts, Jamison Lease Syndicate, supra.*

ships, which under state law are ordinarily required to have at least one general partner whose liability is not limited. Because limitation of liability is not characteristic of other organizations, the existence of this attribute in any type of organization other than a corporation will raise serious questions as to the tax status of such organization. One case of doubtful application has held that the existence of personal liability on the part of participants is not sufficient to prevent the recognition of an association taxable as a corporation.[22]

ASSOCIATIONS IN THE OIL AND GAS INDUSTRY

14.13   Revenue Service Position. The general principles of association developed above should be applicable to the oil industry as well as to other industries. It is essential that the associates engage in the conduct of a trade or business in order to be an association, and for this reason the owners of royalties or any other type of nonoperating interest cannot be taxable as an association. The joint operation of an oil and gas property should result in an association taxable as a corporation only in the event that the three-factor test described in paragraph 14.02 is met. This test contemplates (1) that there be an association of two or more persons, (2) that the association be for the purpose of conducting a business for profit, and (3) that the association bear a substantial resemblance to a corporation. The corporate resemblance test was seen to embody five separate elements of resemblance, the most important of which was the resting place of title to property owned or operated by the association of persons.

Perhaps because it felt that these tests were difficult of application, and because it did not attach significance to the title test of corporate resemblance, the Revenue Service is-

---

[22] *Burk-Waggoner Oil Association* v. *Hopkins, supra; See* discussion in footnote No. 18, *supra.*

sued a ruling [23] regarding associations in the oil and gas industry that does not follow precisely the lines of the tests
developed above. In this ruling the Revenue Service has stated
that an association will be taxable as a corporation if the following four characteristics are found:

1. There must be associates;
2. The association must have a joint profit objective;
3. There must be continuity of existence; and
4. There must be centralized control of group affairs.

When these characteristics are compared with the tests set
forth above, it will be found that the first two correspond with
the general tests or requisites applicable to all businesses conducted by two or more persons for profit. However, the general test of corporate resemblance involved five separate tests,
and the Revenue Service ruling embodies only two of these
tests. The Revenue Service takes the position that the principal elements of corporate resemblance are continuity of
existence, regardless of survival of participants or transfer of
interest, and centralized control or management of the group
affairs. Although it is conceded that these two characteristics
are important attributes of a corporation, the Revenue Service position disregards what is considered to be the most
important test, that is, the resting place of title.

The ruling holds that a mining partnership by its very nature is always made up of associates, that the enterprise has
continuity of existence regardless of survival of partners or
co-owners, and that it has centralized control in that one of
the co-owners or venturers is appointed as operator. The one
corporate attribute that may be missing is the joint profit objective, if, according to the ruling, each of the participants
reserves the right to take the oil or gas produced from the
property in kind, thereby reserving the right to sell the product. The reasoning is that profit arises from the sale of min-

---

[23] I.T. 3930, 1948-2 C.B. 126, modified by I.T. 3933, 1948-2 C.B. 130.

erals, and not from their extraction or processing. Therefore, if each of the participants has the right to sell, he has not entered into a joint operation with a profit objective. On the other hand, if the agreement provides that the operator in his representative capacity irrevocably has authority to extract and to sell the minerals, then the organization created will be considered an association taxable as a corporation. Such an association is considered to be the owner of the depletable economic interest in the oil and gas in place and is entitled to the income derived from the operation. In a later ruling this concept was referred to as "collective irrevocable representative capacity." [24]

14.14   *Collective Irrevocable Representative Capacity.* In effect, the concept of collective irrevocable representative capacity merges into a single test all of the requirements considered necessary by the Revenue Service for an association to become taxable as a corporation. Under this concept, if the operator is given an irrevocable authority to market production, the co-ownership will be considered to be an association taxable as a corporation. According to this ruling, to avoid such classification it is necessary that the joint operating agreement contain either a provision that each co-owner has a right to take his share of production in kind or a provision that the authority of the operator as agent to market the production shall be revocable at the will of the co-owners. Where such revocable representative authority to market production is granted to the operator, or to another person, his authority must be limited in such a way that he is not permitted to enter into any sales contract for a period longer than is required by the minimum needs of the oil and gas industry, and in no event for a period longer than one year.[25] If such provisions are incorporated in the operating agreement, the Revenue

---

[24] I.T. 3948, 1949-1 C.B. 161.
[25] I.T. 3930, *supra;* I.T. 3948, *supra.*

Service will not contend that the association of co-owners is one which is taxable as a corporation.

Another application of this rule is contained in a Revenue Service ruling [26] relative to the custom, prevalent in the oil industry during the years 1942 to 1950, of granting an option to buy oil, known as a call on oil, for an extended period of time. In that situation the ruling concluded that the co-owner had merely disposed of his oil in advance, but it was essential that the co-owner, and not the operator, grant the call. It was also essential that the co-owner grant only the right to take oil, and not the right to find a buyer for the oil. As long as the grantee of the call was acting in its own behalf, no agency was found to exist; but if the call gave the grantee an alternative to take oil or to find a buyer, the ruling held that an agency existed; and if more than one co-owner placed that responsibility in a single agent, an organization embodying collective irrevocable representative capacity existed and constituted an association taxable as a corporation.

In view of the Revenue Service position, particular care should be taken in drafting joint operating agreements in which one of the parties is being carried. In paragraph 8.17, it is pointed out that in a carried interest of the Abercrombie type the carried party must report his share of the income and deductions applicable to the carried interest. Thus, if a carried interest of the Abercrombie type were found to exist, and if the carried party who was not the operator were not entitled to receive his full share of the oil and gas in kind, it is possible that the venture would be held to be an association taxable as a corporation under the Revenue Service rule.

14.15   Conclusion. In the rulings discussed above the Revenue Service has provided a means, relatively simple of application, whereby the operators and co-owners of oil and gas properties can with some assurance avoid classification of the

---

[26] I.T. 3948, *supra.*

joint operation as an association taxable as a corporation. Since the solution offered by the Revenue Service will suffice in most cases, the question of the validity of the ruling may never come before the courts. It is believed, however, that if intentionally or through inadvertence a joint operation fails to comply with the Revenue Service rule, there is still a possibility that such association would not be held taxable as a corporation, if title to the property operated by the joint operation is held in the names of the individual participants. The weight of authority seems to be that title to the property must rest in the entity or in nominees for the benefit of the entity to have an association taxable as a corporation. This view is supported by the Morrissey case, wherein it was stated that one of the essential characteristics of corporate resemblance is that the corporation holds title to property operated by the entity. More directly in point is the Helm and Smith case,[27] where it was held that the operation of oil properties by a trustee who also held title constituted an association taxable as a corporation. The Court distinguished the identical operation by an agent on the basis that the title to the property rested in the co-owners, and held that the operation was a joint venture rather than an association taxable as a corporation. A similar result was reached in a case where legal title to the undivided interests in oil and gas leases was vested in the co-owners individually, and the owners of such interests, by separate instruments, executed a power of attorney to the operator.[28]

[27] *Helm and Smith Syndicate* v. *Commissioner, supra.*
[28] *C. A. Everts, Jamison Lease Syndicate, supra.*

CHAPTER XV

Unitization Agreements

15.01   General. As the name implies, unitization agreements have the effect of combining a number of separate operations into a single operating unit. The owners of leases in a particular oil or gas field may each develop and operate their properties separately, or they may decide to pool their properties into a single operating unit. This pooling is accomplished by means of a unitization agreement.

There are a number of reasons which will cause adjoining property owners to unitize. First, more economical development and operation can be achieved through unitization, because wells can be placed in the most advantageous locations within the unitized area without regard to lease lines. Second, unitization aids conservation, because it results in development fitted to the needs of the pool of oil or gas. Third, the operat-

235

ing problems involved in secondary recovery methods, such as water flooding, are more readily solved if such methods are conducted on a unitized basis.

There are two principal income tax problems arising from unitization agreements: (1) equalization of development costs in the formation of the unit, and (2) adjustment of unit interests after the unit has been operating. If unitization occurs before development has started, there is no problem of equalizing development costs; but if unitization occurs after development has started, various problems arise.

15.02   Formation of Unit. In the establishment of the unit each of the participating property owners receives a percentage of interest in the unitized operation. Fundamentally, the basis for determining each owner's share is the estimated minerals in place. Where the property is partially or fully developed, the percentage participation of each owner will be based on estimated reserves or on acre feet of sand. If the development has not progressed far enough to use this measure for all owners, it may be necessary to base the percentages on surface acreage contributed to the unit. There may be provision for future adjustment of percentage interest after the field is developed to the extent that reserves under each lease are more accurately determinable.

It is customary for one of the property owners to be designated as unit operator or unit manager, or in some instances an operating committee may be appointed. Although authority to operate the unit is vested in a centralized management, customarily each participant is entitled to receive his share of production in kind. The fact that title to the individual interests in the unit remains in each participant, combined with the fact that each owner is entitled to take his production in kind, is important in avoiding classification of the unit operation as an association taxable as a corporation.[1]

---

[1] See Chapter 14.

15.03   *The Property Unit after Unitization.* The unitization agreement may provide for cross assignments or deeds, whereby each participant exchanges his title in a specific property for an undivided interest in the unit, or the unitization may be accomplished merely by pooling production. In either case, the participants will probably have effected some change in the property unit [2] for purposes of the depletion computation. Two theories have been advanced on this subject. One holds that the participant exchanges all of his interest in his property for an undivided interest in the unit. The other theory is to the effect that he retains an interest in his own property equal to his percentage interest in the unit, and exchanges the remainder of the interest in his property for his share of the properties contributed by other participants. For example, if participant A is to have a 10 per cent interest in the unit, according to this second theory he retains a 10 per cent interest in his own property and exchanges 90 per cent of his property for 10 per cent of the property of other participants.

From the standpoint of the effect on the property unit, application of the first theory results in his having a single property for depletion purposes. The second theory results in his having as many property units as there are participants in the unitization, because, although all assignments are made at the same time, each is from a different grantor.[3] It would appear that the first theory is the more tenable of the two, and it has been adopted as a matter of practice, because it is more in accord with the economic realities of the situation, and because it would produce fewer problems in accounting for income from the unit.

If a participant owns two or more separate properties, which are involved in the unitization at its formation, the rule would

---

[2] *See* Chapter 12 for a general discussion of the property unit.

[3] G.C.M. 22106, 1941-1 C.B. 245, modified on other issues, G.C.M. 24094, 1944 C.B. 250; *see also* para. 12.04.

appear to be that he has only a single property in the unit. The situation would be similar to an exchange of two or more leases for a single lease. If, however, one of the participants in the original unitization later exchanges additional acreage for an additional participation in the unit, he would probably be held to have two separate properties for depletion purposes, just as he would be considered to have two separate properties if he purchased one-fourth of the working interest in a lease on one date and another one-fourth on a later date.[4] In either of such instances, however, the taxpayer would have the right to aggregate the interests if he exercises the election described in more detail in paragraph 12.05. If only a portion of a property owned by one of the participants is included in the unit, the participant will have two properties for depletion purposes, one consisting of his interest in the unit, the other consisting of his interest in the property which was not unitized.

15.04   Equalization of Development Costs. Frequently the properties to be combined in the unit have not been proportionately developed. As a consequence, it is necessary for the unitization agreement to provide for some adjustment among the participants to compensate for inequality of development. Such adjustments ordinarily ignore leasehold costs, but take into account both intangible drilling and development costs and equipment costs, even though the former may have been expensed by most or all of the property owners. In general, the exchanges of property interests will be deemed to be exchanges of property of like kind,[5] even though one property may be developed and the other property undeveloped.[6] The general rule is that gain will be recognized only to the extent of any boot received, whether in the form of cash or other property of unlike kind,[7] but that loss from such an exchange

---

[4] G.C.M. 22106, *supra.*

[5] I.R.C., Section 1031(a) [1939 I.R.C., Section 112(b)(1)].

[6] *Kate J. Chrichton*, 42 B.T.A. 490 (1940), acq., 1952-1 C.B. 2, aff'd, 122 F.(2d) 181, 27 A.F.T.R. 824 (5th Cir. 1941); *See also* U.S. Treas. Reg. 118, Section 39.112(b)(1)-1.

[7] I.R.C., Section 1031(b) [1939 I.R.C., Section 112(c)(1)].

is not to be recognized.[8] The working interest consists of real estate and possibly of depreciable property, both of which are used in a trade or business, and any gain or loss recognized from an exchange of such properties held for more than six months would be subject to the provisions of Section 1231 of the Internal Revenue Code [1939 I.R.C., Section 117(j)].[9] Within the framework of these general principles it is necessary to consider each of the possible methods of equalizing development costs, in order to determine the tax consequences to the parties to the unitization agreement.

15.05   *Cash.* If the parties to the unitization agreement elect to equalize development contributions by cash adjustments, the transaction will be taxable to the recipients of cash to the extent of the gain realized, but in an amount not greater than the cash received. For example, assume that five property owners decide to unitize their leases, and that they have incurred the following development expenditures:

Lessee	DEVELOPMENT EXPENDITURES		
	Intangibles	Equipment	Total
A........	$ 300,000	$ 150,000	$ 450,000
B........	150,000	100,000	250,000
C........	....	....	....
D.......	65,000	35,000	100,000
E........	....	....	....
	$ 515,000	$ 285,000	$ 800,000

Notice that no leasehold costs have been included, because ordinarily unitization agreements do not provide for equalization of leasehold investment. Let us assume also that the percentage of interest of each of the participants in the unitization is determined in the following manner:

---

[8] I.R.C., Section 1031(c) [1939 I.R.C., Section 112(e)].
[9] I.T. 3693, 1944 C.B. 272.

Lessee	Surface acreage	Acres in pool	Effective pay (in feet)	Acre feet of sand	Percentage interest in unit
A	120	80	50	4,000	25.0
B	120	100	40	4,000	25.0
C	80	80	50	4,000	25.0
D	80	80	25	2,000	12.5
E	120	100	20	2,000	12.5
				16,000	100.0

The column headed "Effective pay" represents the result of a computation which takes into consideration the depth and potential productivity of the sands as calculated by petroleum engineers. The acre feet of sand allocable to each lessee is determined by multiplying his pooled acreage by the effective pay.

It is apparent that lessees A and B have paid more than their share of development costs, considering the development costs for the unit. On the other hand, lessees C and E have paid no development costs. The following tabulation illustrates the payment of cash to equalize the development expenditures as related to the respective owners' percentage interest in the unit:

Lessee	Total expenditures for development	UNITIZATION		Net development expenditures
		Cash received	Cash paid	
A........	$ 450,000	$ 250,000	$	$ 200,000
B........	250,000	50,000	....	200,000
C........	....	....	200,000	200,000
D........	100,000	....	....	100,000
E........	....	....	100,000	100,000
	$ 800,000	$ 300,000	$ 300,000	$ 800,000

If it is assumed that the fair market value of the interest received by A and B exceeds their basis in the property, and that such excess of value equals or exceeds the amount of cash which they received, A and B will have a taxable gain to the extent of the cash received. D has no gain or loss, having neither given nor received cash, and C and E will have no gain or loss because the giving of boot in an exchange of property of like kind does not give rise to taxable income or deductible loss.

On the assumption that the equipment on the unit is to be jointly owned and that there were no special provisions regarding the interest in the equipment, each of the parties to the unitization agreement will be required to reallocate his basis in proportion to the respective fair market values of equipment and leasehold cost.[10] If the equipment value is equal to 10 per cent of the total value of the property, each lessee would allocate 10 per cent of his basis in the property to equipment costs, and 90 per cent to leasehold cost. In the above example, A, B, and D would be required to allocate 90 per cent of the basis of equipment to leasehold, whereas C and E would allocate 10 per cent of their leasehold cost, if any, to equipment. Reallocation of basis to leasehold may result in a detriment to a taxpayer who has a substantial investment in equipment, because percentage depletion is allowable without regard to basis in the property. Therefore, over the producing life of the property each lessee may lose the benefit of deductions to the extent that the basis of equipment was allocated to leasehold cost. In addition, C and E in the example will be required to allocate 90 per cent of their equalization disbursement to leasehold cost, even though a portion thereof actually represented reimbursement of intangible drilling costs. The tax disadvantages of cash equalization have led to the adoption of other methods of equalization with less adverse tax consequences.

---

[10] U.S. Treas. Reg. 118, Section 39.23(1)-4; *E. C. Laster*, 43 B.T.A. 159 (1940), acq. on another issue, 1941-1 C.B. 7, nonacq. on another issue, 1952-2 C.B. 5, modified on other issues, 128 F.(2d) 4, 29 A.F.T.R. 465 (5th Cir. 1942).

15.06   *Larger Unit Interest.* The unitization agreement might provide that lessees *A* and *B* receive a larger share of future production from the unitized property in order to equalize the development expenditures, instead of receiving a cash adjustment. If such additional share of production is not in the form of an oil payment, the transaction is a nontaxable exchange of properties of like kind, even though *A* and *B* have acquired a disproportionately greater interest. This method of handling the unitization accomplishes the objective of avoiding a tax liability on the part of those parties to the agreement who are to be compensated for their additional development costs. Hence, *A* and *B* would avoid the taxable gain that they realized in the preceding illustration. However, if no special provisions are made regarding the interest in equipment, the parties would be required to allocate their basis between depreciable equipment and leasehold cost, as in the preceding illustration, with a resulting loss of basis in depreciable equipment to several of the parties. This method of equalization would require special calculation of the royalty interests under the *A* and *B* properties, because the royalty owners are not entitled to any larger sum, even though *A* and *B* receive enlarged interests.

15.07   *Oil Payments.* Equalization may be effected by assigning an oil payment, payable out of the unit production, to each participant, such oil payment being equal to the amount of development costs incurred by the participant. Each participant who has incurred development costs exchanges his interest in a property for an interest in the unit, plus an oil payment payable out of the unit. Since the rule presently followed by the Revenue Service is that an exchange of oil payments for other types of interests in oil properties is not an exchange of properties of like kind,[11] the receipt of the oil payment in addition to the interest in the unit would consti-

---

[11] *See* para. 6.04.

tute an exchange in which boot had been received, the boot being represented by the oil payment payable out of unit production. Under this rule the exchange would be only partially tax free, and gain would be realized in an amount not in excess of the fair market value of the oil payment received.[12] A and B, who would receive oil payments, would determine their basis in the unitized property by adding to the basis of the property given up in the exchange the amount of gain realized upon the exchange.[13] If no special provisions are made regarding the equipment, the basis would be allocated between (1) depreciable equipment and depletable leasehold cost, and (2) the oil payment received, in proportion to the fair market values of each. If the courts follow the rule of the Fleming [14] case, which held that an oil payment and other mineral interests were properties of like kind, the exchange would be nontaxable, but the reallocation of basis would still be required.

From the standpoint of the unit, however, an oil payment has been carved out and assigned for a consideration. Under the anticipation of income theory, such a transaction results in the present realization of income equal to the fair market value of the consideration received.[15] It appears that the unit would realize taxable income to the extent of the fair market value of the development costs, and each of the participants would be required to report his share.

It has been suggested as an alternative to the above plan that each participant who has incurred development costs could retain an oil payment equal to such costs upon assignment of his property to the unit. Upon assignment of their interests to the unit all other participants retain an oil payment

---

[12] I.R.C., Section 1031(b) [1939 I.R.C., Section 112(c)(1)].

[13] I.R.C., Section 1031(d) [1939 I.R.C., Section 113(a)(6)].

[14] *Fleming* v. *Campbell*, 205 F.(2d) 549, — A.F.T.R. —, 1953 P-H, Para. 72,611 (5th Cir. June 26, 1953). *See also* para. 6.05.

[15] G.C.M. 24849, 1946-1 C.B. 66; I.T. 4003, 1950-1 C.B. 10; *See also* Chapter 6.

of $100, or some other nominal amount. Each of the oil payments so retained must be payable from the same percentage of production accruing to the individual properties, so that after the unitization the oil payments can be pooled and made payable from the same aggregate percentage of production from the unit. The pooling of retained oil payments may be illustrated by the example below, in which each oil payment has arbitrarily been reserved out of 60 per cent of the leasehold estate:

| Lessee | Lease per cent of unit production | Per cent of unit production applicable to 60 per cent of leasehold interest retained as oil payment | Oil Payments | | Per cent of Unit Production (After Retained Oil Payments Are Pooled so as to Pay Out Simultaneously) Applicable to Satisfaction of: | |
			Amount	Per cent of total	Pooled retained oil payments	Pooled residue leasehold interests
A	25.0	15.0	$ 450,000	56.24	33.75	10.00
B	25.0	15.0	250,000	31.24	18.74	10.00
C	25.0	15.0	100	.01	.005	10.00
D	12.5	7.5	100,000	12.50	7.50	5.00
E	12.5	7.5	100	.01	.005	5.00
	100.0	60.0	$ 800,200	100.00	60.000	40.00

Thus, it will be seen that the economic result of this proposed alternative is the same as the preceding plan, even though in form this transaction is a series of nontaxable exchanges.

15.08 *Unequal Contribution to Subsequent Development.* One means of preventing recognition of gain is a unitization agreement that provides that those lessees who have spent less than their proportionate share for development prior to unitization will pay all future development costs, until such time as they have spent an amount proportionate to that spent by lessees who contributed developed properties. There is some question as to the position of the lessee who pays a disproportionate amount of future drilling and equipping costs. If such costs are incurred in consideration of an assignment of the interest in the property, as they appear to be, the lessees who pay future development costs would be required to capitalize their expenditures to the extent applicable to interests of other parties in the unit.[16] In our illustrative example, A and B would be relieved of the taxability of the gain at formation of the unit. C and E, who would have to pay future development costs for a period of time, probably would not be any worse off than they would have been if the equalization had been made in cash. If no special provisions are made regarding equipment, there should be a reallocation of basis in the manner previously discussed.

15.09 *Delayed Participation in Unit.* Still another method of equalizing development costs is to provide that those lessees whose properties are not proportionately developed at the time of the unitization should withhold the undeveloped properties, develop them proportionately to the other properties contributed, and then contribute the properties to the unit. Under these circumstances it would appear that the lessee would have the right to expense the intangible development costs applicable to his interest in his own property. In addition, the exchange, made at the time that the property has been proportionately developed and is contributed to the unit, would appear to be nontaxable, because it is an exchange of properties of like kind. Here too, however, all of the parties to the unitization agreement will be required to allocate basis between equipment and leasehold costs if no special provision has been made for equipment.

15.10 *Equipment Exchanged Separately.* In each of the foregoing alternatives it has been assumed that the exchange involved a combination of leasehold and equipment. In each

---

[16] U.S. Treas. Reg. 118, Section 39.23(m)-16 (a)(1).

case it was pointed out that it was necessary for the parties to the exchange to reallocate their total basis between depreciable property and depletable property in proportion to the respective market values of each at the time of the exchange. It was also noted that such reallocation sometimes results in a transfer from depreciable basis to depletable basis with a resultant loss of deductions from the property over the period of its productive life. It appears, however, that the parties can deal separately in the equipment and in the lease and, under proper circumstances, avoid this costly reallocation of basis. In the Laster [17] case the taxpayer argued that in an exchange of oil and gas leases the transaction amounted to an exchange of well equipment for well equipment and of leasehold rights for leasehold rights. The Court found no support for this argument in the record. The Court did, however, appear to accept the concept that, if the exchange of equipment had been separated from the exchange of leaseholds, it would not have been necessary to reallocate basis between the two. The rule is well established that when a combination of depreciable and nondepreciable property is acquired for a lump sum, the total consideration must be allocated between the two.[18] It seems desirable that the unitization agreement separate the consideration and the equalization of equipment from equalization of other development costs. If a separate agreement is made providing for assignment of interest in equipment and compensation therefor, it appears that the taxpayers may be able to avoid reallocation of basis.

15.11 *Retention of Equipment.* Equalization of equipment costs might be effected by having those participants who are contributing developed properties retain title to their equipment and contribute only the use of the equipment to the unit.

---

[17] *E. C. Laster, supra.*

[18] *Hazeltine Corporation*, 32 B.T.A. 4 (1935), nonacq., XIV-1 C.B. 30; *Grain King Manufacturing Company*, 14 B.T.A. 793 (1928), appeal dismissed for lack of jurisdiction, 47 F.(2d) 608, 9 A.F.T.R. 951 (2nd Cir. 1931).

Those participants whose properties are not developed would then pay the cost of additional equipment as required and retain title thereto. After costs have been equalized in this manner, additional equipment could be acquired by the unit. This method of equalizing would pose troublesome accounting questions, and it is probable that the lessees who pay for the equipment after unitization would be required to treat as leasehold cost the portion of their expenditures applicable to other participants' interests in the unit.

15.12   Adjustment of Unit Interests. Because the estimated reserves underlying a particular lease cannot be accurately estimated until the property is fully developed and has been operating for some period of time, unitization agreements frequently provide for adjustment of unit interests after development has been completed. In other words, the participants in the unitization agreement reserve for a period of time the right to redetermine the percentage of interest accruing to each participant. Such adjustments may be made only prospectively or they may be made retroactively and prospectively.

15.13   *Prospective*. A prospective adjustment of unit interest contemplates only that the future percentage participation of the various owners will be changed. Two theories as to reallocation of basis may be advanced regarding such an adjustment. The first theory is that since the participants agreed to the adjustment at the time of unitization, there is no exchange but merely a readjustment of participating interests, which is without tax consequence. According to this theory, there would be no gain or loss, and no further reallocation of basis would be necessary. The second theory is that the parties have agreed to make an exchange in the future. Although such an exchange would be tax free, it would appear under this theory that there should be a reallocation of basis, in relation to values at the time of the exchange, between depreciable equipment and depletable leasehold, if no special provisions are made regarding the equipment. This latter theory seems to gather some support where there is only a prospective adjustment, because there is no attempt to correct the percentage participation from the date of the original unitization agreement. It may be possible to avoid the application of either of these theories if the participants make provisions for separate exchanges of leasehold for leasehold and equipment for equipment.

15.14 *Retroactive.* A unitization agreement may provide for both prospective and retroactive adjustment of participating interests. Although both theories discussed above may also be advanced regarding the nature of this transaction, it would seem that the first, that is, a mere readjustment of participating interests without tax consequence, should prevail, because the parties are correcting the participation factors as of the date of the unitization agreement. In the interest of conservatism, however, it might be better for the parties to provide for separate exchanges of leasehold for leasehold and equipment for equipment.

If it is agreed at the time of unitization that such adjustments shall be made on the basis of data which will become available at some later date, the participants will be required to report as income the amounts they receive before the time of adjustment, even though they may later be required to refund a portion of such income. This conclusion appears justified because the income is received under a claim of right and also because of the requirement of accounting for income by annual accounting periods.[19] The same conclusion would be applicable to expenses incurred during the period before the adjustment.

At the time of the adjustment, one or more participants may be required to pay to other participants a sum which

---

[19] *North American Oil Consolidated v. Burnet,* 286 U.S. 417, 11 A.F.T.R. 16 (1932).

represents the difference between income and expenses and development costs applicable to the reduction in interest of the payer. In such case, the adjustment should be broken down into its component income, expense, and capital items. The refund of income would be treated as an allowable loss, but the amount of the loss would be reduced by depletion allowed in respect of such income.[20] The expense items offset against the income would represent income, and capital items offset should be applied to reduce the payer's capital investment of the same classification.[21]

[20] *Maurice P. O'Meara,* 8 T.C. 622 (1947), acq., 1947-2 C.B. 3.

[21] *Arrowsmith* v. *Commissioner,* 344 U.S. 6, 42 A.F.T.R. 649 (1952), reh. den., 344 U.S. 900.

CHAPTER XVI

Special Problems

INTERNAL REVENUE CODE SECTION 270

16.01 General. Section 270 of the Internal Revenue Code [1939 I.R.C., Section 130] was designed to limit the amount of the deduction that individuals could claim for so-called hobby losses.[1] If the deductions exclusive of specially treated deductions attributable to a trade or business carried on by an individual exceed gross income of that particular trade or business by $50,000 a year for a period of five consecutive years, this section provides that the taxpayer's net income for each of the five years should be recomputed by limiting such excess to $50,000. Specially treated deductions include taxes, interest, net operating loss deduction, casualty and abandonment losses connected with a trade or business, losses and expenses of the trade or business of farming that are directly attributable to drought, and expenditures as to which taxpayers are given the option either (1) to deduct or (2) to defer or capitalize. Prior to the enactment of the Internal Revenue Code of 1954 the only specially treated deductions were interest and taxes. The new provision was made applicable retroactively to any year in the five-year period if one year in such period begins after December 31, 1953. If, for example, an individual suffered annual losses of $100,000 from the conduct of a trade or business for five consecutive years, his net income in each of the five years would be recomputed, limiting such loss to $50,000 for each year. Disallowance of the excess loss will result in an additional tax liability if the individual had net income of more than $50,000 from other sources in any of the years adjusted.

16.02   Application to Oil Industry. Although the section was undoubtedly directed primarily at hobby losses, its provisions are so broad that it apparently covers any type of trade or business. Prior to the amendment of the section in 1954, individuals operating in the development phases of the oil industry were confronted with a serious problem, because

---

[1] See Senate Report No. 627, Seventy-Eighth Congress, First Session (December 22, 1943), 1944 C.B. 973 at 994, where the provision is entitled "Hobby Losses." Subsequent references to this section do not limit it to hobby losses, however. See Senate Report No. 627, supra, 1944 C.B. 973 at 1018, and House of Representatives Report No. 1079, Seventy-Eighth Congress, Second Session (February 4, 1944), 1944 C.B. 1059 at 1070.

intangible drilling and development costs and abandonment losses frequently cause substantial losses in the early years of operation. Because both items are now included in the specially treated deductions, which do not have to be considered in determining the loss, the problem is less severe. There are, however, a few situations in the oil industry that are deserving of special attention.

16.03   *Combination of Operations.* The regulations [2] provide that, if an individual conducts several trades or businesses, he shall determine the gross income and deductions of each business separately, and the losses of several businesses shall not be aggregated in determining whether the $50,000 loss limitation has been exceeded. In addition, the regulations provide that the limitation is to be applied only to the same trade or business carried on by the taxpayer in each of five consecutive taxable years. It is conceivable that an individual taxpayer could conduct a fully integrated oil or gas operation, which might embrace the exploration for oil or gas for his own account or for the account of others, the drilling and equipping of oil and gas wells for his own account or for the account of others, the operation of oil and gas properties, the ownership and operation of gathering or trunk pipeline facilities servicing his own properties and the properties of others, the ownership and operation of recycling plants or natural gasoline plants, the ownership and operation of refineries, and the ownership and operation of wholesale and retail marketing facilities. In addition, such a taxpayer might also own nonoperating interests in oil and gas properties such as royalties, overriding royalties, and oil payments. Under the regulations, should the integrated operation be considered as a single trade or business? Or should it be considered as several trades or businesses? If so, which elements should be considered separate? With the possible exception of explora-

---

[2] U.S. Treas. Reg. 118, Section 39.130-1(a).

tion and drilling done for the account of others, all of the activities of the taxpayer might be regarded as part of an integrated effort directed toward the discovery, production, and marketing of oil and gas. All of the activities may be regarded as pointing toward the ultimate objective of deriving income by sale of oil or gas to the ultimate consumers. Although there are no rulings or decisions on this point, there appears to be merit in the argument that all of such operations should be considered together as a single trade or business. The situation regarding exploration and drilling done for others, which might be referred to as contract exploration and contract drilling, is not as clear. If such work is undertaken as an incident to the taxpayer's own operations so as to ulitlize fully the time of his exploration and drilling crews, it seems that the contract income should be combined as part of the income of the taxpayer's oil and gas business. If, however, a major portion of the time of the taxpayer's exploration and drilling crews is spent on contract work, there appears to be less merit in the contention that such income should be combined with the income from the oil and gas business. The principles stated regarding fully integrated operations should also be applicable to one not so fully integrated, where the various activities conducted by the taxpayer have the common objective of producing income from the sale of oil and gas.

16.04   *Partnerships and Joint Ventures.* Another question is presented where an individual is engaged in several oil or gas operations as an individual and through joint ventures, co-partnerships, and cotenancies. Should each of the operations, not carried on by the taxpayer as an individual, be considered as a separate trade or business, or should they also be aggregated for purposes of Section 270? In this connection the Revenue Service has issued two rulings. The first ruling[3] states that for the purposes of Section 270 an individual who is a

---

[3] Rev. Rul. 155, 1953-2 C.B. 180.

member of a partnership is to treat his distributive share of the income or loss of the partnership as income or loss from the conduct of a trade or business carried on by him individually. The second ruling [4] holds that all operations carried on by an individual in a particular line of business, including his distributive share of the income or losses of partnerships, are to be combined and treated as a single trade or business.

The first of these rulings is simple of application until consideration is given to the problem of a single partnership engaged in two or more unrelated business activities. If an individual is engaged in the ranching business and also in the oil business, and neither of the two businesses is the outgrowth of, or incidental to, the other, under the regulation described above he is engaged in two separate trades or businesses, and the $50,000 limitation would be applied to each business separately. Under the described ruling the same activities conducted by a partnership might be considered a single trade or business; therefore, the loss limitation should be applied to the combined operation. Representatives of the Revenue Service have informally expressed the view that if separate businesses are conducted by a partnership, the distributive share of income or loss of the partnership should be broken down to correspond to the separate trades or businesses conducted by the entity.

For the purpose of this ruling, the Revenue Service has adopted the so-called aggregate view of the partnership organization. According to this view, the partnership is regarded as nothing more than the sum of the businesses conducted by a group of individuals. The weight of recent authority dealing with other provisions of the income tax law is to the effect that the partnership should be regarded as an entity for income tax purposes. For example, the Revenue Service has ruled that an interest in a partnership is a capital asset, regardless of the nature of the partnership assets, although this rule is modified by the Internal Revenue Code of 1954 to the extent that the

---

[4] Rev. Rul. 221, 1953-2 C.B. 182.

proportionate part of the partnership interest represented by unrealized receivables and appreciated inventory is not considered as a capital asset.[5] In general, the Internal Revenue Code provides that the partnership and not the individual partners should exercise the various elections available to taxpayers.[6] Further support for this theory may be found in the fact that a partnership may, with the consent of the Secretary, adopt a fiscal year different from that of the partners,[7] and from the fact that a partnership is required to file a return.[8] Despite the number of instances in which the entity theory of partnership is recognized, it is entirely possible that the view of the Revenue Service as expressed in the described ruling will be sustained by the courts because of the difference in the underlying purpose of the statutory provisions.

The second ruling states that the income and deductions of a particular business are to be aggregated whether the business is carried on by an individual, a partnership, or as a joint venture. The taxpayer is required to determine the combined results of the various operations and apply the $50,000 loss limitation to the over-all result. This ruling will ordinarily be detrimental to the individual taxpayer. It is less likely that the taxpayer would be affected by the loss limitation if each prospect or venture were considered as a separate trade or business.

16.05 *Oil and Gas Business Income.* In addition to the problems described above, it is necessary for the taxpayer to decide whether various other types of income related to the oil and gas business are to be considered as income from the conduct of such business. The Revenue Service has issued a ruling[9] that income from oil and gas royalties, and gains and losses arising from the sale or exchange of an oil or gas property are attributable to the oil and gas business for purposes of Section 270. Under the theory of this ruling it appears that

---

[5] G.C.M. 26379, 1950-1 C.B. 58; I.R.C., Section 741.
[6] I.R.C. Section 703(b); *See John G. Scherf, Jr.,* 20 T.C. 346 (May 14, 1953).
[7] I.R.C., Section 706.
[8] I.R.C., Section 6031 [1939 I.R.C., Section 187].
[9] Rev. Rul. 219, 1953-2 C.B. 181.

income from lease bonuses, oil payments, overriding royalties, and net profits interests should be similarly classified; however, the status of delay rentals and payments for exploration rights has not been clarified.

In applying the rule that gains and losses from a sale of real estate and depreciable property used in a trade or business are to be considered in applying Section 270, distinction must be made between the rules applicable to such gains and losses for taxable years ending before October 20, 1951, and years ending on or after that date. For taxable years ending before October 20, 1951,[10] if gains from the sale of Section 1231 [1939 I.R.C., Section 117(j)] assets exceed the losses, only half of such excess is considered as income attributable to the trade or business. For taxable years beginning on or after October 20, 1951, if the gains from sale of Section 1231 assets exceed the losses, all of such excess is considered income attributable to a trade or business, but a deduction of one-half of such amount [11] is also considered attributable to the trade or business. For both groups of years, if the losses from Section 1231 assets exceed the gains, all of the gains and losses are treated as items of income and deduction attributable to the trade or business.

16.06   Methods of Avoiding Section 270. Because Section 270 is applicable if there are five consecutive years of loss in excess of $50,000, it is only necessary to break the chain of losses in one of the five years to avoid its application. For example, if the taxpayer has suffered a loss of $100,000 from the conduct of a single trade or business in each of four years, he may avoid the application of Section 270 by reducing his loss below $50,000 in the fifth year. It may be possible for the taxpayer to reduce his loss in one year by selling an oil payment that results in an anticipation of income, or by selling a property at a profit to offset his loss. If a carved-out oil payment is

---

[10] The date of enactment of the Revenue Act of 1951.
[11] I.R.C., Section 1202 [1939 I.R.C., Sections 23(ee) and 117(b)].

sold, it must be in an amount sufficient to reduce the loss below $50,000 after giving effect to the depletion allowable against such oil payment. If a property which is a Section 1231 asset is sold, the profit must be large enough to reduce the loss below $50,000 after giving effect to the deduction from gross income of one-half of the profit.[12]

16.07 Community Property. Residents of community property states are confronted with additional problems under Section 270. Are the husband and wife who file separate returns limited to a combined loss of $50,000, or may each spouse claim a loss of $50,000 on his or her separate return? Would the answer be changed if the taxpayers filed joint returns? These issues were squarely before the Tax Court in the MacMurray case,[13] where the husband and wife, who were residents of California, a community property state, filed separate returns for five years and in the sixth year filed a joint return. The losses in the conduct of the community business had exceeded $50,000 in each of the six years. The Court made no distinction between the joint and the separate returns in holding that each spouse was entitled to a loss of $50,000 before Section 270 was applicable. The Court stated that Section 270 referred to losses of an individual and that the Court was not at liberty to rewrite the law for citizens of community property states.

OIL AND GAS INCOME AND THE SELF-EMPLOYMENT TAX [14]

16.08 General. A general discussion of the self-employment tax is beyond the scope of this book, but it should be observed

---

[12] *See* paragraph 16.05.

[13] *Fred MacMurray*, 21 T.C. 15 (October 9, 1953), acq., I.R.B. No. 21, p. 4 (May 24, 1954); *See also* Rev. Rul. 54-179, I.R.B. No. 21, p. 6 (May 24, 1954).

[14] A detailed discussion of the Self-Employment Tax is contained in Prentice-Hall Social Security Tax Service, Volume 1, Para. 31,950 *et seq.*, and Prentice-Hall Federal Tax Service, Volume 1, Para. 4,161 *et seq. See also* I.R.C.,

that certain oil and gas income may be considered self-employment income. The self-employment tax is imposed upon the net
income of an individual derived from nonexempt trades or
businesses. If the taxpayer owns all or a fraction of the working
interest in an oil or gas property he would be considered as
carrying on a trade or business,[15] and the income therefrom
would be considered self-employment income. The ownership
of a gas royalty has been held not to constitute the conduct of
a trade or business for purposes of the self-employment tax so
long as the owner was not otherwise engaged in the gas business.[16] It may be assumed from this ruling that the income
derived from ownership of nonoperating interests in oil and
gas properties, such as lease bonuses, oil payments, royalties,
overriding royalties, and net profits interests would not be subject to self-employment tax. A different question is presented
where the taxpayer is the owner of both operating and nonoperating interests in oil and gas properties. It is clear that the
net income from his operating interests should be considered
as self-employment income, but it is not clear whether the net
income from his nonoperating interests should be combined
with the income from the operating interests. The Revenue
Service has ruled,[17] for purposes of Section 270 of the Internal
Revenue Code [1939 I.R.C., Section 130], that the income of
operating and nonoperating interests should be combined in
determining the net income of the taxpayer's trade or business.
By analogy to this ruling, it might be inferred that income from
both types of interest should be combined for purposes of the
self-employment tax.

Sections 1401 *et seq.* [1939 I.R.C., Sections 480 *et seq.*] and U.S. Treas. Reg.
118, Sections 39.480 *et seq.*

   [15] *Helvering* v. *Combs,* 296 U.S. 365, 16 A.F.T.R. 1272 (1935); *See also* I.T.
3693, 1944 C.B. 272.

   [16] Special Ruling, February 11, 1952, signed by E. I. McLarney, Deputy
Commissioner.

   [17] Rev. Rul. 219, *supra.*

INTERNAL REVENUE CODE, SECTION 632

16.09   Application of Section. Section 632 of the Internal Revenue Code [1939, I.R.C., Section 105] limits the surtax on gains realized from certain sales of oil or gas properties to an amount equal to 30 per cent of the selling price of such properties. The section is of limited application, because 30 per cent of the selling price will normally result in a higher tax than the limited tax provided by Section 1201 of the Internal Revenue Code [1939 I.R.C., Section 117(c)]. Section 632 may, however, afford some relief where an oil property held for less than six months is sold. To qualify for the application of Section 632, the transaction must meet two tests: [18]

1. There must have been a bona fide sale of an oil or gas property, or any interest therein, and

2. the principal value of the property must have been demonstrated by prospecting, exploration, or discovery work done by the taxpayer selling the property.

Presumably the word "sale" is used in this section in the same sense as described in Chapter 5, and would include a taxable exchange. The term would not include a leasing transaction such as is described in Chapter 4,[19] and it is probable that the Revenue Service would not consider the section applicable to the sale of a carved-out oil payment. An oil or gas property, as distinguished from oil or gas production, must be sold.[20]

The requirement that the value of the property be demonstrated by activities of the taxpayer is also strictly construed. A discovery or demonstration of value by a lessee of the property will not satisfy the requirement of this section in respect

---

[18] I.R.C., Section 632 [1939 I.R.C., Section 105].

[19] *McLean* v. *Commissioner*, 120 F.(2d) 942, 27 A.F.T.R. 544 (5th Cir. 1941), cert. den., 314 U.S. 670, reh. den., 314 U.S. 710, aff'g on this issue 41 B.T.A. 565 (1940), acq. and nonacq. on other issues, 1942-1 C.B. 12, 26. *See also* Chapter 4.

[20] O.D. 658, 3 C.B. 74 (1920).

of the lessor.[21] The Revenue Service has also ruled that the limitation does not apply where individuals transfer property to a corporation that demonstrates the value of the property and liquidates, transferring the property back to the individuals who then sell it.[22]

In applying the limitation under Section 632, the taxpayer first computes the surtax upon his entire net income. The surtax attributable to the sale of the property is that proportion of the total surtax that the net income from the sale of the property bears to total net income.[23] In determining the net income attributable to sale of the property, the regulations provide [24] that all expenses directly allocable to such sale shall be deducted; in addition, any general expenses, losses, and deductions that are not properly allocated otherwise must be ratably apportioned to the income from all sources, including the income from the sale of the property. If the fraction of the ordinary surtax so computed exceeds 30 per cent of the selling price of the property, the surtax attributable thereto is to be reduced to that amount.[25]

CORPORATE EARNINGS AND PROFITS

16.10   General Rule. In order to determine the taxability of corporate distributions, it is necessary to compute the corporation's earnings and profits for the taxable year in which the distribution is made, as well as the accumulated earnings and profits at the beginning of the year of distribution.[26] In making

---

[21] I.T. 1568, II-1 C.B. 115 (1923); *See also Anna Taylor,* 3 B.T.A. 1201 (1926).

[22] T.B.R. 8, 1 C.B. 57 (1919).

[23] U.S. Treas. Reg. 118, Section 39.105-1(a).

[24] U.S. Treas. Reg. 118, Section 39.105-1(b).

[25] U.S. Treas. Reg. 118, Section 39.105-1(a); *See also Fowler* v. *United States,* 11 F.(2d) 895, 5 A.F.T.R. 5920 (N.D. Tex. 1926), aff'd, 16 F.(2d) 925, 6 A.F.T.R. 6473 (5th Cir. 1927).

[26] *See* in general I.R.C., Section 316 [1939 I.R.C., Section 115] and the corresponding sections of U.S. Treas. Reg. 118; Prentice-Hall Federal Tax Service, Volume 1, Para. 9,000 *et seq.*

such computations, depletion is to be computed without regard to percentage depletion,[27] but the depletion computation is not what has been referred to as tax cost depletion, nor does it necessarily correspond to book cost depletion. The difference, if any, between book cost depletion and depletion for computation of earnings and profits arises from possible differences in the depletable bases. One of the reasons that the depletable bases might differ is that the corporation may capitalize intangibles as depletable, or amortizable, cost on the books and expense such costs on its tax return. Other costs may also be handled differently for book and tax purposes. In computing earnings and profits, intangible drilling and development costs are treated in the same manner in which the corporation has elected to treat them for income tax purposes.[28]

Depletion for earnings and profits is computed on the cost or other basis of the property, but such cost or other basis is not reduced by any prior depletion allowances based on percentage of income or discovery value. Depletion for income tax purposes, on the other hand, is computed on the cost or other basis of the property, reduced by the allowed or allowable depletion, whether computed on the basis of cost, percentage of income, or discovery value.[29] It becomes apparent that the Internal Revenue Code and regulations contemplate two different depletion computations based on cost, one for the determination of taxable income and one for the determination of earnings and profits, and that neither will necessarily correspond with book depletion. Under these circumstances, it is also apparent that a company owning producing oil or gas properties must make an independent computation of earnings and profits for each year, and on an accumulated basis; it cannot rely on taxable income or loss or surplus, or book income or loss or surplus, in determining the taxability of its distribution.

---

[27] U.S. Treas. Reg. 118, Section 39.115(a)-2(c)(1).
[28] U.S. Treas. Reg. 118, Section 39.115(a)-2(a).
[29] I.R.C., Section 1016(a)(2) [1939 I.R.C., Section 113(b)(1)(B)] and 167(f) [1939 I.R.C., Section 114(a)].

16.11   *Distribution from Depletion or Depreciation Reserves.* Corporations in the extractive industries sometimes declare dividends from depletion or depreciation reserves. Under the following circumstances such distributions may represent a return of capital to the shareholders: [30] (1) the reserve must have been accumulated on the cost depletion basis as computed for the determination of earnings and profits, and (2) the corporation must have exhausted its earnings and profits.[31] In view of this latter requirement the provisions are not of particular significance, because they do not change the general rule applicable to corporate distributions.

PERSONAL HOLDING COMPANIES

16.12   **General.** If not more than five individuals own, directly or indirectly, 50 per cent or more of the value of the outstanding stock of a corporation at any time during the last half of the corporation's taxable year, and if 80 per cent of the corporation's gross income for the taxable year consists of personal holding company income, the corporation will be classified as a personal holding company and will be subject to extremely high surtax rates.[32] Under certain circumstances prior to 1954, a corporation might have qualified as a personal holding company if only 70 per cent of the income consists of personal holding company income.[33]

Personal holding company income consists of what would ordinarily be considered investment income. Included in this category are mineral, oil, or gas royalties, unless the aggregate amount of such royalties constitutes 50 per cent or more of the gross income of the corporation, and the allowable deduction for ordinary and necessary trade or business expenses under

---

[30] I.R.C., Section 301 [1939 I.R.C., Section 115(d)].
[31] U.S. Treas. Reg. 118, Section 39.115(d)-2.
[32] I.R.C., Section 542 [1939 I.R.C., Section 501].
[33] 1939 I.R.C., Section 501.

Section 162 of the Internal Revenue Code [1939 I.R.C., Section 23(a)], other than compensation for personal services rendered by the shareholders, constitutes 15 per cent or more of the gross income of the corporation.[34] The term mineral, oil, or gas royalties excludes overriding royalties, if such overriding royalties represent "amounts received from the sublessee by the operating company which originally leased and developed the natural resource property in respect of which such overriding royalties are paid."[35] Since working interests and oil payments do not constitute royalties,[36] income from such sources is not considered personal holding company income.

16.13   Oil Payments. Under the rule[37] presently followed by the Revenue Service, a production payment created from the working interest is not regarded as an overriding royalty or as a royalty, because the payment is not co-extensive with the life of the lease. Such limited payments have never been considered royalties as that term is used in the oil and gas industry.[38]

Companies otherwise classifiable as personal holding companies may escape such classification by purchasing an oil payment. The entire proceeds of such oil payment may be included in the gross income of the corporation in applying the 80 per cent test with reference to personal holding company income; and, since oil payments do not constitute a type of personal holding company income, it is possible to avoid personal holding company classification in this manner. In applying the income test, it is the gross receipts from the oil payment that are included in the corporate gross income and not the receipts less depletion, because depletion allowances

---

[34] I.R.C., Section 543(a)(8) [1939 I.R.C., Section 502(h)].

[35] U.S. Treas. Reg. 118, Section 39.502-1(k)(2).

[36] *See* Chapter 2.

[37] G.C.M. 24849, 1946-1 C.B. 66; I.T. 4003, 1950-1 C.B. 10.

[38] Compare *Palmer* v. *Bender*, 287 U.S. 551, 11 A.F.T.R. 1106 (1933); *Thomas* v. *Perkins*, 301 U.S. 655, 19 A.F.T.R. 538 (1937); *Anderson* v. *Helvering*, 310 U.S. 404, 24 A.F.T.R. 967 (1940).

are ordinarily not deductible in determining gross income.[39] The Revenue Service has ruled [40] that a taxpayer may elect to subtract cost depletion in determining gross income by filing its return in that manner. Thus, a corporation that might otherwise be a personal holding company should take either cost or percentage depletion as a deduction, in preference to treating cost depletion as an element of cost of goods sold. The oil payment should be in an amount large enough so that the proceeds in a given taxable year will constitute more than 20 per cent of the total gross income. If a corporation, never classified as a personal holding company, received during a taxable year $80,000 of income classifiable as personal holding company income, it could avoid the personal holding company surtax by purchasing an oil payment that would produce more than $20,000 of gross income in the same taxable year. The gross receipts from the oil payment would be included in gross income, and the personal holding company income of $80,000 would, therefore, constitute less than 80 per cent of the taxpayer's entire gross income.

CARVED-OUT OIL PAYMENTS IN TAX PLANNING

16.14   General. As pointed out in Chapter 6, the sale of a carved-out oil payment is considered to result in the immediate realization of income from the property subject to depletion. This fact has caused the oil payment to become an important tool in tax planning. By selling an oil payment for an appropriate amount and carefully selecting the property or properties out of which it is carved, the taxpayer can (a) avoid the application of Section 270 of the Internal Revenue Code [1939

---

[39] U.S. Treas. Reg. 118, Section 39.22(a)-5. The deduction for depletion under I.R.C., Section 611 [1939 I.R.C., Section 23(m)] is ordinarily a deduction from gross income in determining net income.

[40] Rev. Rul. 141, 1953-2 C.B. 101.

I.R.C., Section 130], as discussed in paragraphs 16.01 *et seq.*, and (b) obtain higher depletion allowances by increasing income from a property so that the 50 per cent of net income limitation on percentage depletion is not applicable.

16.15 *The 50 Per Cent of Net Income Limitation.* As more fully explained in Chapter 11, percentage depletion allowable in respect of an oil and gas property is equal to 27½ per cent of the gross income from that property, but cannot exceed 50 per cent of the net income from the property. If it is foreseen that 50 per cent of net income from a property for the taxable year will be less than 27½ per cent of gross income, the taxpayer can sell an oil payment carved out of that property and increase both gross and net income by equal amounts. In effect, the additional depletion allowable due to the sale of the oil payment will be 50 per cent of the proceeds, limited to the extent indicated in the formula below, instead of the normal 27½ per cent. For example, assume that the operator of an oil property has elected to expense intangible drilling and development costs and for that reason, and also because of percentage depletion taken in prior years, has a very low basis for depletion. He estimates that his gross income from the property will be $300,000 and that, because of additional development costs, his deductions other than depletion will amount to $247,500. The depletion allowable under these circumstances, compared with those in which he sells a carved-out oil payment for $250,000, is computed as follows:

	No Oil Payment Sold	*Oil Payment Sold for $250,000*
Gross income from property..........	$ 300,000	$ 550,000
Deductions	247,500	247,500
Net income from the property	$ 52,500	$ 302,500
27½% of gross income	$ 82,500	$ 151,250
50% of net income	$ 26,250	$ 151,250
Allowable depletion	$ 26,250	$ 151,250

The additional depletion attributable to the oil payment sold is

$125,000 ($151,250 less $26,250) or 50 per cent of the oil payment.

It should be noted that the percentage depletion allowance is based upon the sales proceeds of the oil payment, its face value being immaterial for this purpose. Every dollar of sales proceeds from a carved-out oil payment increases the percentage depletion based on gross income by $.275. At the same time, it increases net income by one dollar and the limitation on percentage depletion (50 per cent of net income) by $.50. Thus, every dollar of oil payment sales proceeds reduces the difference between the two depletion limitations by $.225. In order to compute the amount which should be realized from the sale of an oil payment, the difference between 27½ per cent of the expected gross and 50 per cent of the expected net income from the property should be divided by .225. In the example set out above the difference between 27½ per cent of expected gross and 50 per cent of expected net income is $56,250 ($82,500 less $26,250). Dividing $56,250 by .225 gives $250,000, which is the optimum amount to be received from the sale of the carved-out oil payment. If more than $250,000 were realized from the sale of the oil payment in this case, depletion would be increased by 50 per cent of the amount realized up to $250,000 and by only 27½ per cent of the excess over $250,000.

CHAPTER XVII

Canadian Income Taxes

CANADIAN INCOME TAX RULES

17.01   General. This chapter will set forth the Canadian income tax rules, as contrasted to the United States income tax rules applicable specifically to the oil and gas industry. It should be observed that Canadian taxation related specifically to this industry is in its infancy, and there is very little jurisprudence on the subject. As a consequence, it is not always possible to present the Canadian rules applicable in all circumstances.

One fundamental difference between the tax laws of the two countries, which affects almost every transaction, is the difference in the treatment of capital gains. In the United States capital gains are accorded a preferential tax treatment, whereas in Canada there is no tax on capital gains. Since there is no capital gains tax, any gain is either taxable as ordinary income or not taxable at all.[1]

The effect of this difference in the fundamental plan of taxation may be illustrated by the following examples:

1. In Canada, a bona fide exploration company may sell a reservation property for a profit without the profit being subjected to tax; or, if a loss is incurred on the sale, no deduction is allowed. Since there is no capital gains tax, it is not necessary to determine the holding period of the property sold.

2. A taxpayer, other than a dealer in securities, pays no tax when shares of stock are sold for a price in excess of cost and is entitled to no taxable deduction when there is a loss. There is no six months rule regarding the holding period.

3. The sale of royalty not held in trust is accorded the same treatment as securities in 2 above.

17.02   Property Interests. Property interests found in Canada are in general the same as those found in the United States. Thus, Canadian law recognizes the landowner's royalty (commonly called a gross royalty), the working interest, the overriding royalty, the net profits interest (usually called a net royalty), and the carried interest. As a general rule oil payments are not used in Canada because of undesirable income tax consequences, which will be discussed in a later connection.

---

[1] Income Tax Act, Section 2.

Although the general character of property interests is the same in Canada and the United States, their origin may differ because of historical differences in the two countries. In the United States a large proportion of potentially oil-bearing lands is privately owned, whereas in Canada a large proportion of such lands is owned, or the mineral rights therein are controlled, by the provincial and federal governments. For example, in the Province of Alberta, which embraces approximately 163 million acres, private owners hold the mineral rights to only some 16 million acres, which are called freehold lands. The remainder of the mineral rights is controlled by the provincial government. Of the 16 million acres of freehold land, 13 million acres are owned by railways and 2.4 million acres are owned by the Hudson's Bay Company, thus leaving a very minor interest in the hands of private individuals and other companies.[2] The methods of acquiring mineral rights differ between the so-called freehold lands and the governmental properties.

17.03   Reservations and Leases. The usual method of acquiring mineral rights in Canada is by securing a reservation or a permit from the provincial government for geological and geophysical surveys. Although the procedure is not uniform in all provinces, the provisions in the Province of Alberta may be considered typical. In that province a person or a company may not acquire and hold more than two reservations at one time. The reservation, which may not cover more than 100,000 acres, is obtained for a fee of $250 plus a deposit in cash or certain specified bonds for each 20,000 acres or part thereof contained in the reservation. The bond is required to guarantee that a certain minimum amount of work will be performed on the reservation in accordance with the requirements of the provincial government. The holder of a reservation must,

---

[2] *See* the booklet issued by Canadian Bank of Commerce, *For Oil and Allied Industries* (1952), p. 23.

within 90 days after its acquisition, submit a detailed plan of his proposed examination to the Department of Mines and Minerals for approval. If the plan is approved, the reservation may be renewed every four months for the first year and every three months for the second and third years, upon payment of a small rental charge. Under abnormal circumstances a reservation may be extended to cover a period not exceeding 4½ years. Any reservation or permit or part thereof that is abandoned reverts to the provincial government. The deposit made is refunded upon completion of the planned exploratory work and the filing of a report giving the details of the examination.

The holder of a reservation who has complied with all of the regulations has a right to convert a part of the holdings under the reservation to leases. Although the regulations vary in the different provinces, approximately one-half of the holdings may be so converted; the remainder of the acreage reverts to the government. The holdings converted into leases may not all be in one block, but are subject to checkerboard regulations. The lease received upon conversion of a reservation is for 21 years, and is renewable for successive periods of 21 years so long as oil or gas is produced from the property. The portion of the reservation which reverts to the government may, in the Province of Alberta, be put up for public auction and sold to the highest bidder who bids a lump sum amount. Bids may be submitted by any person or company, including the holder of the original reservation.

Under the usual form of lease, the lessee is required to pay annual rentals, usually at the rate of $1.00 per acre per year, and to pay a royalty to the governmental body, which may range from 5 per cent to 16⅔ per cent of the production from the property. The lessee also undertakes to drill a well within one year from the granting of the lease and to commence a new well within 90 days after the successful completion of each well. There are also certain requirements regarding the drilling of offset wells.

17.04 *Freehold Lands.* The procedure for leasing freehold land in Canada is almost identical with the procedure in the United States as outlined in Chapter 1. The provisions of the lease are, in general, similar to those used in the United States, and the landowner's royalty or gross royalty is usually ⅛ of the total production.

17.05 **Conveyances.** Under United States tax law, as has been described in previous chapters, in order to determine the tax consequences to the parties resulting from an assignment or grant of an interest in mineral property it is necessary to determine whether the transaction constitutes a sale, a lease, anticipation of income, or a sharing arrangement. In Canada, however, there is no need to distinguish between these types of transaction to determine whether the disposition of oil and gas rights gives rise to capital gain or ordinary income.

If the contract is, in effect, a sale of property, and the vendor wishes to receive the proceeds as a capital gain to minimize his tax, it is necessary that an amount and term certain be stipulated in the contract. If the contract contains a reservation of a certain amount of production, the purchaser would want it clearly stipulated that he is neither receiving this part of the production as his income nor making a capital purchase; to insure that this is understood, the contract should clearly state that a royalty interest is being paid.

Assuming that the grantor is not in the business of buying and selling mineral rights, and assuming that any initial consideration paid to the grantor does not constitute a prepayment of delay rentals, any initial payment made for the grant or assignment of an interest in the mineral property constitutes a nontaxable recovery of capital or capital gain. The payer of such sums must treat them as nondeductible capital expenditures. Thus bonus payments made to the owner of mineral rights for the granting of a lease constitute a nondeductible capital expenditure to the grantee and are not taxable income to the grantor.

There is one exception, however, to the preceding paragraph. If a lease (not a reservation) was directly acquired from a governmental body after December 31, 1952, and is later abandoned without any production having been obtained therefrom, the cost may be claimed as a deduction for income tax purposes at the time of abandonment, provided no part of the cost has been recovered. This regulation applies only to the taxpayer who originally acquired the lease from the governmental body.[3]

Payments of rentals for reservations, permits, and leases are allowable deductions up to $1.00 an acre a year. Any payment in excess of that amount is considered a capital expenditure.[4] Payments of surface rentals, regardless of the amount per acre, are fully deductible by the lessee. Regardless of amount, both delay rentals and surface rentals are income to the lessor.[5] If the original payment to a mineral owner includes prepaid delay rentals, the lessee is entitled to deduct the rental over the term of the lease, up to $1.00 an acre a year. In this situation, it is necessary that the contract stipulate clearly that the payment is a prepayment of rentals, or the full amount may be treated as a capital expenditure. When delay rental is prepaid, the entire amount is taxable to the lessor as income in the year the payment is received.

If any portion of the proceeds from the sale or other grant of a mineral interest is contingent upon production from or use of the property, such amounts are treated as ordinary income. The Canadian Income Tax Act provides: [6]

Amounts received by the taxpayer in the year that were dependent upon use of or production from property whether or not they

[3] Statutes of Canada, 1949, Chapter 25, Section 53(3A).
[4] Statutes of Canada, 1949, Chapter 25, Section 53(2A).
[5] Income Tax Act, Sections 3 and 4.
[6] Income Tax Act, Section 6(j).

were installments of the sales price of the property [shall be included in computing the income of a taxpayer for a taxation year] but installments of the sale price of agricultural land shall not be included by virtue of this paragraph.

This provision was added to the Income Tax Act in 1934, after the Privy Council decided that royalty payments to the vendor of an oil lease were part of the sales price of the property and hence did not constitute income to the grantor of the lease.[7] Because of this provision the grantor realizes ordinary income, regardless of the legal form of the transaction, if payments received by him can be construed to be contingent upon production. When it is considered that the capital cost of an interest in a property cannot be charged directly as an expense against production income, it will be apparent that the vendor or grantor of an interest in a property will attempt to avoid any payment contingent upon production from the property. It is this fact which renders the oil payment ineffectual in Canada.

In order to avoid having future payments treated as ordinary income, the grantor of a property will require that such payments be set up on a definite and fixed basis, without regard to whether petroleum or natural gas is produced from the property and without regard to the amount produced. In order to protect the grantor against depletion of his security in the event that production is obtained more quickly than had been anticipated, or in greater amounts than had been anticipated, it might be permissible to provide, in addition to the fixed payments, an amount payable in respect of production without the adverse tax consequence mentioned above.

17.06   Taxpayers Entitled to Deductions. Before considering the deductibility of certain types of exploration and development costs, it should be noted that right to the deductions is granted only to certain types of taxpayers. Such deductions

---

[7] *Spooner* v. *Minister of National Revenue,* 1933 A.C. 684, aff'g 1931 S.C.R. 399.

may only be claimed for income tax purposes by corporations whose principal business is (a) production, refining, or marketing of petroleum, petroleum products, or natural gas, (b) exploring or drilling for petroleum or natural gas, or (c) mining or exploring for minerals;[8] or by associations, partnerships, or syndicates formed for the purpose of exploring or drilling for oil or natural gas;[9] or by individuals in regard to drilling costs that are incurred in connection with producing wells only, and only to the extent that the income from each well equals or exceeds the cost of drilling that well.[10] An individual who is a member of two or more partnerships that qualify for such deductions cannot offset his share of the excess expenses from one partnership against the net income received from another partnership.

17.07   Exploration and Development Costs. Under the Canadian tax law, geological, geophysical, drilling, and development costs are accorded the same treatment for tax purposes, except in the case of individuals, as referred to in the preceding paragraph. All such expenditures must be claimed as deductions for tax purposes when incurred to the extent that income is available; if they are not claimed as income becomes available, then the right to such deduction is lost.[11] If the expenditures of this class exceed the income available, they are deferred to the next year or to subsequent years, until sufficient income has been received to offset the expense. Any expenses deferred under the foregoing provisions of the law may be carried forward for an indefinite number of years,[12] but only if there is no income available against which to offset the expenses.

---

[8] Statutes of Canada, 1949, Chapter 25, Section 53(1A).

[9] Statutes of Canada, 1949, Chapter 25, Section 53(2).

[10] Income Tax Regulations, Part XII, Section 1204(2).

[11] Statutes of Canada, 1949, Chapter 25, Section 53(1A), (2).

[12] Statutes of Canada, 1949, Chapter 25, Section 53(3); Sub-section (3) was extended by Section 32 of Chapter 57 of the Statutes of 1954 to cover expenditures incurred in the calendar year of 1957. The present practice of the government is to amend Section 53(3) to extend the operation of the section for one year.

In other words, it is not permissible for a taxpayer to record a loss for tax purposes by claiming such expenses in excess of the income from oil operations for a given taxable year. The result of these provisions is that neither corporations nor other business organizations that do not come within the scope of those entitled to deductions as set forth in paragraph 17.06, nor individuals under any circumstances, can reduce taxable income from other sources by means of exploration or drilling costs. Such provisions obviously reduce considerably the source of funds available for oil exploration. The Canadian government has taken the position that it does not intend to enter into the business of exploring for oil and gas and that it would be entering into such business if permission were granted to charge exploration and drilling costs against income received from sources other than petroleum or natural gas or mining operations, except by the organizations referred to above, which are specifically allowed such deductions.

Taxwise, drilling and exploration expenses cannot be passed on from one taxpayer to another. If Company A has spent $100,000 drilling a well which it sells to Company B, Company A retains the right to claim the $100,000 as expense, and Company B has made a nondeductible capital expenditure.

It is not necessary to charge off drilling and exploration expenses on the books or in the financial statements to be entitled to claim such expenses taxwise.

The applicable Canadian statutes further restrict the deductibility of geological, geophysical and general exploration costs to those expenditures made within the boundaries of Canada.[13] Similar expenditures made outside of the boundaries of Canada are treated as capital expenditures and are not deductible for tax purposes. Drilling costs for producing wells may be claimed against the income of the well; drilling costs of one well cannot be claimed against the income of any other well inside or outside Canada; cost of drilling a dry hole outside Canada cannot be recovered.[14] For this reason, a Canadian

[13] Statutes of Canada, 1949, Chapter 25, Section 53(1), (2).
[14] Income Tax Regulations, Section 1204(1).

national that desires to conduct operations in the United States or in a foreign country will usually form a corporation to operate in such countries, in order to avoid having the income from the foreign operation included in taxable income without allowance of a deduction for all expenses incurred in earning such income.

17.08   *Dry-Hole and Bottom-Hole Contributions.* Expenditures incurred as dry-hole or bottom-hole payments are treated in the same manner as deductible drilling costs. These payments are income to the recipient, and are usually offset against well costs to which they are applicable. Such expenditures incurred outside Canada are not allowed nor are they allowed to individuals in Canada.

17.09   *Sharing Arrangements.* The Canadian tax treatment of exploration and drilling costs in connection with sharing arrangements is different from that in the United States, because the Canadian rules do not contain the provision regarding capitalization of a portion of the costs where the taxpayer drills one or more wells for a portion of the working interest in a lease. As in the United States, only the taxpayer who actually incurs the cost or makes the expenditure for drilling is entitled to any tax benefit therefrom. However, such costs are deductible by the party who incurs them, even though he acquires only part of the working interest in the property in consideration for such expenditures. For example, if Company A agrees to assign a 50 per cent interest in a lease to Company B in consideration for B's drilling the first well, the cost of such drilling is fully deductible by Company B. Company A could obtain a deduction if Company B made a payment of one-half of the estimated cost of drilling the well to Company A for a 50 per cent interest in the lease, and then each company paid one-half of the actual drilling cost. In this case, each company would be entitled to a deduction for its share of the drilling costs, but Company B would have made a nondeductible payment to Company A to the extent of the cash paid for the interest in the lease.

17.10 *Special Credit for Deep Test Wells.* A special credit may be allowed in the case of expenditures, other than geological and geophysical expenditures, made in drilling deep test wells which prove nonproductive.[15] If the project has been approved by the Minister of Mines and Technical Surveys, the taxpayer may deduct 35 per cent of certified deep test drilling costs from the tax otherwise payable in the year that the expenditure is incurred. This tax credit is allowed in addition to claiming the drilling costs of the deep test well as an expense in the same manner as other drilling costs. If the tax credit available is in excess of the amount of tax due for the year, the unused portion of the tax credit may be carried forward to future taxable years.

17.11 *Salt Water Disposal Wells.* The costs of drilling salt water disposal wells and water or gas injection wells are treated as ordinary expenditures, and not as drilling and exploration costs. To date there have been no court cases to determine whether or not these expenditures can be classified as drilling and exploration costs. Since ordinary expenditures are deducted from revenue before drilling and exploration costs, and since a company is almost certain to have revenue when it is engaged in drilling salt water disposal wells or water or gas injection wells, the question may quite likely remain of academic interest only.

17.12 **Depletion Allowance.** Depletion for tax purposes in Canada is based on profits and bears no relation to cost of the property. Percentage depletion is allowed under Section 11(1)(b) of the Income Tax Act and Part XII of the Income Tax Regulations. The depletion regulations are not included in the Income Tax Act proper, but were issued originally under an Order in Council. They can be changed by further amendments to the regulations by Orders in Council without the approval of Parliament. Part XII of the Regulations provides as follows:

---

[15] Statutes of Canada, 1949, Chapter 25, Section 53(5), (5A)(6).

1201(1) Where the taxpayer operates an oil or gas well the deduction allowed is 33⅓% of the aggregate of the profits minus the aggregate of the losses of the taxpayer for the taxation year reasonably attributable to the production of oil or gas for such wells.

1201(3) In computing the profits reasonably attributable to the production of oil or gas, for the purposes of this section a deduction shall be made equal to the aggregate of the amount, if any, deducted in computing the taxpayer's income for the taxation year under the provisions of subsection (10) of Section 141 of the Act and Section 1204 of these regulations.

1202(1) Where a person other than the operator has an interest in the proceeds from the sale of the products of an oil or gas well or receives a rental or royalty computed by reference to the amount or value of the production from such a well, the deduction allowed is 25% of the amount in respect of such interest included in computing his income for the year.

1202(2) Where the amount received in respect of an interest in the income from a well is a dividend or is deemed to be a dividend, subsection (1) does not apply.

Section 141(10) of the Income Tax Act provides as follows:

There may be deducted in computing income for a taxation year under Part 1 the amount that would be deductible under Section 53 of Chapter 25 of the Statutes of 1949 (Second Session) in computing income under the 1948 Income Tax Act if that Act were applicable to the taxation year.

The depletion allowance is computed on the basis of the taxpayer's net profit, which is the excess of all income over all expense. There is no allowance for depletion computed on the basis of cost or gross income. If a taxpayer purchases a proven lease and has no other oil operations, he claims depletion as soon as income from that lease exceeds allowable expenses incurred on that lease. If the taxpayer is incurring expenses on any other lease or in any other field or area in Canada, he must also charge off these other expenses before he is in a net income position. Until he is in a net income position he is not entitled to claim a depletion allowance. However, if income is received from royalty interests, a depletion allowance of 25 per cent may be claimed immediately.[16] Royalty depletion is

---

[16] Under Regulations Section 1202(1).

computed before the deduction of expenses under Section 53.

The regulations presently in force state that where the tax-payer "operates" an oil or gas well the deduction allowed is 33⅓ per cent, whereas a person "other than the operator" is allowed 25 per cent. Regulation 1201(5) enacted September 1, 1954 and applicable to 1953 and subsequent taxation years reads as follows:

> For the purposes of this Part, a taxpayer who has an interest in the proceeds of production from an oil or gas well under an agreement which provides that he shall share in the profits remaining after deducting the costs of operating the well, shall be deemed to be a person who operates a well.

A carried interest is entitled to depletion only on a 25 per cent basis, so it may be preferable to have a joint interest rather than a carried interest in order to obtain the additional 8⅓ per cent depletion allowance. To avoid a conflict in terminology with the depletion regulations it would be wise to avoid the use of terms "operator" and "nonoperator" in contracts in the petroleum industry such as joint operating agreements, farm-out agreements, and so on, and to use instead the terms "joint operator" for all parties and "manager" for the actual operator.

17.13 *Depletion Allowance on Dividends.* A shareholder who files a Canadian income tax return may claim depletion of from 10 per cent to 20 per cent on dividends received from companies engaged in the production of petroleum or natural gas; the percentage depends on the ratio of the company's income from petroleum and natural gas to its total income from all sources.[17] Income from refining, marketing, or transporting petroleum or natural gas is not classed as income from production.

The depletion allowance on dividends is determined by the following rules as set forth in the Regulations. [18]

1. Dividends from a corporation carrying on business in Canada:
   (a) An allowance equal to 10 per cent of the dividend where the mineral profits of the corporation are equal to not less than 25 per cent but less than 50 per cent of its income;
   (b) An allowance equal to 15 per cent of the dividend where

---

[17] Income Tax Act, Section 11(2).
[18] Income Tax Regulations XIII, Section 1300 to 1302.

the mineral profits of the corporation are equal to not less than 50 per cent but less than 75 per cent of its income;

(c) An allowance equal to 20 per cent of the dividend where the mineral profits of the corporation are equal to not less than 75 per cent of its income.

2. Dividends from a corporation not carrying on business in Canada:

(a) An allowance equal to 15 per cent of the dividend if the mineral profits of the corporation are equal to not less than 50 per cent of its income.

17.14   Depreciation Allowances. Prior to 1949 a deduction for depreciation was not allowed, except such amount as the Minister might allow. Under the present Income Tax Act, the taxpayer has the right to claim a deduction for depreciation as allowed by regulations.[19] As a general rule, depreciation in Canada is computed by the diminishing balance method.[20] Any amount from nil to stated maxima can be claimed for depreciation; this allowance is not restricted to the amounts recorded on the books and reported in the annual financial statements. The maximum rate for most equipment used in the oil producing and exploring business is 30 per cent. This percentage applies to all equipment normally used above ground, such as drilling rigs, automotive equipment, and tubing. Oil pipelines are depreciated at a rate of 6 per cent unless the field from which the oil is produced has a limited life of less than 15 years, in which case a rate of 20 per cent is allowed.

Contrary to practice in the United States, casing is not a depreciable asset, but is treated as a drilling and development cost. If any casing is salvaged, such salvage must be included in income. Drill pipe may be handled in one of two ways. The cost of the drill pipe may be added to the cost of the drilling rig and depreciated as part of that rig, in which case the replacement of pipe is charged to expense as purchased; the other method is to inventory the drill pipe at the end of each fiscal year, so that all pipe is charged to expense when con-

---

[19] Income Tax Act, Section 11(1)(a).
[20] Income Tax Regulations XI, Section 1100.

sumed. If the latter method is used, no depreciation rate is involved. Tubing, however, is a depreciable asset.

In the United States, when depreciable business assets are sold, any gain is treated as capital gain, and loss is treated as ordinary loss.[21] In Canada the provisions are quite different.[22] If depreciable assets such as buildings, plant, and equipment are sold at a price in excess of their original cost, such excess is a nontaxable capital gain. If the sales price is greater than the depreciated value, the excess up to the original cost is treated as recaptured depreciation and is deducted from the undepreciated capital cost of other assets of the same class. If the sales price is less than the depreciated value, the loss may be added to the undepreciated capital cost of other assets of the same class. In the two latter cases, the net result is to reduce or increase the amount of depreciation which may be claimed in the subsequent years, rather than to recognize income or a loss at the time of disposition of a particular asset. If all assets of one class are sold and a credit results, the credit may be spread back over the five immediately preceding taxable years.[23] If an entire class of assets is disposed of, but an undepreciated balance remains after applying the proceeds from disposition, such balance may be claimed as an expense.

CANADIAN NATIONALS WITH UNITED STATES OPERATIONS

17.15   General. It was stated above that Canadian taxpayers are not allowed a deduction in Canada for geological, geophysical and general exploration costs incurred outside the boundaries of that country;[24] they are allowed only drilling costs to the extent that income is received for each well up to the amount of such costs; costs of one well cannot be claimed against income of another well. All costs not allowed are treated as nondeductible capital costs. As a consequence, no Canadian

---

[21] I.R.C., Section 1231 [1939 I.R.C., Section 117(j)].
[22] Income Tax Act, Section 12(1)(b).
[23] Income Tax Act, Section 43.
[24] Statutes of Canada, 1949, Chapter 25, Section 53(1), (2). *See also* paragraph 17.07.

taxpayer can afford to engage directly in oil and gas operations in the United States, because any income derived from such operation would be taxable, but the geological, geophysical and general exploratory and some or all drilling costs might not be deducted. A Canadian national, whether an individual, a partnership, a syndicate, or a corporation, should, therefore, conduct operations in the United States through a corporation formed in one of the states of the United States.

As a domestic corporation in the United States, such a company would be subject to the United States income tax laws in their entirety. The applicable income tax rules for United States oil operations conducted by such a company are set forth in the preceding chapters. The company would not, however, be subject to Canadian income taxes, assuming that it had no Canadian operations.

The Canadian income tax would be imposed only upon dividends paid by the United States company to Canadian stockholders, and such dividends would also be subject to United States income tax to the extent provided in the Canada-United States Reciprocal Tax Convention. However, the dividends would not be taxable in the hands of a Canadian company that owned 25 per cent or more of the voting shares of the United States company.[25] The Canadian tax would be imposed at regular rates but after allowance of depletion as described in paragraph 17.13. United States tax must be withheld at the time of payment of the dividend. Under the Tax Convention, the withholding tax rate is 15 per cent of the dividend, except in the case of dividends paid by a subsidiary to a parent company that owns 95 per cent or more of the shares carrying full voting rights at all times, where the withholding rate is 5 per cent.[26]

Another type of Canadian corporation subject to special treatment is the "foreign business corporation." Its business

---

[25] Income Tax Act, Section 28(1).
[26] Canada-United States Reciprocal Tax Convention, Art. XI.

operations must be of an industrial, mining, commercial, public utility, or public service nature, and such business must be carried on entirely outside of Canada.[27] A corporation which meets the above requirements and wishes to qualify as a foreign business corporation for a taxation year may either:[28]

(i) Within 120 days from the end of the year file a return and pay a fee of $100, or

(ii) Within 370 days from the end of the year file a return and pay a fee of $100 plus a penalty for late filing equal to $10 for each day of delay in filing beyond 120 days from the end of the year.

Corporations which qualify as foreign business corporations are not subject to Canadian income tax, and certain shareholders of foreign business corporations which directly or indirectly operate public utilities outside Canada are exempted from the Canadian withholding tax on dividends paid by such companies.[29]

UNITED STATES NATIONALS WITH CANADIAN OPERATIONS

17.16   General. It is not intended that this book attempt to consider all phases of Canadian income tax law, but certain of the general provisions are of interest to the United States national who contemplates the development and operation of oil and gas properties in Canada. The following observations are not exhaustive, but merely suggest some of the possibilities to be considered. Where reference is made to "subsidiary," the discussion would be, for the main part, equally applicable to any corporation owned by United States individuals.

17.17   Form of Organization. If a United States national intends to commence oil and gas operations in Canada it may do so in one of the following ways: as an individual or partnership, a branch of a United States corporation, a United States

---

[27] Income Tax Act, Section 71(2).
[28] Income Tax Act, Section 71(2)(b).
[29] Income Tax Act, Section 107(1).

subsidiary, or a Canadian subsidiary. Each of such organizations may be subjected to both United States and Canadian taxes, as outlined in more detail below.

17.18   *Individual or Partnership.* A citizen of the United States may be considered as carrying on a business in Canada whether he is a resident or a nonresident. "Carrying on business" includes engaging in a profession, calling, trade, manufacture, or undertaking of any kind whatsoever with the purpose of making a profit.[30] A person is considered a resident for Canadian tax purposes if he resides in Canada more than 183 days in a calendar year.[31] However, under Section 2(1) of the Income Tax Act, even if a person has been present in Canada for less than 183 days, he may still be deemed a resident, depending upon his intent and purpose. If an individual was resident in Canada during part of a taxable year, and the other part of the taxable year was not resident in Canada, was not employed in Canada, and was not carrying on business in Canada, he is taxable in Canada only on the income received from all sources while present in Canada minus those deductions which are reasonably applicable to such income.[32] If an individual resides in Canada for the entire taxable year, he is taxable as a Canadian resident: he must report all of his income from whatever source received, and is taxed at regular individual tax rates. A resident taxpayer has certain advantages not available to a nonresident taxpayer. He is entitled to claim a tax credit up to 20 per cent of dividends received from a Canadian company that is subject to Canadian income taxes.[33] He is entitled to deplete dividends received from a corporation engaged in the production of oil and gas at rates which range from 10 to 20 per cent.[34] To avoid double taxation, the Canadian Income Tax Act provides that a resident taxpayer is

---

[30] Income Tax Act, Section 139(1)(e).
[31] Income Tax Act, Section 139(3).
[32] Income Tax Act, Section 29.
[33] Income Tax Act, Section 38(1).
[34] Income Tax Act, Section 11(2).

entitled to a tax credit for the taxes paid to the United States,[35] but such tax credit cannot exceed the Canadian tax on the amount involved.

Any amount paid or credited to a nonresident person is subject to a 15 per cent withholding tax on gross income, and no deductions are allowed from such income.[36] A nonresident may have an agent in Canada to carry on business for him, in which case he is subject to tax. The Canadian agent is required to withhold 15 per cent of any amount paid to a nonresident. If the income was not taxable under the Income Tax Act, the nonresident must file a return indicating the amount withheld and apply for a refund. In cases where no withholding tax was deducted at source, the nonresident is required to file a Canadian tax return for taxable income earned in Canada.

In Canada a partnership as such is exempt from tax and is not required to file a return.[37] Individual partners are taxed on their respective shares of the partnership profits, and must include in their returns a statement of the partnership profits for the partnership fiscal year. If a partnership doing business in Canada has a nonresident partner, that nonresident is required to file an annual tax return on a prescribed form and is taxed upon his share of the partnership profits. Partnerships, associations, or syndicates are not taxable as corporations in Canada under any circumstances; consequently, arrangements required in the United States to avoid taxation as a corporation are unnecessary in Canada. Canada formerly had such a provision, but it was repealed effective in 1950.

It is not advisable for an individual to engage in the oil and gas business in Canada, since an individual may not offset expenses of exploration and drilling against income for Canadian income tax purposes,[38] except drilling costs to the limited extent set forth above. An association, partnership, or syndi-

---

[35] Income Tax Act, Section 41(1).
[36] Income Tax Act, Section 108.
[37] Income Tax Act, Section 6(c).
[38] Statutes of Canada, 1949, Chapter 25, Section 53(1), (2); Income Tax Regulations 1204.

cate formed for the purpose of exploring or drilling for oil or natural gas is entitled to such deductions; [39] therefore, an individual as a member of one of these organizations would receive benefit from these expenses.

17.19   *Branch of a United States Corporation.* If a United States corporation carries on business in Canada at any time during the year, it is taxable under the Canadian Income Tax Act upon the income allocable to such business at regular corporation rates. Any engagement in the oil and gas industry in Canada by a United States corporation is deemed as carrying on business in Canada by the terms of the Tax Convention between the United States and Canada.[40] The United States corporation may operate in Canada by opening a branch office in Canada, or it can operate through an agent.

The nonresident company must maintain separate books and records covering the Canadian operation. These may be maintained in Canada or at such other place as may be designated by the Minister of National Revenue. If the nonresident taxpayer gives all information requested, the books and records may be maintained in its office in the United States. The company is required to forward annually complete and comprehensive statements to the proper Director of Taxation in Canada, or it may send a duly authorized officer or accountant with such records, vouchers, statements, and accounts to the Director's office in Canada in order to make a full disclosure of the Canadian business.[41]

A United States corporation operating a branch business in Canada pays Canadian taxes only on its Canadian operations, but pays United States taxes on all its operations. To avoid double taxation, the United States corporation would have the benefit of the provisions of Section 901 of the Internal Revenue

[39] Statutes of Canada, 1949, Chapter 25, Section 53(2).
[40] Article I of Canada-United States Reciprocal Tax Convention, Section 3(f) of the Protocol.
[41] Income Tax Act, Section 125(1).

Code [1939 I.R.C., Section 131], which allows a credit against the United States tax for taxes paid to a foreign country, or Section 164(b)(6) of the Internal Revenue Code, [1939 I.R.C., Section 23(c)(1)(C)], which allows the taxpayer the election to deduct the Canadian taxes in lieu of the tax credit.

17.20 *United States Subsidiary.* The United States corporation could form a United States subsidiary whose entire operations would be carried on in Canada. The head office, records, and directors could all be located in the United States, and all directors' and stockholders' meetings could be held in the United States. The subsidiary must furnish annually complete and comprehensive statements to the proper authority in Canada and such records must be made available to the Director of Taxation's office in Canada if required, as discussed in paragraph 17.19. The taxable income of this company would be subject to normal Canadian corporation tax rates. The United States subsidiary is not required to withhold Canadian taxes on dividends, as would be required of a Canadian corporation. Since it operates as an entity separate from its parent, there is no problem of allocation of income and expenses between Canadian and United States operations, as in the case of a branch operation.

The United States subsidiary would also be subject to United States taxes, and may qualify as a Western Hemisphere Trade Corporation as defined in Section 921 of the Internal Revenue Code [1939 I.R.C., Section 109].

Section 922 of the Internal Revenue Code [1939 I.R.C., Section 26(i)] provides that such a corporation is allowed a special deduction against net income, which is computed by multiplying net income by a fraction the numerator of which is 14 per cent, and the denominator of which is a percentage that equals the sum of the normal tax rate and surtax rate for the taxable year. This deduction is in addition to the tax credit or deduction allowed for taxes paid to a foreign country under

Section 901 of the Internal Revenue Code. The 2 per cent additional surtax applicable generally to consolidated returns does not apply to any portion of the consolidated corporation net income attributable to a Western Hemisphere Trade Corporation.

17.21 *Canadian Subsidiary.* The United States corporation could incorporate a Canadian subsidiary corporation, which could be operated from the United States but would have to maintain a head office in Canada. The requirements as to organization, directors, stockholders' meetings, and other corporate matters differ in the various provinces.

The subsidiary is subject to the same tax provisions as a resident-owned Canadian corporation. Its income would not be subject to United States corporation taxes unless it also carried on business in the United States. Any dividends paid by a Canadian subsidiary to its United States parent company that owns 95 per cent or more of the shares carrying full voting rights at all times are subject to a 5 per cent withholding tax, or, if the dividends are paid to individuals in the United States, they would be subject to a 15 per cent withholding tax.

The Canadian subsidiary could be operated as a "nonresident-owned investment corporation" [42] if the company qualifies and proper election is made with the Department of National Revenue. A corporation incorporated in Canada qualifies as a nonresident-owned investment corporation if at least 95 per cent of the aggregate value of its issued shares and all of its bonds, debentures, and other funded indebtedness are held by nonresident persons, including corporations. Its income must be derived from specified sources that include, among others, royalty income. Such a company is taxed at the special rate of 15 per cent on its taxable income for the year. In computing the taxable income of a nonresident-owned investment corporation the only deductions allowed are (1) dividends and in-

---

[42] Income Tax Act, Section 70(1)-(4).

terest received in the year from other nonresident-owned investment corporations, and (2) taxes paid to a foreign government other than Canada in respect of any part of the income of the corporation for the year derived from sources therein. Such a company is prohibited from deducting from tax the amount of any taxes paid to foreign countries. In computing its income, no deductions are allowed for interest payable or paid on its bonds, debentures, securities, or other indebtedness. Dividends paid by a company that is a subsidiary of a nonresident corporation that owns 95 per cent or more of the shares carrying full voting rights at all times would be subject to withholding tax of only 5 per cent; if not so owned, the nonresident shareholders would be subject to the withholding of 15 per cent. The result of operating a company as a nonresident-owned investment corporation is that the Canadian taxes may be limited to a maximum of 27¾ per cent.

Dividends received by a Canadian corporation that is subject to tax under the Income Tax Act are not included as taxable income of the recipient company, provided the recipient does not control the payer.[43] In the case of controlled companies the same treatment applies, unless the dividend is paid out of income that was earned prior to the date of control.[44]

There is no provision in the Canadian Income Tax Act to force a company to distribute its accumulated surplus, nor is there any provision to tax accumulated surplus if it is not distributed by paying dividends, as is provided under Section 531 of the Internal Revenue Code [1939 I.R.C., Section 102] of the United States.

The present corporation tax rates in Canada are 20 per cent on the first $20,000 of taxable income and 49 per cent on taxable income in excess of that amount. If two or more corporations are related to each other in a taxation year, then the lower rate of 20 per cent may be applied only on $20,000 of

---

[43] Income Tax Act Section 28(1).
[44] Income Tax Act Section 28(2).

their combined incomes; the companies may elect to have one company obtain the full benefit or they may divide the $20,-000 between them.[45] One corporation is considered to be related to another in a taxation year if, at any time in the year, (a) one of them owned 70 per cent or more of all issued common stock of the other, or (b) 70 per cent or more of all the issued common stock of the corporations is owned by one person, or by two or more persons jointly, or by persons not dealing at arm's length if such persons own stock of both companies. Related companies have no privilege of filing consolidated tax returns in Canada.[46]

---

[45] Income Tax Act, Section 39(3), (3A), and (4).

[46] Under former Section 75, a parent corporation resident in Canada could elect to file consolidated returns with its wholly-owned subsidiary corporation that carried on the same general class of business as the parent and had the same taxation year as the parent. However, this section was repealed by Statutes of Canada, 1951, Chapter 51, Section 26, which is applicable to 1952 and subsequent taxation years.

APPENDIX

U.S. Treasury Regulations

U.S. Treasury Regulations	Article or Section	Paragraph Number
118	39.112(c)-1	5.03
118	39.112(e)-1	5.03
118	39.113(a)(6)-1(c)(1)	4.05
118	39.115(a)-2(a)	16.10
118	39.115(a)-2(c)(1)	16.10
118	39.115(d)-2	16.11
118	39.130-1(a)	16.03
118	39.480 *et seq.*	16.08
118	39.502-1(k)(2)	16.12
118	39.3797-1	14.01
118	39.3797-2	14.02
118	39.3797-3	14.05

1939 I.R.C. Sections

1939 I.R.C. Section	1954 I.R.C. Section	Paragraph Number
23(a)	162	16.12
23(a)(1)(A)	162(a)	8.05, 9.01, 9.02
23(c)(1)(C)	164(b)(6)	17.19
23(e)	165(a), (c)	8.09, 9.05, 11.01
23(f)	165(a)	8.09, 9.05, 11.01
23(l)	167	8.18
23(m)	611	8.18, 10.02, 11.02, 11.07, 16.13
23(cc)	616	10.02
23(ee)	None	16.05
24(a)(2)	263, 263(a)	9.01, 10.02
24(a)(7)	266	8.05, 11.16
26(i)	922	17.20
102	531	17.21
105	632	16.09
109	921	17.20
112(b)(1)	1031(a)	5.03, 15.04
112(c)(1)	1031(b)	5.03, 15.04, 15.07
112(e)	1031(c)	15.04
113(a)(6)	1031(d)	15.07
113(b)	1011	8.18, 12.01
113(b)(1)	1016	12.01
113(b)(1)(A)	1016(a)(1)	11.01
113(b)(1)(B)	1016(a)(2)	11.02, 11.21, 16.10
113(b)(1)(B)(ii)	1016(a)(2)(B)	8.18, 11.02
113(d)	1020	8.18, 11.02
114(a)	167(f)	8.18, 16.10
114(b)(1)	612	11.02, 12.01
114(b)(3)	613	11.02, 11.07, 11.14, 11.20, 12.01
115	316	16.10
115(d)	301	16.11
117(a)(1)(A)	1221(l)	5.05

1939 I.R.C. Section	1954 I.R.C. Section	Paragraph Number
117(b)	1202	16.05
117(c)	1201	16.09
117(j)	1231	5.05, 15.04, 16.05, 16.06, 17.14
130	270	16.01, 16.04, 16.05, 16.06, 16.07, 16.08, 16.14
131	901	17.19, 17.20
187	6031	16.04
188	706(a)	13.12, 16.04
433(b)(9)(B)	None	10.02
480 *et seq.*	1401 *et seq.*	16.08
501	None	16.12
502(h)	543(a)(8)	16.12
711(b)(1)	None	10.02
3797(a)(1)	7701(a)(1)	14.03
3797(a)(3)	7701(a)(3)	14.01, 14.02, 14.08

1954 I.R.C. Sections

1954 I.R.C. Section	1939 I.R.C. Section	Paragraph Number
162	23(a)	16.12
162(a)	23(a)(1)(A)	8.05, 9.01, 9.02
164(b)(6)	23(c)(1)(C)	17.19
165	23(e) & (f)	12.01
165(a)	23(e) & (f)	8.09, 9.05, 11.01
165(c)	23(e)	8.09, 9.05, 11.01
167	23(l)	8.18, 8.19
167(f)	114(a)	8.18, 16.10
263	24(a)(2)	10.02
263(a)	24(a)(2)	9.01
263(c)	None	10.02
266	24(a)(7)	8.05, 11.16
270	130	16.01, 16.04, 16.05, 16.06, 16.07, 16.08, 16.14
301	115(d)	16.11
316	115	16.10
337	None	2.12
452	None	4.03, 6.04
531	102	17.21
542	501	16.12
543	502	13.06
543(a)(8)	502(h)	16.12
611	23(m)	8.18, 10.02, 11.07, 16.13
612	114(b)(1)	11.02, 12.01
613	114(b)(3)	11.02, 11.07, 11.14, 11.20, 12.01
614(a)	None	12.02
614(b)	None	12.05
614(b)(3)	None	12.07
614(c)	None	10.07
616	22(cc)	10.02
632	105	16.09
703(b)	None	10.05, 13.04, 16.05

1954 I.R.C. Section	1939 I.R.C. Section	Paragraph Number
704(a)	None	13.16
704(b)	None	13.16
706(a)	188	13.12, 16.04
706(b)(1)	None	13.03
741	None	15.05
761(a)	None	13.06, 13.09
771(b)(1)	None	13.03
901	131	17.19, 17.20
921	109	17.20
922	26(i)	17.20
1011	113(b)	8.18, 12.01
1016	113(b)(1)	12.01
1016(a)(1)	113(b)(1)(A)	11.01
1016(a)(2)	113(b)(1)(B)	11.02, 11.21, 16.10
1016(a)(2)(B)	113(b)(1)(B)(ii)	8.18, 11.02
1020	113(d)	8.18, 11.02
1031(a)	112(b)(1)	5.03, 15.04
1031(b)	112(c)(1)	5.03, 15.04, 15.07
1031(c)	112(e)	15.04
1031(d)	113(a)(6)	15.07
1201	117(c)	16.09
1202	117(b)	16.05
1221(l)	117(a)(1)(A)	5.05
1231	117(j)	5.05, 15.04, 16.05, 16.06, 17.14
1361	None	13.06
1401 *et seq.*	480 *et seq.*	16.08
6031	187	16.04
7701(a)(1)	3797(a)(1)	14.03
7701(a)(3)	3797(a)(3)	14.01, 14.02, 14.08
7851	None	10.02

Canadian References

Citations

Citation	Paragraph Number
Abercrombie Co., J. S., 7 T.C. 120 (1946)	2.08, 8.14
Abercrombie Co., J. S.; Commissioner v., 162 F.(2d) 338, 35 A.F.T.R. 1467 (5th Cir. 1947)	2.08, 8.14
Allen, Leland J., 5 T.C. 1232 (1945)	8.12
Alworth-Stephens Co.; Lynch v., 267 U.S. 364, 5 A.F.T.R. 5258 (1925)	2.09
American National Realty Company, 47 B.T.A. 653 (1942)	11.02, 11.21
American National Realty Company, 136 F.(2d) 486, 31 A.F.T.R. 189 (5th Cir. 1943)	11.02
Anderson v. Helvering, 310 U.S. 404, 24 A.F.T.R. 967 (1940) 2.09, 2.10, 2.11, 2.12, 11.02, 11.09, 11.11, 16.13	
Appleby, Estate of Edgar S., 41 B.T.A. 18 (1940)......	13.07
Appleby, Estate of; Commissioner v., 123 F.(2d) 700, 28 A.F.T.R. 396 (2nd Cir. 1941)	13.07
Arkansas-Oklahoma Gas Co. v. Commissioner, 201 F.(2d) 98, 43 A.F.T.R. 120 (8th Cir. 1953) ..	10.09
Armstrong, William M., 25 B.T.A. 928 (1932)	8.14
Armstrong; Helvering v., 69 F.(2d) 370, 13 A.F.T.R. 695 (9th Cir. 1934)	8.14
Arrowsmith v. Commissioner, 344 U.S. 6, 42 A.F.T.R. 649 (1952)	15.14
Badger Oil Co. v. Commissioner, 118 F.(2d) 791, 26 A.F.T.R. 910 (5th Cir. 1941)	12.03
Bailey, Vern W., 21 T.C.—(No. 76) February 9, 1954) .	7.01
Bankline Oil Co.; Helvering v., 303 U.S. 362, 20 A.F.T.R. 782 (1938) 2.11, 8.12, 11.11	
Bennett v. Scofield, 170 F.(2d) 887, 37 A.F.T.R. 570 (5th Cir. 1948)	8.05
Bentex Oil Corporation, 20 T.C. 565 (May 29, 1953) ...	10.05, 13.07

Index

(Bold face numbers in parentheses refer to paragraphs in the book; the light face numbers refer to pages.)

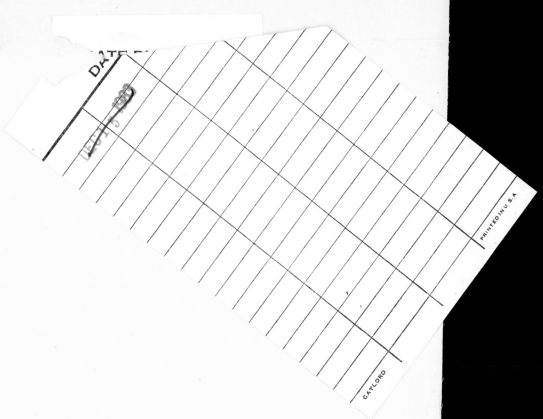

DATE
GAYLORD

PRINTED IN U.S.A.